THE BOOK

This edition contains the complete texts
of *THE SOCIAL CONTRACT* (1762)
and *DISCOURSE ON THE ORIGIN
OF INEQUALITY* (1755) in translations
noted for their adherence to the flavor
and style of Rousseau's own writings.

THE AUTHOR

Although it is for his political writings
that Rousseau is best remembered today,
he also achieved success with his operas,
novels, and *CONFESSIONS*. Rousseau
died in 1778; in 1794 his remains were
placed with Voltaire's in the Pantheon.

THE ACCLAIM

THE SOCIAL CONTRACT, Rousseau's
materpiece, has been called the "bible"
of the French Revolution.

Jean-Jacques Rousseau

The Social Contract and Discourse on the Origin of Inequality

Edited and with an Introduction by Lester G. Crocker

WASHINGTON SQUARE PRESS
PUBLISHED BY POCKET BOOKS NEW YORK

Back cover photograph from the Bettmann Archive, Inc.

A Washington Square Press Publication of
POCKET BOOKS, a division of Simon & Schuster, Inc.
1230 Avenue of the Americas, New York, N.Y. 10020

ISBN: 0-671-62858-5

First Pocket Books printing June, 1967

23   22   21   20   19   18   17   16   15   14

WASHINGTON SQUARE PRESS, WSP and colophon are
registered trademarks of Simon & Schuster, Inc.

Printed in the U.S.A.

Contents

BOOK IV

Discourse on the Origin and Foundation of Inequality Among Mankind

Introduction

DESPITE ENEMIES and persecutions, Jean-Jacques Rousseau (1712-1778) conquered most of his age. He conquered some by the force of his ideas, others by his literary style and his personal, emotional conviction, still others by the myth that grew up around him toward the end of his life. And he sowed a seed that was to continue its germination, beyond his time and into our own. In fact, as Henri Peyre has remarked, the two French writers of the past who are most alive in the mind of twentieth-century men are Pascal and Rousseau. One part of Rousseau's influence was expended nourishing the blossoms of romanticism. Another part—his feeling of anguish in a hostile world and his primary need to experience existence—long lay dormant for lack of men to whom it could speak. It has become fresh with importance to our own generation. A third phase of his work has been continuously active, from his day to ours—his social and political thought. The men of the American Revolution and the French Revolution, Marx and his followers, modern theorists of democracy and of totalitarian collectivism, all have found vital matter in his writings.

Out of some ten pieces which contain Rousseau's thinking on society and politics, two are of outstanding importance, the *Discourse on the Origin of Inequality* and *The Social Contract*. They are the most brilliant, and the most profound; they form the two poles of the axis of his work. The first is a radical criticism of society; the second contains his theoretical reconstruction of a just and good society.

In the autumn of 1749, while Rousseau was trudging to the prison of Vincennes to visit his friend, Diderot, a stroke of chance roused him from the aimlessness and discouragement in which he had been floundering. Leafing through the pages of the *Mercure de France* during a brief rest on the roadside, he fell upon the subject of a prize essay, announced by the Academy of Dijon: "Has the reestablishment of sciences and arts contributed to purifying or corrupting morals?" He was rooted to the spot, inflamed by his great inspiration. In a moment, he had set upon the unique path he was thereafter to follow, stubbornly and alone, through bitterness and misery, until the end of his days. "The instant I read it," he tells us in his *Confessions,* "I saw another universe and I became another man." To be more exact, he became the man that he really was, the maladjusted rebel. At the age of thirty-seven, he had found the identity he had been seeking in all his adventures and wanderings.* No longer did he have to try to conform to a society in which he was unhappy, no longer feel himself a failure. It was society that was wrong, society and "progress" that have corrupted the natural good in men, the good (we must understand implicitly) that *he* embodied. The separateness to which his nature, and the corruption of other men, condemned him, was not something to escape from, he now understood; it was something to live.

Rousseau set down his ideas with an eloquence and personal feeling that were new to his time. He won the prize. His friends, the *philosophes,* headed by Diderot and d'Alembert, rejoiced with him. They saw nothing in this *Discourse on the sciences and the arts* (1750) but a clever and impertinent paradox. They were to learn that Rousseau was in deadly earnest. They were to discover that they, the proponents of progress, scientific technique, the "natural rights" of man, and capitalism—

---

* *The Confessions of Jean-Jacques Rousseau,* ed. Lester G. Crocker (New York: Washington Square Press, 1965), Book VIII.

the philosophy of the Enlightenment—were his target and his natural foes. Resentment and rage followed, for all who were involved.

In the *Preface to Narcissus* (1753), Rousseau continued his critique of a culture based on competition and science. The sciences, industry, and the arts, he proclaimed, link men by bonds of self-interest instead of benevolence and mutual esteem. From this perversion of human relationships flow the ills and false values of our competitive society. Shortly thereafter, when the *Mercure de France* announced the subject of a new essay contest: "What is the origin of inequality among men and whether it is authorized by natural law," Rousseau again took up his pen. The question of inequality struck him as basic. It led him inevitably to the twin problems of man's "original nature" and the origin of society. Brooding alone in the forest of Saint-Germain, he believed he saw the cause of the corrupting influence of civilization. The social structure itself perverted human nature, our way of life, our search for happiness.

The result of Rousseau's meditations was his *Discourse on the Origin of Inequality,* published in 1755. It did not win the prize, but it brought him much notoriety and a swarm of attacks from *philosophes* and devout Christians alike. Voltaire was not the least caustic. "I have received, sir," he wrote Rousseau, "your new book against mankind. You will please men when you tell them the truth about themselves, but you will not improve them. It is impossible to paint in stronger colors the horrors of human society, from which we in our ignorance and weakness expect so much consolation. Never has so much cleverness been used in trying to turn us into beasts; it makes one feel like walking on all fours, when one reads your work. However, it being more than sixty years since I lost the habit, I feel unfortunately that it is impossible for me to get it back, and I leave that natural gait to those who are worthier of it than you or I." Palissot, in his sharply satirical comedy, *Les Philosophes,* grouped Rousseau with his enemies and represented him, much as Voltaire had suggested, walking on the stage on all fours, munching lettuce. The *Discourse,* then, was misunderstood, as too often it is in our own day, as an appeal for a "return to nature."

To ask how inequality came to be is to inquire how society came to be, since inequality is a social relationship. Rousseau's cardinal assumption, then, is that society "came to be," as an act of human will, and that it is possible to conceive of a "natural man" living in isolation. On this assumption all the rest stands. If it is not historically true (Rousseau cautiously avoids the commitment to fact, though his reasoning proceeds as if his hypotheses were factual), it is at least a theoretical truth, both valid and necessary.

In the drama of the establishment of civil society, the villain in the piece is property; from it grew all the inequalities and moral ills of mankind. But property itself was a rather late institution, one that "came to be" as a result of increasing population, the discovery of metallurgy and consequent division of labor. To determine how all this may have developed, Rousseau paints an unforgettable picture of man in the "state of nature," and then describes the steps which led to what might be called a secular version of his "Fall" and expulsion from the "Garden of Eden." While much of Rousseau's anthropology is false, some of it is quite valid. It little matters, for it is his philosophy that is a constant provocation and challenge.

What is man? What is nature? These are the ultimate questions at stake. Rousseau tries to reconstruct the logic of human development. In so doing, he posits a "man" who lacks qualities we consider necessary to the human status; moral notions, language, thought, the need for others, and a continuing relationship with others. His "original man" is human only by virtue of his feeling of pity, his freedom, and his fatal perfectibility (once again, the transposed myth of the Fall). Historically, this "natural" man is completely artificial. Yet the picture

has a strong appeal to our imagination, and upon it
Rousseau builds his theory.

It is also possible to consider Rousseau's natural man,
although he never so states, as a pseudo-historical trans-
position of a psychological reality. This is the "original
nature" we bring with us at birth, before the awakening
of moral responses and the molding process of social
patterns. Again it might be objected that "human"
beings have never existed and never could exist without
others, nor, consequently, without judgments of right
and wrong. This was the common eighteenth-century
opinion. But Rousseau really escapes this criticism, since
the creature he paints is admittedly not human, but pre-
human, living "in a state of animality." If we should
object further that even this animal is a purely mythical
construct, as unreal as a faun or a phoenix, Rousseau
might reply that it is a necessary hypothetical construct
for his purpose, leading to valid conclusions.

We must remember that Rousseau is striving to show
that man, naturally good, has been corrupted and perverted by society. To demonstrate this, he must obviously
find a way of revealing a man who is outside of society,
and prior to it. Such, then, is his artificial "natural man"—
"natural" only in the sense of a nature which is purely
metaphysical, absolute, or essential. The real difficulty
in Rousseau's argument is that he cannot stay on this
level. To make his point he must also consider man in
an empirical nature and in a historical order. His "trick"
is to make it seem that there is no break; that the historical man is the logical and actual development of the
other, the abstract "original" man. In the first situation,
man is good, or at least, not evil; in the second he is,
inevitably, evil. So the conclusion becomes inescapable:
society has corrupted man!

Yet is there not a basic truth in all this? Rousseau's
logic and anthropology, to be sure, break down. He errs
in conceiving of social relationships as external to man,
as an accidental and unnecessary accretion. He is wrong
in thinking that human nature can be abstracted from

these relationships and considered "in itself." He is right, however, in thinking that our human qualities are unfolded by social experience; that we are born with little baggage other than some basic drives, freedom from the fixity of animal instinct, and "perfectibility," or certain "faculties" which we can develop. He is right again, in large measure, in attributing to society the development of man as a moral being, a being who is moral not only in the acquisition of a particular code of ethics, but even more basically, inasmuch as he experiences spiritual love and the need for power, security, and prestige. In society, man comes to feel the insatiable restlessness of curiosity and increasing needs. In society, he inevitably knows, does, and suffers evil—as well as good. In this sense, society corrupts man, and man in society is inevitably evil. But both good and evil were already in him, as potentialities; and as he cannot exist or properly be considered philosophically without society, man, we must conclude—despite Rousseau's refusal to admit it—is necessarily evil, *naturally* evil. There is no "lost innocence."

Rousseau's own conclusion, however, is precisely a rejection of the doctrine that man is naturally evil. He eludes it, not only by his concept of a presocial "natural man," but by semantic juggling or trickery. He speaks often of human nature being "naturally good." Actually, all he has shown is a picture of a pre-human who is also pre-moral. This pre-human is incapable of moral goodness, or virtue, which requires moral judgment and self-sacrifice—of which man is capable, he freely admits, only in society. The germs of what in society will become moral good and moral evil are both present in Rousseau's natural men. They will not restrain their ego or self-interest in any way; but they are free of the compulsive desires, which society develops, to hurt others. When they hurt others, they do so in innocence, knowing no moral judgments. On the other hand, their "goodness" is also a mere biological impulse, one of pity; it will not lead them to help others, much less to risk their own well-being or to make any sacrifice. Consequently, the most Rousseau could logically claim is that society has developed the potential *moral* good, which is naturally in man, far less than the potential *moral* evil, which is naturally in him—both of these qualities existing equally in "natural man" as biological, non-moral sources of action.

Building upon this devastating basic assault, Rousseau draws up a more detailed indictment of society. Luxury and property are shown to be evils. The perversion of self-love to selfishness; the flight from the self into a formalized, mechanized, therefore empty existence; the loss of freedom and equality—these are other parts of the dark picture of a competitive society. A competitive society is one whose values are perverted by a false notion of "progress" and "good," one in which men have every interest in hating each other and in hurting each other.

Rousseau's apparent "primitivism" had a powerful appeal to his contemporaries, as well as to men of later times. Others followed the logic of his *Discourse* to its obvious end, dreamed of an equalitarian, communistic society, or even of an anarchistic social state. But Rousseau himself, as he turned to the constructive part of his work and sought a way out of man's dilemma, rejected primitivism. While he urged a simple way of living for the individual and abjured none of his criticisms of society, he realized that the simplistic solutions of "abolition" were pure fantasy. Evolution is an irreversible process. The question is, Where can we go from here?

For Rousseau, society is the original sin, but it is also the testing place, as earthly life is in the Christian tradition. The direction man must take is not a "return to nature"—neither the hypothetical, metaphysical nature of "natural man," nor the empirical, historical nature which obtains around us. We must leave all this behind and forge a new destiny, utterly unknown to nature, one that is truly man's own. The paths are mapped out in three books, *La Nouvelle Héloïse* (1761), *Emile* (1762), and *The Social Contract* (1762). To be sure, Rousseau still speaks of "natural" ways of living; but in *Emile* he clearly says, "We must not confuse what is natural to the savage state and what is natural to the civil state." It is the latter he is concerned with now. Montesquieu, he thought, had made this error, overlooking the opposition between the natural order of things and the civil order. In physical nature, man depends on things, which have necessity and stability. In society, man depends on men. Rousseau's hope, expressed and exemplified in *La Nouvelle Héloïse* and in *Emile,* is to give to human laws the necessity and inflexibility of physical laws; in this way, "we would unite in the Republic all the advantages of the natural state to those of the civil state." But in order to accomplish this, we must, precisely, overcome what is "natural" in man—impulses and self-centered passions. Many natural impulses that are harmless in the original state are deadly in society. We must "denature man." Only in this way will he be able to satisfy his natural needs in an artificial social existence.

The Social Contract opens with a famous first sentence. "Man was born free, and everywhere he is in chains." It would be wrong to take these words as a protest. They are only the statement of a fact, that man in society no longer enjoys the freedom of "natural man." The prime purpose of Rousseau's inquiry will be to determine what conditions justify this civil status; in other words, what are the foundations of a legitimate political society. Here he breaks cleanly with most other thinkers of his time who, like Montesquieu, were seeking to found the body politic on natural laws, or else on a rational "Natural Law." Following his view that society is not natural to man, he looks elsewhere, to artificial and deliberate conventions. In this, Hobbes' influence was doubtless great. In nature, argues Rousseau, there is only force. In society, men create right, which, though using force, supersedes it. Force under law is quite different from force without law. Right comes into being by the convention of the social compact.

Rousseau's version of the social contract theory is

brilliantly original.* For him, as for Hobbes, it completely terminates the state of nature, with its natural freedom and equality. But a legitimate political society gives men, in their stead, something new and far more precious, political liberty (as Rousseau understands it) and civil equality. The compact is the one unanimous act which obviates the need for further unanimity in voting. It creates the obligation to submit to the will of the majority: legally, since the individual has agreed to its rule; morally, since he is still obeying his true will, which is that the general will shall rule. Rousseau shows in detail what is lost forever on accepting the compact, and the gains which, point by point, are substituted for the losses. Possession, for instance, a usurpation which is limited only by strength, becomes property, a right which is both secured and limited by the community. Further, society is assumed, in Rousseau's theory, to be prior to government. The consequence is revolutionary. The so-called rulers of men have no part in the contract; they are only the instruments and servants of the people, in whom all sovereignty inalienably resides, and they may be dispossessed by the simple will of the sovereign people.

This summary points to the two great problems of *The Social Contract* which have puzzled and exercised the minds of countless commentators. The first is the expression of the will of the community, which is to be the determinant of justice and social control. This involves Rousseau's famous notion of the "general will." The general will is to be ascertained or formulated by the process of majority vote, that is, a process of cancellation, in accordance with what Rousseau considered to be the workings of the mathematical laws of probability. But we must not err, as many commentators do, by confusing the nature of the general will with this positivistic process of its expression. The "general will" is essentially a rationalistic notion and involves the same type of hypothesis as the "natural man" or the "state of nature."

* Book I, ch. VI.

Rousseau does not deny what we might call "empirical man," man as he is, fighting primarily for his own interest. But beyond this he assumes a rational unity among all men, consisting of what their reason would desire if all individual passions and desires could be stilled. This is the "general will." It is questionable whether in the majority rule Rousseau has found a procedure that would realize it, or that he was really convinced he had. It is on the supposititious general will, and on the participation of each citizen in the voting process, that he bases his theory that political and civil liberty consist not in doing what we want, but in doing what this hypothetical or metaphysical "general will" wants. Thus, when we suppress the individual's protest, even the protest of his conscience, we merely force him to be free, force him to do what he *really* wants to do. Again, Rousseau's error was to mingle in one concept a real, empirical situation (the will one experiences as his own) and a purely metaphysical postulate (the will which, the citizen is told, is really his own).

Rousseau conceives of the State as a unanimous *moi commun* ("corporate self," or "collective self"), whose will creates right and justice and supersedes the individual conscience in matters of public concern. The concept is obviously a dangerous and disturbing one to those who favor pluralistic or "open" societies.

This brings us to the second difficult problem, the new relationship of the individual citizen to the State. Is Rousseau's thought totalitarian or liberal? A remarkable quantity of ink has flowed in the attempt to prove it one or the other. Rousseau of course was not thinking of political labels or philosophies that did not exist, nor would he have approved of any of our twentieth-century societies, totalitarian or other. He wanted only to secure men's happiness, through a legitimate, just political society; and this could not be done without sacrifice and control. If we are to make the transition from a natural state of force to a civil state of right a successful one for mankind, we must think of men as citizens who have become part of a greater whole, and not as independent, self-centered individuals. The mutuality of the sacrifice, the application of laws to all (the two conditions of Rousseau's "equality," for he does not demand economic equality, but only a narrowing of the gap), the respecting of others as we wish them to respect us, and the limitation of the sacrifice as determined by the sovereign people itself—this is the theoretical foundation.

In the working out of Rousseau's plan, however, both individual dissent and political parties are excluded. Not only are there no minority rights; there cannot even be minorities. Rousseau constantly uses the word "liberty," but for him it does not have the same meaning as for us. Liberty, for him, is first of all the independence or sovereignty of the State. Second, it is the independence of any individual from all others, or from group pressures. This is achieved by the complete dependence of all on the collective self—an impersonal, inflexible force like that of nature in the original state of nature.* Third, it is law self-given, or consented to. A liberal society assumes that we sacrifice part of our freedom in order that the remainder of it may be protected. Rousseau demands a total alienation of all rights to the State (the sovereign may not be limited by a Bill of Rights, a Constitution, custom, or precedent). Yet he claims that the individual in his society is as totally free as in the state of nature. What is changed is the meaning of liberty and the nature of the self. Liberty is now the freedom to do the "ought"; and the will he "freely" obeys is no longer that of his egoistic self (in several writings, Rousseau calls it, deprecatingly, the "human self"), but that of a new social self (called *le moi commun,* or "collective self"). Now liberty, though it certainly means obedience to majority rule as expressed in the law, must mean

---

* Rousseau's political vocabulary has not been adequately studied. The idea of liberty is frequently associated with words such as "docile," "docility," "submissive to the yoke"—words that constitute a *leitmotif* and an implicit definition.

more than this. The liberal view, as developed in the eighteenth century and thereafter, fears and rejects Rousseau's concept of a "total alienation" of the individual to the collectivity, with the latter returning only what it wishes—even if he does keep an equal voice in the expression of its will. Liberalism fears the tyranny of the majority, even the tyranny of the "whole" which it supposedly expresses. Can a people be called "free" if it freely decides to be enslaved? Rousseau, it seems, fails to discriminate between the promotion of individual good through collective action and the sacrifice of the individual to the collective whole.

Still more important, we must not forget the lesson of the *Discourse on Inequality*. Historical or social man, because of the very conditions of social living, is inevitably evil—that is, he is impelled to selfish actions that will hurt others. The more civilized the society, the more evil he will be. The development of virtue (as contrasted with natural man's merely instinctive "goodness" or sympathy) is therefore Rousseau's principal consideration. He has no confidence in good will, reason, or "Natural Law." Virtue is placing the general good above one's own. It is *against* nature, and can be attained only through social discipline. We must "form" citizens. Social man is an artificial man, and social life must not be confused with the state of nature: its rights, its morality, its conditions of interdependence, man himself—all are radically different. Natural freedom was good in the state of nature, because then men had only natural needs. But where men are exposed to all sorts of artificial needs and urges, individual liberty would lead to luxury, acquisitiveness, power drives, and all the other evils of a competitive society which it is precisely Rousseau's intention to eliminate, as destructive to the true happiness of the individual. We must therefore overcome the natural in man, in order to give human affairs "the necessity and inflexibility" of natural events. We must create a new, artificial man, a "social" man, and a society of harmony and cooperation, not of competition for power and prestige, not of war between men and within each man.

When we realize what kind of society Rousseau is dreaming of, we can better understand the function of the political processes outlined in *The Social Contract*. The voting process, for instance, has no resemblance to that of Western, liberal democracies. Its purpose is not to find a consensus among opposing group interests, each of which freely expresses its will, but to abolish all group interests, or "particular wills," by "discovering" the general will. There is no debate or discussion, and each citizen must deliberate in isolation. The proposition cannot be amended, and the citizen is called on only to say "Yes" or "No"—and to say it (if we may interpolate a statement from the *Proposal for a Constitution for Corsica*) openly, in front of all. Even more significant, the citizens may not vote until they are sufficiently "informed" by a "guide," who apparently knows the general will *before* the vote. After the vote, as we have seen, no dissent or contrary will is allowed. The citizen who has voted the wrong way was "mistaken," and he must surrender his own will, his own ideas, his own conscience.

Rousseau's condition that the people be the sole judge of whether the will of the Legislator or guide is the general will simply cannot be fulfilled. As one scholar has put it, "It is precisely because the people does not in fact judge according to the general good that the Legislator is necessary in the first place; how then can it judge whether or not the Legislator's will is really the general will?"

We must look beyond the voting process itself for its ultimate function. In the main, its purpose is to obtain the total participation and the total commitment of all individuals to the general will, and thus to achieve a unanimous, cooperative society in which individuals will think of themselves as part of the Whole, rather than as self-centered units. This is probably the real reason for Rousseau's opposition to representative government, in which participation and commitment are only partial, never total. Second, the vote is one factor in the more complex process of "remaking" the individual, which is the Legislator's principal task. There is an important element of duplicity in this. But a reading of *La Nouvelle Héloïse* and of *Emile* will show that duplicity is a constant and conscious mechanism in Rousseau's methodology for conditioning and indoctrinating the individual. Many a time he says that the best way to control men is to capture their will, and that control is most complete when they think they are doing freely what their guide wants them to do, and makes them do.

The method of duplicity, or what Rousseau calls "the hidden hand," may even lead us to suspect that still another function of the vote—in addition to its principal purpose of creating the *moi commun*—is to give the citizenry the illusion of self-government. (Rousseau not infrequently speaks of the beneficent utility of illusion.) Indeed he seems to "give the game away" when, reiterating one of his most constant beliefs, he writes that law is inadequate: At best, it can control actions, but it cannot control wills, opinions, or passions. It cannot change men. And it is this control, he says, without which laws are futile, that must be the constant preoccupation of the legislator, the work he must unremittingly carry on *in secret*. (II,12, II,7.) We remember that Rousseau has assured us that his citizens are free because they obey only the law. But in view of these later statements in *The Social Contract,* is it not obvious that they will be obeying something other than the law—the whole secret process of control, which is the *really* important thing?

In view of his theory of human nature and society, Rousseau was bound to fear individual liberty. The remaking of the individualistic, ego-centered personality involves both the repression of natural competitive instincts (or better, their harnessing to the collective purposes), and a process of coercive conditioning through education and law. All the forces of the collectivity are brought to bear to assure the socialization of the egoistic self. The most important—though Rousseau strangely neglects it in *The Social Contract*—is education. Another mechanism developed in other writings is the institution of popular festivals and demonstrations; these create patriotism, pride of citizenship, emotional involvement, and a feeling of belonging to one unanimous body. (The vote, too, may be regarded as a kind of *fête*.) Two other mechanisms are carefully described in *The Social Contract*. One is censorship, which is Rousseau's word for what we now call thought control, a force he complains statesmen have always overlooked, and one he deems essential. Here, too, we have duplicity and the fostering of an illusion of freedom. The people must believe that the censorial tribunal is not the arbiter of their opinions, but only the means of expressing them. But again no dissent is permitted, and the censors' judgments are not subject to debate or revision. It is not unjust to infer that from "censorship" would flow the State control of publications, and the regimentation of art, the theater, and all means of communication. Here and elsewhere, Rousseau demands public inspection of private actions, or the abolition of privacy. Nothing must be allowed to rupture the unity of the collectivity, or to impede the State in its work of socializing or "denaturing" refractory individuals. Rousseau, in the *Confessions,* declares that morals and politics are inseparable. In his system, both become politics, and every phenomenon has a political significance. Nothing is neutral or indifferent.

The other force that must be harnessed to the total effort is religion. We shall not discuss here Rousseau's opposition to Christianity or the tenets of his "civil religion." The essential point is the intolerance and persecution that are implied. He does indeed demand toleration of all faiths, for intolerance would only promote the dissensions and disharmonies he is eager to suppress. After all, what matters to him is not the truth of religion, but its coercive and emotional power. However, two categories are excluded from toleration. One consists of religions that are themselves intolerant, particularly Roman Catholicism. The other comprises those individuals who either refuse to take an oath that they believe in the civil religion, or who, having taken the oath, violate it. The former are banished, the latter put to death. This imposition of a religious test will recall to Americans the loyalty oaths of the McCarthy period. It is obvious that Rousseau's intention is to control consciences, beliefs, and opinions. Beliefs become a matter for punishment. Implied are the rights of inspection and inquisition. Still worse, Rousseau speaks of punishing those who *act* as if they did not believe. The potentialities of this statement are immeasurable. It would allow the State to interpret actions—or non-action—as indicative of belief or opinion. The effect of such a state of affairs on people's conduct can only be imagined from the worst excesses of the Terror, of Stalinism, or of Chinese communism. We are reminded of the fact that Rousseau, in *La Nouvelle Héloïse,* establishes a system of spying and informing, and that in a personal letter (to M. de Beaumont), he declares that "everyone has the right to inform himself as to whether another man believes himself obliged to be just, and the sovereign has the right to examine the reasons on which each one bases that obligation."

The foregoing discussions point to two final conclusions. One is the falsity of the accusation leveled against Rousseau by his enemies, that he was a romantic who wanted the anarchy of popular sovereignty. On the contrary, the individual and the mass are controlled, in his system, to the very depths of their being. The second is the importance of reading all of Rousseau's socio-political writings in order to understand the true meaning of *The Social Contract.* His article, "Political Economy," lays the basis for the monistic State and control of the individual. In *La Nouvelle Héloïse* and *Emile,* we see this control carried out by various means of indoctrination, operant conditioning, and duplicity (hidden control, or *la main cachée*). His novel is, in fact, the first manual of "cultural engineering." His theory of "education" is developed in *Considerations on the Government of Poland;* while the *Proposal for a Constitution for Corsica,* in which we see the total control of private lives, reveals the meaninglessness of his contradictory assurance, in *The Social Contract,* that the individual surrenders only those of his rights which the State judges to be of social importance.

Democracy and totalitarianism are not exclusive terms. Democracy is rule by the people. Totalitarianism is the attempt to impose a single pattern upon the thought, feelings, and actions of a community. The opposite of totalitarianism is not democracy, but the pluralistic society, in which people are free to differ and in which complete conformity is not the test of good citizenship. The liberal, then, cannot accept Rousseau's total submergence into a higher unity. He will cry out with the *romantic* Rousseau (for there was this other Rousseau), "I am I, a sacred I. Thus far do I surrender myself, thus far do I *belong,* but no further." He will not accept Rousseau's "people's democracy."

It would be hard to imagine a more dramatic contrast than that between the *Discourse on Inequality* and *The Social Contract.* Little wonder that many critics, in Rousseau's lifetime and in later years, have accused him of inconsistency. Yet there is no basic contradiction between the two works, for their frames of reference, their controlling concepts of nature and man are different. The basic value, man's happiness, remains unchanged. Freedom, however defined, is in both an instrumental value. The independence of natural man assured his freedom and his happy existence. The imposition of society on this natural man created a situation of conflict, inequality, distorted values, and misery. The substitution of interdependence for natural independence makes dependence on the collective whole the necessary condition for independence from oppressive individuals or groups. Happiness can come only from the good society, one in which men would be made to live according to virtue. Its realization depends on the factors which make up Rousseau's disputable concept of political liberty, on equality, and control; these in turn must inhere in the organization of a legitimate human polity.

The *Discourse on Inequality* tells us what men may have been, in their remote origins, or what they still are in their fundamental sub-structure, and what has happened to them because of social experience. *The Social Contract* was written as a theoretical work, not as a practical program—Rousseau does not believe that corrupted societies can be redeemed. Nevertheless, it indicates a direction. It tells us how to overcome and transform this "natural man" within us. It tells us what men may become—or rather, what Rousseau thought they must become, if the unique *human* experiment in a *natural* universe is to succeed and to survive.

Lester G. Crocker

Western Reserve University

Suggested Readings

C. E. Vaughan. *The Political Writings of Jean-Jacques Rousseau*. 2 vols. Cambridge, 1915. (The important Introduction has remained valuable.)

Ernst Cassirer. *The Question of Jean-Jacques Rousseau*. New York, 1954.

G. H. Sabine. *A History of Political Theory*. New York, 1950.

J. L. Talmon. *The Rise of Totalitarian Democracy*. Boston, 1952.

J. Plamenatz. *Man and Society*. 2 vols. New York, 1963.

R. Derathé. *Rousseau et la science politique de son temps*. Paris, 1950.

L. G. Crocker. *Nature and Culture*. Baltimore, 1963. Also, "Rousseau et la voie du totalitarisme," in *Rousseau et la philosophie politique, Annales de philosophie politique*, No. 5 (1965). 137–152.

L. Gossman. "Rousseau's Idealism," *Romanic Review*, Vol. 57 (1961), 173–182.

J. I. McAdam. "Rousseau and the Friends of Despotism," *Ethics*, Vol. 74 (1963), 34–43.

D. Thomson. "The Dream of Unanimity," *Fortnightly Review* (Feb., 1953), 75–80.

The serious student will find many articles of interest in the volume *Études sur le "Contrat Social" de Jean-Jacques Rousseau*, Paris, 1964, and in various volumes of the *Annales de la Société Jean-Jacques Rousseau* (Geneva).

A Note on the Text

There have been only four translations of the *Discourse on Inequality*. The first, an anonymous version published in 1761, conserves the full eighteenth-century flavor, but abounds in inaccuracies. The second, appearing in a five-volume edition *The Miscellaneous Works of J. J. Rousseau* published in 1767, differs significantly from the earlier translation, although it too reflects a literal rendering of the original and is by an anonymous translator. A twentieth-century version by G. D. H. Cole, which is commonly used, feels a bit remote from Rousseau's style; it also has numerous inaccuracies, though many fewer than the earliest translation. The most recent, brought to my attention after I completed my own work, is by Roger D. Masters.

For this edition, I have used the anonymous translation of 1761 as a base, and have attempted to keep as much of it as possible, while submitting it to a thorough revision. Since I have been unable to obtain the Dedication in this translation, I have used that of 1767 as a base and have revised it within the spirit of the earlier translation.

The Social Contract is presented in the excellent nineteenth-century version of Henry J. Tozer.

The text of both works is complete, except that in the *Discourse* many of the notes and a few sentences added in a posthumous printing (1782) are omitted. The notes which have been kept are referred to by the same letters as in the original.

The Social
Contract

Prefatory Note

THIS little treatise is extracted from a larger
work undertaken at an earlier time without consideration of my capacity, and long
since abandoned. Of the various fragments
that might be selected from what was ac-
complished, the following is the most considerable, and appears to me the least
unworthy of being offered to the public.
The rest of the work is no longer
in existence.

BOOK I

~~~~~~~~~~

Introductory Note

I WISH to inquire whether, taking men as they are and laws as they can be made, it is possible to establish some just and certain rule of administration in civil affairs. In this investigation I shall always strive to reconcile what right permits with what interest prescribes, so that justice and utility may not be severed.

I enter upon this inquiry without demonstrating the importance of my subject. I shall be asked whether I am a prince or a legislator that I write on politics. I reply that I am not; and that it is for this very reason that I write on politics. If I were a prince or a legislator, I should not waste my time in saying what ought to be done; I should do it or remain silent.

Having been born a citizen of a free State, and a member of the sovereign body, however feeble an influence my voice may have in public affairs, the right to vote upon them is sufficient to impose on me the duty of informing myself about them; and I feel happy, whenever I meditate on governments, always to discover in my researches new reasons for loving that of my own country.

CHAPTER I

Subject of the First Book

MAN was born free, and everywhere he is in chains. Many a one believes himself the master of others, and yet he is a greater slave than they. How has this change come about? I do not know. What can render it legitimate? I believe that I can settle this question.

If I considered only force and the results that proceed from it, I should say that so long as a people is compelled to obey and does obey, it does well; but that, so soon as it can shake off the yoke and does shake it off, it does better; for, if men recover their freedom by virtue of the same right by which it was taken away, either they are justified in resuming it, or there was no justification for depriving them of it. But the social order is a sacred right which serves as a foundation for all others. This right, however, does not come from nature. It is therefore based on conventions. The question is to know what these conventions are. Before coming to that, I must establish what I have just laid down.

CHAPTER II

Primitive Societies

THE earliest of all societies, and the only natural one, is the family; yet children remain attached to their father only so long as they have need of him for their own preservation. As soon as this need ceases, the natural bond is dissolved. The children being freed from the obedience which they owed to their father, and the father from the cares which he owed to his children, become equally independent. If they remain united, it is no longer naturally but voluntarily; and the family itself is kept together only by convention.

This common liberty is a consequence of man's nature. His first law is to attend to his own preservation, his first cares are those which he owes to himself; and as soon as he comes to years of discretion, being sole judge of the means adapted for his own preservation, he becomes his own master.

The family is, then, if you will, the primitive model of political societies; the chief is the analogue of the father, while the people represent the children; and all, being born free and equal, alienate their liberty only for their own advantage. The whole difference is that, in the family, the father's love for his children repays him for the care that he bestows upon them; while, in the State, the pleasure of ruling makes up for the chief's lack of love for his people.

Grotius denies that all human authority is established for the benefit of the governed, and he cites slavery as an instance. His invariable mode of reasoning is to establish right by fact.* A juster method might be employed, but none more favorable to tyrants.

It is doubtful, then, according to Grotius, whether the human race belongs to a hundred men, or whether these hundred men belong to the human race; and he appears throughout his book to incline to the former opinion, which is also that of Hobbes. In this way we have mankind divided like herds of cattle, each of which has a master, who looks after it in order to devour it.

Just as a herdsman is superior in nature to his herd, so chiefs, who are the herdsmen of men, are superior in nature to their people. Thus, according to Philo's account, the Emperor Caligula reasoned, inferring truly enough from this analogy that kings are gods, or that men are brutes.

The reasoning of Caligula is tantamount to that of Hobbes and Grotius. Aristotle, before them all, had likewise said that men are not naturally equal, but that some are born for slavery and others for dominion.

Aristotle was right, but he mistook the effect for the cause. Every man born in slavery is born for slavery; nothing is more certain. Slaves lose everything in their bonds, even the desire to escape from them; they love their servitude as the companions of Ulysses loved their brutishness.† If, then, there are slaves by nature, it is because there have been slaves contrary to nature. The first slaves were made such by force; their cowardice kept them in bondage.

I have said nothing about King Adam nor about Emperor Noah, the father of three great monarchs who shared the universe, like the children of Saturn with whom they are supposed to be identical. I hope that my

---

* "Learned researches in public law are often nothing but the history of ancient abuses; and to devote much labor to studying them is misplaced pertinacity" (*Treatise on the Interests of France in Relation to Her Neighbours,* by the Marquis d'Argenson). That is exactly what Grotius did.

† See a small treatise by Plutarch, entitled *That Brutes Employ Reason.*

moderation will give satisfaction; for, as I am a direct descendant of one of these princes, and perhaps of the eldest branch, how do I know whether, by examination of titles, I might not find myself the lawful king of the human race? Be that as it may, it cannot be denied that Adam was sovereign of the world, as Robinson was of his island, so long as he was its sole inhabitant; and it was an agreeable feature of that empire that the monarch, secure on his throne, had nothing to fear from rebellions, or wars, or conspirators.

CHAPTER III

The Right of the Strongest

THE strongest man is never strong enough to be always master, unless he transforms his power into right, and obedience into duty. Hence the right of the strongest—a right apparently assumed in irony, and really established in principle. But will this phrase never be explained to us? Force is a physical power; I do not see what morality can result from its effects. To yield to force is an act of necessity, not of will; it is at most an act of prudence. In what sense can it be a duty?

Let us assume for a moment this pretended right. I say that nothing results from it but inexplicable nonsense; for if force constitutes right, the effect changes with the cause, and any force which overcomes the first succeeds to its rights. As soon as men can disobey with impunity, they may do so legitimately; and since the strongest is always in the right, the only thing is to act in such a way that one may be the strongest. But what sort of a right is it that perishes when force ceases? If it is necessary to obey by compulsion, there is no need to obey from duty;

and if men are no longer forced to obey, obligation is at an end. We see, then, that this word *right* adds nothing to force; it here means nothing at all.

Obey the powers that be. If that means, Yield to force, the precept is good but superfluous; I reply that it will never be violated. All power comes from God, I admit; but every disease comes from Him too; does it follow that we are prohibited from calling in a physician? If a brigand should surprise me in the recesses of a wood, am I bound not only to give up my purse when forced, but am I also morally bound to do so when I might conceal it? For, in effect, the pistol which he holds is a superior force.

Let us agree, then, that might does not make right, and that we are bound to obey none but lawful authorities. Thus my original question ever recurs.

CHAPTER IV

Slavery

SINCE no man has any natural authority over his fellow men, and since force is not the source of right, conventions remain as the basis of all lawful authority among men.

If an individual, says Grotius, can alienate his liberty and become the slave of a master, why should not a whole people be able to alienate theirs, and become subject to a king? In this there are many equivocal terms requiring explanation; but let us confine ourselves to the word *alienate*. To alienate is to give or sell. Now, a man who becomes another's slave does not give himself; he sells himself at the very least for his subsistence. But why does a nation sell itself? So far from a king supplying his subjects with their subsistence, he draws his from them; and, according to Rabelais, a king does not live on a little. Do subjects, then, give up their persons on condition that their property also shall be taken? I do not see what is left for them to keep.

It will be said that the despot secures to his subjects civil peace. Be it so; but what do they gain by that, if the wars which his ambition brings upon them, together with his insatiable greed and the vexations of his administration, harass them more than their own dissensions would? What do they gain by it if this tranquillity is itself one of their miseries? Men live tranquilly also in dungeons; is that enough to make them contented there? The Greeks confined in the cave of the Cyclops lived peacefully until their turn came to be devoured.

To say that a man gives himself for nothing is to say what is absurd and inconceivable; such an act is illegitimate and invalid, for the simple reason that he who performs it is not in his right mind. To say the same thing of a whole nation is to suppose a nation of fools; and madness does not confer rights.

Even if each person could alienate himself, he could not alienate his children; they are born free men; their liberty belongs to them, and no one has a right to dispose of it except themselves. Before they have come to years of discretion, the father can, in their name, stipulate conditions for their preservation and welfare, but not surrender them irrevocably and unconditionally; for such a gift is contrary to the ends of nature, and exceeds the rights of paternity. In order, then, that an arbitrary government might be legitimate, it would be necessary that the people in each generation should have the option of accepting or rejecting it; but in that case such a government would no longer be arbitrary.

To renounce one's liberty is to renounce one's quality as a man, the rights and also the duties of humanity. For him who renounces everything there is no possible compensation. Such a renunciation is incompatible with man's nature, for to take away all freedom from his will is to take away all morality from his actions. In short, a convention which stipulates absolute authority on the one side and unlimited obedience on the other is vain and contradictory. Is it not clear that we are under no obligations whatsoever towards a man from whom we have a right to demand everything? And does not this single condition, without equivalent, without exchange, involve the nullity of the act? For what right would my slave have against me, since all that he has belongs to me? His rights being mine, this right of me against myself is a meaningless phrase.

Grotius and others derive from war another origin for the pretended right of slavery. The victor having, according to them, the right of slaying the vanquished, the latter may purchase his life at the cost of his freedom; an agreement so much the more legitimate that it turns to the advantage of both.

But it is manifest that this pretended right of slaying the vanquished in no way results from the state of war. Men are not naturally enemies, if only for the reason that, living in their primitive independence, they have no mutual relations sufficiently durable to constitute a state of peace or a state of war. It is the relation of things and not of men which constitutes war; and since the state of war cannot arise from simple personal relations, but only from real relations, private war—war between man and man—cannot exist either in the state of nature, where there is no settled ownership, or in the social state, where everything is under the authority of the laws.

Private combats, duels, and encounters are acts which do not constitute a state of war; and with regard to the private wars authorized by the Establishments of Louis IX, king of France, and suspended by the Peace of God, they were abuses of the feudal government, an absurd system if ever there was one, contrary both to the principles of natural right and to all sound government.

War, then, is not a relation between man and man, but a relation between State and State, in which individuals are enemies only by accident, not as men, nor even as citizens,* but as soldiers; not as members of the fatherland, but as its defenders. In short, each State can have as enemies only other States and not individual men, inasmuch as it is impossible to fix any true relation between things of different kinds.

This principle is also conformable to the established maxims of all ages and to the invariable practice of all civilized nations. Declarations of war are not so much warnings to the powers as to their subjects. The foreigner, whether king, or nation, or private person, that robs, slays, or detains subjects without declaring war against the government, is not an enemy, but a brigand. Even in open war, a just prince, while he rightly takes possession of all that belongs to the State in an enemy's country, respects the person and property of individuals; he respects the rights on which his own are based. The aim of war being the destruction of the hostile State, we have a right to slay its defenders so long as they have arms in their hands; but as soon as they lay them down and surrender, ceasing to be enemies or instruments of the enemy, they become again simply men, and no one has any further right over their lives. Sometimes it is possible to destroy the State without killing a single one

---

* The Romans, who understood and respected the rights of war better than any nation in the world, carried their scruples so far in this respect that no citizen was allowed to serve as a volunteer without enlisting expressly against the enemy, and by name against a certain enemy. A legion in which Cato the younger made his first campaign under Popilius having been re-formed, Cato the elder wrote to Popilius that, if he consented to his son's continuing to serve under him, it was necessary that he should take a new military oath, because, the first being annulled, he could no longer bear arms against the enemy (Cicero, *De Officiis* I, 11). And Cato also wrote to his son to abstain from appearing in battle until he had taken this new oath. I know that it will be possible to urge against me the siege of Clusium and other particular cases; but I cite laws and customs (Livy, V. 35-37). No nation has transgressed its laws less frequently than the Romans, and no nation has had laws so admirable.

of its members; but war confers no right except what is necessary to its end. These are not the principles of Grotius; they are not based on the authority of poets, but are derived from the nature of things, and are founded on reason.

With regard to the right of conquest, it has no other foundation than the law of the strongest. If war does not confer on the victor the right of slaying the vanquished, this right, which he does not possess, cannot be the foundation of a right to enslave them. If we have a right to slay an enemy only when it is impossible to enslave him, the right to enslave him is not derived from the right to kill him; it is, therefore, an iniquitous bargain to make him purchase his life, over which the victor has no right, at the cost of his liberty. In establishing the right of life and death upon the right of slavery, and the right of slavery upon the right of life and death, is it not manifest that one falls into a vicious circle?

Even if we grant this terrible right of killing everybody, I say that a slave made in war, or a conquered nation, is under no obligation at all to a master, except to obey him so far as compelled. In taking an equivalent for his life the victor has conferred no favor on the slave; instead of killing him unprofitably, he has destroyed him for his own advantage. Far, then, from having acquired over him any authority in addition to that of force, the state of war subsists between them as before, their relation even is the effect of it; and the exercise of the rights of war supposes that there is no treaty of peace. They have made a convention. Be it so; but this convention, far from terminating the state of war, supposes its continuance.

Thus, in whatever way we regard things, the right of slavery is invalid, not only because it is illegitimate, but because it is absurd and meaningless. These terms, *slavery* and *right,* are contradictory and mutually exclusive. Whether addressed by a man to a man, or by a man to a nation, such a speech as this will always be equally foolish: "I make an agreement with you wholly at your expense and wholly for my benefit, and I shall observe it as long as I please, while you also shall observe it as long as I please."

CHAPTER V

That It Is Always Necessary To Go Back to a First Convention

IF I should concede all that I have so far refuted, those who favor despotism would be no farther advanced. There will always be a great difference between subduing a multitude and ruling a society. When isolated men, however numerous they may be, are subjected one after another to a single person, this seems to me only a case of master and slaves, not of a nation and its chief; they form, if you will, an aggregation, but not an association, for they have neither public property nor a body politic. Such a man, had he enslaved half the world, is never anything but an individual; his interest, separated from that of the rest, is never anything but a private interest. If he dies, his empire after him is left disconnected and disunited, as an oak dissolves and becomes a heap of ashes after the fire has consumed it.

A nation, says Grotius, can give itself to a king. According to Grotius, then, a nation is a nation before it gives itself to a king. This gift itself is a civil act, and presupposes a public resolution. Consequently, before examining the act by which a nation elects a king, it would be proper to examine the act by which a nation becomes a nation; for this act, being necessarily anterior to the other, is the real foundation of the society.

In fact, if there were no anterior convention, where, unless the election were unanimous, would be the obligation upon the minority to submit to the decision of the majority? And whence do the hundred who desire a master derive the right to vote on behalf of ten who do not desire one? The law of the plurality of votes is itself established by convention, and presupposes unanimity once at least.

CHAPTER VI

The Social Pact

I ASSUME that men have reached a point at which the obstacles that endanger their preservation in the state of nature overcome by their resistance the forces which each individual can exert with a view to maintaining himself in that state. Then this primitive condition can no longer subsist, and the human race would perish unless it changed its mode of existence.

Now, as men cannot create any new forces, but only combine and direct those that exist, they have no other means of self-preservation than to form by aggregation a sum of forces which may overcome the resistance, to put them in action by a single motive power, and to make them work in concert.

This sum of forces can be produced only by the combination of many; but the strength and freedom of each man being the chief instruments of his preservation, how can he pledge them without injuring himself, and without neglecting the cares which he owes to himself? This difficulty, applied to my subject, may be expressed in these terms:—

"To find a form of association which may defend and protect with the whole force of the community the person and property of every associate, and by means of which each, coalescing with all, may nevertheless obey only himself, and remain as free as before." Such is the fundamental problem of which the social contract furnishes the solution.

The clauses of this contract are so determined by the nature of the act that the slightest modification would render them vain and ineffectual; so that, although they have never perhaps been formally enunciated, they are everywhere the same, everywhere tacitly admitted and recognized, until, the social pact being violated, each man regains his original rights and recovers his natural liberty, while losing the conventional liberty for which he renounced it.

These clauses, rightly understood, are reducible to one only, viz., the total alienation to the whole community of each associate with all his rights; for, in the first place, since each gives himself up entirely, the conditions are equal for all; and, the conditions being equal for all, no one has any interest in making them burdensome to others.

Further, the alienation being made without reserve, the union is as perfect as it can be, and an individual associate can no longer claim anything; for, if any rights were left to individuals, since there would be no common superior who could judge between them and the public, each, being on some point his own judge, would soon claim to be so on all; the state of nature would still subsist, and the association would necessarily become tyrannical or useless.

In short, each giving himself to all, gives himself to nobody; and as there is not one associate over whom we do not acquire the same rights which we concede to him over ourselves, we gain the equivalent of all that we lose, and more power to preserve what we have.

If, then, we set aside what is not of the essence of the social contract, we shall find that it is reducible to the following terms: "Each of us puts in common his person and his whole power under the supreme direction of the general will; and in return we receive every member as an indivisible part of the whole."

Forthwith, instead of the individual personalities of all the contracting parties, this act of association produces a moral and collective body, which is composed of as many members as the assembly has voices, and which receives from this same act its unity, its common self (*moi*), its life, and its will. This public person, which is thus formed by the union of all the individual members, formerly took the name of *city*,* and now takes that of *republic* or *body politic,* which is called by its members *State* when it is passive, *sovereign* when it is active, *power* when it is compared to similar bodies. With regard to the associates, they take collectively the name of *people,* and are called individually *citizens,* as participating in the sovereign power, and *subjects,* as subjected to the laws of the State. But these terms are often confused and are mistaken one for another; it is sufficient to know how to distinguish them when they are used with complete precision.

---

* The real meaning of this word has been almost completely effaced among the moderns; the majority take a town for a city, and a burgess for a citizen. They do not know that houses make the town, and that citizens make the city. This very mistake cost the Carthaginians dear. I have never read of the title citizens (*cives*) being given to the subjects of a prince, not even in ancient times to the Macedonians, nor, in our days, to the English, although nearer liberty than all the rest. The French alone employ familiarly this name *citizen,* because they have no true idea of it, as we can see from their dictionaries; but for this fact, they would, by assuming it, commit the crime of high treason. The name, among them, expresses a virtue, not a right. When Bodin wanted to give an account of our citizens and burgesses he made a gross blunder, mistaking the one for the other. M. d'Alembert has not erred in this, and, in his article *Geneva,* has clearly distinguished the four orders of men (even five, counting mere foreigners) which exist in our town, and of which two only compose the republic. No other French author that I know of has understood the real meaning of the word *citizen.*

CHAPTER VII

The Sovereign

WE see from this formula that the act of association contains a reciprocal engagement between the public and individuals, and that every individual, contracting so to speak with himself, is engaged in a double relation, viz., as a member of the sovereign towards individuals, and as a member of the State towards the sovereign. But we cannot apply here the maxim of civil law that no one is bound by engagements made with himself; for there is a great difference between being bound to oneself and to a whole of which one forms part.

We must further observe that the public resolution which can bind all subjects to the sovereign in consequence of the two different relations under which each of them is regarded cannot, for a contrary reason, bind the sovereign to itself; and that accordingly it is contrary to the nature of the body politic for the sovereign to impose on itself a law which it cannot transgress. As it can only be considered under one and the same relation, it is in the position of an individual contracting with himself; whence we see that there is not, nor can be, any kind of fundamental law binding upon the body of the people, not even the social contract. This does not imply that such a body cannot perfectly well enter into engagements with others in what does not derogate from this contract; for, with regard to foreigners, it becomes a simple being, an individual.

But the body politic or sovereign, deriving its existence only from the sanctity of the contract, can never bind itself, even to others, in anything that derogates from the original act, such as alienation of some portion of itself, or submission to another sovereign. To violate the act by which it exists would be to annihilate itself; and what is nothing produces nothing.

So soon as the multitude is thus united in one body, it is impossible to injure one of the members without attacking the body, still less to injure the body without the members feeling the effects. Thus duty and interest alike oblige the two contracting parties to give mutual assistance; and the men themselves should seek to combine in this twofold relationship all the advantages which are attendant on it.

Now, the sovereign, being formed only of the individuals that compose it, neither has nor can have any interest contrary to theirs; consequently the sovereign power needs no guarantee towards its subjects, because it is impossible that the body should wish to injure all its members; and we shall see hereafter that it can injure no one as an individual. The sovereign, for the simple reason that it is so, is always everything that it ought to be.

But this is not the case as regards the relation of subjects to the sovereign, which, notwithstanding the common interest, would have no security for the performance of their engagements, unless it found means to ensure their fidelity.

Indeed, every individual may, as a man, have a particular will contrary to, or divergent from, the general will which he has as a citizen; his private interest may prompt him quite differently from the common interest; his absolute and naturally independent existence may make him regard what he owes to the common cause as a gratuitous contribution, the loss of which will be less harmful to others than the payment of it will be burdensome to him; and, regarding the moral person that constitutes the State as an imaginary being because it is not a man, he would be willing to enjoy the rights of a citizen without being willing to fulfil the duties of a subject. The progress of such injustice would bring about the ruin of the body politic.

In order, then, that the social pact may not be a vain formulary, it tacitly includes this engagement, which can alone give force to the others—that whoever refuses to obey the general will shall be constrained to do so by the whole body; which means nothing else than that he shall be forced to be free; for such is the condition which, uniting every citizen to his native land, guarantees him from all personal dependence, a condition that ensures the control and working of the political machine, and alone renders legitimate civil engagements, which, without it, would be absurd and tyrannical, and subject to the most enormous abuses.

CHAPTER VIII

The Civil State

THE passage from the state of nature to the civil state produces in man a very remarkable change, by substituting in his conduct justice for instinct, and by giving his actions the moral quality that they previously lacked. It is only when the voice of duty succeeds physical impulse, and law succeeds appetite, that man, who till then had regarded only himself, sees that he is obliged to act on other principles, and to consult his reason before listening to his inclinations. Although, in this state, he is deprived of many advantages that he derives from nature, he acquires equally great ones in return; his faculties are exercised and developed; his ideas are expanded; his feelings are ennobled; his whole soul is exalted to such a degree that, if the abuses of this new condition did not often degrade him below that from which he has emerged, he ought to bless without ceasing the happy moment that released him from it for ever, and transformed him from a stupid and ignorant animal into an intelligent being and a man.

Let us reduce this whole balance to terms easy to compare. What man loses by the social contract is his natural liberty and an unlimited right to anything which tempts him and which he is able to attain; what he gains is civil liberty and property in all that he possesses. In order that we may not be mistaken about these compensations, we must clearly distinguish natural liberty, which is limited only by the powers of the individual, from civil liberty, which is limited by the general will; and possession, which is nothing but the result of force or the right of first occupancy, from property, which can be based only on a positive title.

Besides the preceding, we might add to the acquisitions of the civil state moral freedom, which alone renders man truly master of himself; for the impulse of mere appetite is slavery, while obedience to a self-prescribed law is liberty. But I have already said too much on this head, and the philosophical meaning of the term *liberty* does not belong to my present subject.

CHAPTER IX

Real Property

EVERY member of the community at the moment of its formation gives himself up to it, just as he actually is, himself and all his powers, of which the property that he possesses forms part. By this act, possession does not change its nature when it changes hands, and become property in those of the sovereign; but, as the powers of the State (*cité*) are incomparably greater than those of an individual, public possession is also, in fact, more secure and more irrevocable, without being more legitimate, at least in respect of foreigners; for the State, with regard to its members, is owner of all their property by the social contract, which, in the State, serves as the basis of all rights; but with regard to other powers, it is owner only by the right of first occupancy which it derives from individuals.

The right of first occupancy, although more real than that of the strongest, becomes a true right only after the establishment of that of property. Every man has by nature a right to all that is necessary to him; but the positive act which makes him proprietor of certain property excludes him from all the residue. His portion having been allotted, he ought to confine himself to it, and he has no further right to the undivided property. That is why the right of first occupancy, so weak in the state of nature, is respected by every member of a State. In this right men regard not so much what belongs to others as what does not belong to themselves.

In order to legalize the right of first occupancy over any domain whatsoever, the following conditions are, in general, necessary: first, the land must not yet be inhabited by any one; secondly, a man must occupy only the area required for his subsistence; thirdly, he must take possession of it, not by an empty ceremony, but by labor and cultivation, the only mark of ownership which, in default of legal title, ought to be respected by others.

Indeed, if we accord the right of first occupancy to necessity and labor, do we not extend it as far as it can go? Is it impossible to assign limits to this right? Will the mere setting foot on common ground be sufficient to give an immediate claim to the ownership of it? Will the power of driving away other men from it for a moment suffice to deprive them for ever of the right of returning to it? How can a man or a people take possession of an immense territory and rob the whole human race of it except by a punishable usurpation, since other men are deprived of the place of residence and the sustenance which nature gives to them in common? When Núñez de Balboa on the seashore took possession of the Pacific Ocean and of the whole of South America in the name of the crown of Castille, was this sufficient to dispossess all the inhabitants, and exclude from it all the princes in the world? On this supposition, such ceremonies might have been multiplied vainly enough; and the Catholic king in his cabinet might, by a single stroke, have taken possession of the whole world, only cutting off afterwards from his empire what was previously occupied by other princes.

We perceive how the lands of individuals, united and contiguous, become public territory, and how the right of sovereignty, extending itself from the subjects to the land which they occupy, becomes at once real and personal; which places the possessors in greater dependence, and makes their own powers a guarantee for their fidelity—an advantage which ancient monarchs do not appear to have clearly perceived, for, calling themselves only kings of the Persians or Scythians or Macedonians, they seem to have regarded themselves as chiefs of men rather than as owners of countries. Monarchs of today call themselves more cleverly kings of France, Spain, England, etc.; in thus holding the land they are quite sure of holding its inhabitants.

The peculiarity of this alienation is that the community, in receiving the property of individuals, so far from robbing them of it, only assures them lawful possession, and changes usurpation into true right, enjoyment into ownership. Also, the possessors being considered as depositaries of the public property, and their rights being respected by all the members of the State, as well as maintained by all its power against foreigners, they have, as it were, by a transfer advantageous to the public and still more to themselves, acquired all that they have given up—a paradox which is easily explained by distinguishing between the rights which the sovereign and the proprietor have over the same property, as we shall see hereafter.

It may also happen that men begin to unite before they possess anything, and that afterwards occupying territory sufficient for all, they enjoy it in common, or share it among themselves, either equally or in proportions fixed by the sovereign. In whatever way this acquisition is made, the right which every individual has over his own property is always subordinate to the right which the community has over all; otherwise there would be no stability in the social union, and no real force in the exercise of sovereignty.

I shall close this chapter and this book with a remark which ought to serve as a basis for the whole social system; it is that instead of destroying natural equality, the fundamental pact, on the contrary, substitutes a moral and lawful equality for the physical inequality which nature imposed upon men, so that, although unequal in strength or intellect, they all become equal by convention and legal right.*

---

* Under bad governments this equality is only apparent and illusory; it serves only to keep the poor in their misery and the rich in their usurpations. In fact, laws are always useful to those who possess and injurious to those that have nothing; whence it follows that the social state is advantageous to men only so far as they all have something, and none of them has too much.

BOOK II

~~~~~~~~~~~~~~~~~~~~~~~~

CHAPTER I

That Sovereignty Is Inalienable

THE first and most important consequence of the principles above established is that the general will alone can direct the forces of the State according to the object of its institution, which is the common good; for if the opposition of private interests has rendered necessary the establishment of societies, the agreement of these same interests has rendered it possible. That which is common to these different interests forms the social bond; and unless there were some point in which all interests agree, no society could exist. Now, it is solely with regard to this common interest that the society should be governed.

I say, then, that sovereignty, being nothing but the exercise of the general will, can never be alienated, and that the sovereign power, which is only a collective being, can be represented by itself alone; power indeed can be transmitted, but not will.

In fact, if it is not impossible that a particular will should agree on some point with the general will, it is at least impossible that this agreement should be lasting and constant; for the particular will naturally tends to preferences, and the general will to equality. It is still more impossible to have a security for this agreement; even though it should always exist, it would not be a result of art, but of chance. The sovereign may indeed say: "I will now what a certain man wills, or at least what he says that he wills"; but he cannot say: "What that man wills tomorrow, I shall also will," since it is absurd that the will should bind itself as regards the future, and since it is not incumbent on any will to consent to anything contrary to the welfare of the being that wills. If, then, the nation simply promises to obey, it dissolves itself by that act and loses its character as a people; the moment there is a master, there is no longer a sovereign, and forthwith the body politic is destroyed.

This does not imply that the orders of the chiefs cannot pass for decisions of the general will, so long as the sovereign, free to oppose them, refrains from doing so. In such a case the consent of the people should be inferred from the universal silence. This will be explained at greater length.

CHAPTER II

That Sovereignty Is Indivisible

FOR the same reason that sovereignty is inalienable it is indivisible; for the will is either general,* or it is not; it is either that of the body of the people, or that of only a portion. In the first case, this declared will is an act of sovereignty and constitutes law; in the second case, it is only a particular will, or an act of magistracy—it is at most a decree.

But our publicists, being unable to divide sovereignty in its principle, divide it in its object. They divide it into

---

* That a will may be general, it is not always necessary that it should be unanimous, but it is necessary that all votes should be counted; any formal exclusion destroys the generality.

force and will, into legislative power and executive power; into rights of taxation, of justice, and of war; into internal administration and power of treating with foreigners— sometimes confounding all these departments, and sometimes separating them. They make the sovereign a fantastic being, formed of connected parts; it is as if they composed a man of several bodies, one with eyes, another with arms, another with feet, and nothing else. The Japanese conjurers, it is said, cut up a child before the eyes of the spectators; then, throwing all its limbs into the air, they make the child come down again alive and whole. Such almost are the jugglers' tricks of our publicists; after dismembering the social body, by a deception worthy of the fair, they recombine its parts, nobody knows how.

This error arises from their not having formed exact notions about the sovereign authority, and from their taking as parts of this authority what are only emanations from it. Thus, for example, the acts of declaring war and making peace have been regarded as acts of sovereignty, which is not the case, since neither of them is a law, but only an application of the law, a particular act which determines the case of the law, as will be clearly seen when the idea attached to the word *law* is fixed.

By following out the other divisions in the same way, it would be found that, whenever the sovereignty appears divided, we are mistaken in our supposition; and that the rights which are taken as parts of that sovereignty are all subordinate to it, and always suppose supreme wills of which these rights are merely executive.

It would be impossible to describe the great obscurity in which this want of precision has involved the conclusions of writers on the subject of political right when they have endeavored to decide upon the respective rights of kings and peoples on the principles that they had established. Every one can see, in chapters III and IV of the first book of Grotius, how that learned man and his translator Barbeyrac become entangled and embarrassed in their sophisms, for fear of saying too much or not saying enough according to their views, and so offending the interests that they had to conciliate. Grotius, having taken refuge in France through discontent with his own country, and wishing to pay court to Louis XIII, to whom his book is dedicated, spares no pains to despoil the people of all their rights, and, in the most artful manner, bestow them on kings. This also would clearly have been the inclination of Barbeyrac, who dedicated his translation to the king of England, George I. But unfortunately the expulsion of James II, which he calls an abdication, forced him to be reserved and to equivocate and evade, in order not to make William appear a usurper. If these two writers had adopted true principles, all difficulties would have been removed, and they would have been always consistent; but they would have spoken the truth with regret, and would have paid court only to the people. Truth, however, does not lead to fortune, and the people confer neither embassies, nor professorships, nor pensions.

CHAPTER III

Whether the General Will Can Err

It follows from what precedes that the general will is always right and always tends to the public advantage; but it does not follow that the resolutions of the people have always the same rectitude. Men always desire their own good, but do not always discern it; the people are never corrupted, though often deceived, and it is only then that they seem to will what is evil.

There is often a great deal of difference between the will of all and the general will; the latter regards only the common interest, while the former has regard to private interests, and is merely a sum of particular wills; but take away from these same wills the pluses and minuses which cancel one another,* and the general will remains as the sum of the differences.

If the people came to a resolution when adequately informed and without any communication among the citizens, the general will would always result from the great number of slight differences, and the resolution would always be good. But when factions, partial associations, are formed to the detriment of the whole society, the will of each of these associations becomes general with reference to its members, and particular with reference to the State; it may then be said that there are no longer as many voters as there are men, but only as many voters as there are associations. The differences become less numerous and yield a less general result. Lastly, when one of these associations becomes so great that it predominates over all the rest, you no longer have as the result a sum of small differences, but a single difference; there is then no longer a general will, and the opinion which prevails is only a particular opinion.

It is important, then, in order to have a clear declaration of the general will, that there should be no partial association in the State, and that every citizen should express only his own opinion.† Such was the unique and

---

* "Every interest," says the Marquis d'Argenson, "has different principles. The accord of two particular interests is formed by opposition to that of a third." He might have added that the accord of all interests is formed by opposition to that of each. Unless there were different interests, the common interest would scarcely be felt and would never meet with any obstacles; everything would go of itself, and politics would cease to be an art.

† "It is true," says Machiavelli, "that some divisions injure the State, while some are beneficial to it; those are injurious to it which are accompanied by cabals and factions; those assist it which are maintained without cabals, without factions. Since, therefore, no founder of a State can provide against enmities in it, he ought at least to provide that there shall be no cabals" (*History of Florence*, Book VII).

sublime institution of the great Lycurgus. But if there are partial associations, it is necessary to multiply their number and prevent inequality, as Solon, Numa, and Servius did. These are the only proper precautions for ensuring that the general will may always be enlightened, and that the people may not be deceived.

CHAPTER IV

The Limits of the Sovereign Power

IF the State or city is nothing but a moral person, the life of which consists in the union of its members, and if the most important of its cares is that of self-preservation, it needs a universal and compulsive force to move and dispose every part in the manner most expedient for the whole. As nature gives every man an absolute power over all his limbs, the social pact gives the body politic an absolute power over all its members; and it is this same power which, when directed by the general will, bears, as I said, the name of sovereignty.

But besides the public person, we have to consider the private persons who compose it, and whose life and liberty are naturally independent of it. The question, then, is to distinguish clearly between the respective rights of the citizens and of the sovereign,* as well as between the duties which the former have to fulfill in their capacity as subjects and the natural rights which they ought to enjoy in their character as men.

It is admitted that whatever part of his power, property,

---

* Attentive readers, do not, I beg you, hastily charge me with contradiction here. I could not avoid it in terms owing to the poverty of the language, but wait.

and liberty each one alienates by the social compact is only that part of the whole of which the use is important to the community; but we must also admit that the sovereign alone is judge of what is important.

All the services that a citizen can render to the State he owes to it as soon as the sovereign demands them; but the sovereign, on its part, cannot impose on its subjects any burden which is useless to the community; it cannot even wish to do so, for, by the law of reason, just as by the law of nature, nothing is done without a cause.

The engagements which bind us to the social body are obligatory only because they are mutual; and their nature is such that in fulfilling them we cannot work for others without also working for ourselves. Why is the general will always right, and why do all invariably desire the prosperity of each, unless it is because there is no one but appropriates to himself this word *each* and thinks of himself in voting on behalf of all? This proves that equality of rights and the notion of justice that it produces are derived from the preference which each gives to himself, and consequently from man's nature; that the general will, to be truly such, should be so in its object as well as in its essence; that it ought to proceed from all in order to be applicable to all; and that it loses its natural rectitude when it tends to some individual and determinate object, because in that case, judging of what is unknown to us, we have no true principle of equity to guide us.

Indeed, so soon as a particular fact or right is in question with regard to a point which has not been regulated by an anterior general convention, the matter becomes contentious; it is a process in which the private persons interested are one of the parties and the public the other, but in which I perceive neither the law which must be followed, nor the judge who should decide. It would be ridiculous in such a case to wish to refer the matter for an express decision of the general will, which can be nothing but the decision of one of the parties, and which, consequently, is for the other party only a will that is foreign, partial, and inclined on such an occasion to injustice as well as liable to error. Therefore, just as a particular will cannot represent the general will, the general will in turn changes its nature when it has a particular end, and cannot, as general, decide about either a person or a fact. When the people of Athens, for instance, elected or deposed their chiefs, decreed honors to one, imposed penalties on another, and by multitudes of particular decrees exercised indiscriminately all the functions of government, the people no longer had any general will properly so called; they no longer acted as a sovereign power, but as magistrates. This will appear contrary to common ideas, but I must be allowed time to expound my own.

From this we must understand that what generalizes the will is not so much the number of voices as the common interest which unites them; for, under this system, each necessarily submits to the conditions which he imposes on others—an admirable union of interest and justice, which gives to the deliberations of the community a spirit of equity that seems to disappear in the discussion of any private affair, for want of a common interest to unite and identify the ruling principle of the judge with that of the party.

By whatever path we return to our principle we always arrive at the same conclusion, viz., that the social compact establishes among the citizens such an equality that they all pledge themselves under the same conditions and ought all to enjoy the same rights. Thus, by the nature of the compact, every act of sovereignty, that is, every authentic act of the general will, binds or favors equally all the citizens; so that the sovereign knows only the body of the nation, and distinguishes none of those that compose it.

What, then, is an act of sovereignty properly so called? It is not an agreement between a superior and an inferior, but an agreement of the body with each of its members;

a lawful agreement, because it has the social contract as its foundation; equitable, because it is common to all; useful, because it can have no other object than the general welfare; and stable, because it has the public force and the supreme power as a guarantee. So long as the subjects submit only to such conventions, they obey no one, but simply their own will; and to ask how far the respective rights of the sovereign and citizens extend is to ask up to what point the latter can make engagements among themselves, each with all and all with each.

Thus we see that the sovereign power, wholly absolute, wholly sacred, and wholly inviolable as it is, does not, and cannot, pass the limits of general conventions, and that every man can fully dispose of what is left to him of his property and liberty by these conventions; so that the sovereign never has a right to burden one subject more than another, because then the matter becomes particular and his power is no longer competent.

These distinctions once admitted, so untrue is it that in the social contract there is on the part of individuals any real renunciation, that their situation, as a result of this contract, is in reality preferable to what it was before, and that, instead of an alienation, they have only made an advantageous exchange of an uncertain and precarious mode of existence for a better and more assured one, of natural independence for liberty, of the power to injure others for their own safety, and of their strength, which others might overcome, for a right which the social union renders inviolable. Their lives, also, which they have devoted to the State, are continually protected by it; and in exposing their lives for its defense, what do they do but restore what they have received from it? What do they do but what they would do more frequently and with more risk in the state of nature, when, engaging in inevitable struggles, they would defend at the peril of their lives their means of preservation? All have to fight for their country in case of need, it is true; but then no one ever has to fight for himself. Do we not gain, moreover, by incurring, for what insures our safety, a part of the risks that we should have to incur for ourselves individually, as soon as we were deprived of it?

CHAPTER V

The Right of Life and Death

It may be asked how individuals who have no right to dispose of their own lives can transmit to the sovereign this right which they do not possess. The question appears hard to solve only because it is badly stated. Every man has a right to risk his own life in order to preserve it. Has it ever been said that one who throws himself out of a window to escape from a fire is guilty of suicide? Has this crime, indeed, ever been imputed to a man who perishes in a storm, although, on embarking, he was not ignorant of the danger?

The social treaty has as its end the preservation of the contracting parties. He who desires the end desires also the means, and some risks, even some losses, are inseparable from these means. He who is willing to preserve his life at the expense of others ought also to give it up for them when necessary. Now, the citizen is not a judge of the peril to which the law requires that he should expose himself; and when the prince has said to him: "It is expedient for the State that you should die," he ought to die, since it is only on this condition that he has lived in security up to that time, and since his life is no longer merely a gift of nature, but a conditional gift of the State.

The penalty of death inflicted on criminals may be regarded almost from the same point of view; it is in order not to be the victim of an assassin that a man consents to die if he becomes one. In this treaty, far from disposing of his own life, he thinks only of securing it, and it is not to be supposed that any of the contracting parties contemplates at the time being hanged.

Moreover, every evildoer who attacks social rights becomes by his crimes a rebel and a traitor to his country; by violating its laws he ceases to be a member of it, and even makes war upon it. Then the preservation of the State is incompatible with his own—one of the two must perish; and when a guilty man is executed, it is less as a citizen than as an enemy. The proceedings and the judgment are the proofs and the declaration that he has broken the social treaty, and consequently that he is no longer a member of the State. Now, as he has acknowledged himself to be such, at least by his residence, he ought to be cut off from it by exile as a violator of the compact, or by death as a public enemy; for such an enemy is not a moral person, he is simply a man; and this is a case in which the right of war is to slay the vanquished.

But, it will be said, the condemnation of a criminal is a particular act. Granted; but this condemnation does not belong to the sovereign; it is a right which that power can confer, though itself unable to exercise it. All my ideas are connected, but I could not expound them all at once.

Again, the frequency of capital punishments is always a sign of weakness or indolence in the government. There is no man so worthless that he cannot be made good for something. We have a right to kill, even for example's sake, only those who cannot be preserved without danger.

As regards the right to pardon or to exempt a guilty man from the penalty imposed by the law and inflicted by the judge, it belongs only to a power which is above both the judge and the law, that is to say, the sovereign; still its right in this is not very plain, and the occasions for exercising it are very rare. In a well-governed State there are few punishments, not because many pardons are granted, but because there are few criminals; the multitude of crimes insures impunity when the State is decaying. Under the Roman Republic neither the Senate nor the consuls attempted to grant pardons; the people even did not grant any, although they sometimes revoked their own judgments. Frequent pardons proclaim that crimes will soon need them no longer, and every one sees to what that leads. But I feel my heart murmuring and restraining my pen; let us leave these questions to be discussed by the just man who has not erred, and who never needed pardon himself.

CHAPTER VI

The Law

BY the social compact we have given existence and life to the body politic; the question now is to endow it with movement and will by legislation. For the original act by which this body is formed and consolidated determines nothing in addition as to what it must do for its own preservation.

What is right and conformable to order is such by the nature of things, and independently of human conventions. All justice comes from God, He alone is the source of it; but could we receive it direct from so lofty a source, we should need neither government nor laws. Without doubt there is a universal justice emanating from reason alone; but this justice, in order to be admitted among us, should be reciprocal. Regarding things from a human standpoint, the laws of justice are inoperative among men for want of a natural sanction; they only bring good to the wicked and evil to the just when the latter observe them with every one, and no one observes them in return. Conventions and laws, then, are necessary to couple rights with duties and apply justice to its object. In the state of nature, where everything is in common, I owe nothing to those to whom I have promised nothing; I recognize as belonging to others only what is useless to me. This is not the case in the civil state, in which all rights are determined by law.

But then, finally, what is a law? So long as men are content to attach to this word only metaphysical ideas, they will continue to argue without being understood; and when they have stated what a law of nature is, they will know no better what a law of the State is.

I have already said that there is no general will with reference to a particular object. In fact, this particular object is either in the State or outside of it. If it is outside the State, a will which is foreign to it is not general in relation to it; and if it is within the State, it forms part of it; then there is formed between the whole and its part a relation which makes of it two separate beings, of which the part is one, and the whole, less this same part, is the other. But the whole less one part is not the whole, and so long as the relation subsists, there is no longer any whole, but two unequal parts; whence it follows that the will of the one is no longer general in relation to the other.

But when the whole people decree concerning the whole people, they consider themselves alone; and if a relation is then constituted, it is between the whole object under one point of view and the whole object under another point of view, without any division at all. Then the matter respecting which they decree is general like the will that decrees. It is this act that I call a law.

When I say that the object of the laws is always general, I mean that the law considers subjects collectively, and actions as abstract, never a man as an individual nor a particular action. Thus the law may indeed decree that there shall be privileges, but cannot confer them on any person by name; the law can create several classes of citizens, and even assign the qualifications which shall entitle them to rank in these classes, but it cannot nominate such and such persons to be admitted to them; it can establish a royal government and a hereditary succession, but cannot elect a king or appoint a royal family; in a word, no function which has reference to an individual object appertains to the legislative power.

From this standpoint we see immediately that it is no longer necessary to ask whose office it is to make laws, since they are acts of the general will; nor whether the prince is above the laws, since he is a member of the State; nor whether the law can be unjust, since no one is unjust to himself; nor how we are free and yet subject to the laws, since the laws are only registers of our wills.

We see, further, that since the law combines the universality of the will with the universality of the object, whatever any man prescribes on his own authority is not a law; and whatever the sovereign itself prescribes respecting a particular object is not a law, but a decree, not an act of sovereignty, but of magistracy.

I therefore call any State a republic which is governed by laws, under whatever form of administration it may be; for then only does the public interest predominate and the commonwealth count for something. Every legitimate government is republican; * I will explain hereafter what government is.

Laws are properly only the conditions of civil associations. The people, being subjected to the laws, should be the authors of them; it concerns only the associates to determine the conditions of association. But how will they be determined? Will it be by a common agreement, by a sudden inspiration? Has the body politic an organ for expressing its will? Who will give it the foresight

---

* I do not mean by this word an aristocracy or democracy only, but in general any government directed by the general will, which is the law. To be legitimate, the government must not be combined with the sovereign power, but must be its minister; then monarchy itself is a republic. This will be made clear in the next book.

necessary to frame its acts and publish them at the outset? Or how shall it declare them in the hour of need? How would a blind multitude, which often knows not what it wishes because it rarely knows what is good for it, execute of itself an enterprise so great, so difficult, as a system of legislation? Of themselves, the people always desire what is good, but do not always discern it. The general will is always right, but the judgment which guides it is not always enlightened. It must be made to see objects as they are, sometimes as they ought to appear; it must be shown the good path that it is seeking, and guarded from the seduction of private interests; it must be made to observe closely times and places, and to balance the attraction of immediate and palpable advantages against the danger of remote and concealed evils. Individuals see the good which they reject; the public desire the good which they do not see. All alike have need of guides. The former must be compelled to conform their wills to their reason; the people must be taught to know what they require. Then from the public enlightenment results the union of the understanding and the will in the social body; and from that the close cooperation of the parts, and, lastly, the maximum power of the whole. Hence arises the need of a legislator.

CHAPTER VII

The Legislator

In order to discover the rules of association that are most suitable to nations, a superior intelligence would be necessary who could see all the passions of men without experiencing any of them; who would have no affinity with our nature and yet know it thoroughly; whose happiness would not depend on us, and who would nevertheless be quite willing to interest himself in ours; and, lastly, one who, storing up for himself with the progress of time a far-off glory in the future, could labor in one age and enjoy in another.* Gods would be necessary to give laws to men.

The same argument that Caligula adduced as to fact, Plato put forward with regard to right, in order to give an idea of the civil or royal man whom he is in quest of in his work the *Statesman*. But if it is true that a great prince is a rare man, what will a great legislator be? The first has only to follow the model which the other has to frame. The latter is the mechanician who invents the machine, the former is only the workman who puts it in readiness and works it. "In the birth of societies," says Montesquieu, "it is the chiefs of the republics who frame the institutions, and afterwards it is the institutions which mold the chiefs of the republics."

---

* A nation becomes famous only when its legislation is beginning to decline. We are ignorant during how many centuries the institutions of Lycurgus conferred happiness on the Spartans before they were known in the rest of Greece.

He who dares undertake to give institutions to a nation ought to feel himself capable, as it were, of changing human nature; of transforming every individual, who in himself is a complete and independent whole, into part of a greater whole, from which he receives in some manner his life and his being; of altering man's constitution in order to strengthen it; of substituting a social and moral existence for the independent and physical existence which we have all received from nature. In a word, it is necessary to deprive man of his native powers in order to endow him with some which are alien to him, and of which he cannot make use without the aid of other people. The more thoroughly those natural powers are deadened and destroyed, the greater and more durable are the acquired powers, the more solid and perfect also are the institutions; so that if every citizen is nothing, and can be nothing, except in combination with all the rest, and if the force acquired by the whole be equal or superior to the sum of the natural forces of all the individuals, we may say that legislation is at the highest point of perfection which it can attain.

The legislator is in all respects an extraordinary man in the State. If he ought to be so by his genius, he is not less so by his office. It is not magistracy nor sovereignty. This office, which constitutes the republic, does not enter into its constitution; it is a special and superior office, having nothing in common with human government; for, if he who rules men ought not to control legislation, he who controls legislation ought not to rule men; otherwise his laws, being ministers of his passions, would often serve only to perpetuate his acts of injustice; he would never be able to prevent private interests from corrupting the sacredness of his work.

When Lycurgus gave laws to his country, he began by abdicating his royalty. It was the practice of the majority of the Greek towns to entrust to foreigners the framing of their laws. The modern republics of Italy often imitated this usage; that of Geneva did the same and found it advantageous.* Rome, at her most glorious epoch, saw all the crimes of tyranny spring up in her bosom, and saw herself on the verge of destruction, through uniting in the same hands legislative authority and sovereign power.

Yet the Decemvirs themselves never arrogated the right to pass any law on their sole authority. Nothing that we propose to you, they said to the people, can pass into law without your consent. Romans, be yourselves the authors of the laws which are to secure your happiness.

He who frames laws, then, has, or ought to have, no legislative right, and the people themselves cannot, even if they wished, divest themselves of this incommunicable right, because, according to the fundamental compact, it is only the general will that binds individuals, and we can never be sure that a particular will is conformable to the general will until it has been submitted to the free votes of the people. I have said this already, but it is not useless to repeat it.

Thus we find simultaneously in the work of legislation two things that seem incompatible—an enterprise surpassing human powers, and, to execute it, an authority that is a mere nothing.

Another difficulty deserves attention. Wise men who want to speak to the vulgar in their own language instead of in a popular way will not be understood. Now, there are a thousand kinds of ideas which it is impossible to translate into the language of the people. Views very general and objects very remote are alike beyond its reach; and each individual, approving of no other plan of government than that which promotes his own in-

---

* Those who consider Calvin only as a theologian are but little acquainted with the extent of his genius. The preparation of our wise edicts, in which he had a large share, does him as much credit as his *Institutes*. Whatever revolution time may bring about in our religion, so long as love of country and of liberty is not extinct among us, the memory of that great man will not cease to be revered.

terests, does not readily perceive the benefits that he is to derive from the continual deprivations which good laws impose. In order that a newly formed nation might approve sound maxims of politics and observe the fundamental rules of state-policy, it would be necessary that the effect should become the cause; that the social spirit, which should be the work of the institution, should preside over the institution itself, and that men should be, prior to the laws, what they ought to become by means of them. Since, then, the legislator cannot employ either force or reasoning, he must needs have recourse to an authority of a different order, which can compel without violence and persuade without convincing.

It is this which in all ages has constrained the founders of nations to resort to the intervention of heaven, and to give the gods the credit for their own wisdom, in order that the nations, subjected to the laws of the State as to those of nature, and recognizing the same power in the formation of man and in that of the State, might obey willingly, and bear submissively the yoke of the public welfare.

The legislator puts into the mouths of the immortals that sublime reason which soars beyond the reach of common men, in order that he may win over by divine authority those whom human prudence could not move.* But it does not belong to every man to make the gods his oracles, nor to be believed when he proclaims himself their interpreter. The great soul of the legislator is the real miracle which must give proof of his mission. Any man can engrave tables of stone, or bribe an oracle, or pretend secret intercourse with some divinity, or train a bird to speak in his ear, or find some other clumsy

---

* "It is true," says Machiavelli, "there never was in a nation any promulgator of extraordinary laws who had not recourse to God, because otherwise they would not have been accepted; for there are many advantages recognized by a wise man which are not so self-evident that they can convince others" (*Discourses on Titus Livius,* Book I, chapter 11).

means to impose on the people. He who is acquainted with such means only will perchance be able to assemble a crowd of foolish persons; but he will never found an empire, and his extravagant work will speedily perish with him. Empty deceptions form but a transient bond; it is only wisdom that makes it lasting. The Jewish law, which still endures, and that of the child of Ishmael, which for ten centuries has ruled half the world, still bear witness today to the great men who dictated them; and while proud philosophy or blind party spirit sees in them nothing but fortunate impostors, the true statesman admires in their systems the great and powerful genius which directs durable institutions.

It is not necessary from all this to infer with Warburton that politics and religion have among us a common aim, but only that, in the origin of nations, one serves as an instrument of the other.

CHAPTER VIII

The People

As an architect, before erecting a large edifice, examines and tests the soil in order to see whether it can support the weight, so a wise lawgiver does not begin by drawing up laws that are good in themselves, but considers first whether the people for whom he designs them are fit to endure them. It is on this account that Plato refused to legislate for the Arcadians and Cyrenians, knowing that these two peoples were rich and could not tolerate equality; and it is on this account that good laws and worthless men were to be found in Crete, for Minos had only disciplined a people steeped in vice.

A thousand nations that have flourished on the earth could never have borne good laws; and even those that might have done so could have succeeded for only a very short period of their whole duration. The majority of nations, as well as of men, are tractable only in their youth; they become incorrigible as they grow old. When once customs are established and prejudices have taken root, it is a perilous and futile enterprise to try and reform them; for the people cannot even endure that their evils should be touched with a view to their removal, like those stupid and cowardly patients that shudder at the sight of a physician.

But just as some diseases unhinge men's minds and deprive them of all remembrance of the past, so we sometimes find, during the existence of States, epochs of violence, in which revolutions produce an influence upon nations such as certain crises produce upon individuals, in which horror of the past supplies the place of forgetfulness, and in which the State, inflamed by civil wars, springs forth so to speak from its ashes, and regains the vigour of youth in issuing from the arms of death. Such was Sparta in the time of Lycurgus, such was Rome after the Tarquins, and such among us moderns were Holland and Switzerland after the expulsion of their tyrants.

But these events are rare; they are exceptions, the explanation of which is always found in the particular constitution of the excepted State. They could not even happen twice with the same nation; for it may render itself free so long as it is merely barbarous, but can no longer do so when the resources of the State are exhausted. Then commotions may destroy it without revolutions being able to restore it, and as soon as its chains are broken, it falls in pieces and ceases to exist; henceforward it requires a master and not a deliverer. Free nations, remember this maxim: "Liberty may be acquired but never recovered."

Youth is not infancy. There is for nations as for men

a period of youth, or, if you will, of maturity, which they must await before they are subjected to laws; but it is not always easy to discern when a people is mature, and if the time is anticipated, the labor is abortive. One nation is governable from its origin, another is not so at the end of ten centuries. The Russians will never be really civilized, because they have been civilized too early. Peter had an imitative genius; he had not the true genius that creates and produces anything from nothing. Some of his measures were beneficial, but the majority were ill-timed. He saw that his people were barbarous, but he did not see that they were unripe for civilization; he wished to civilize them, when it was necessary only to discipline them. He wished to produce at once Germans or Englishmen, when he should have begun by making Russians; he prevented his subjects from ever becoming what they might have been, by persuading them that they were what they were not. It is in this way that a French tutor trains his pupil to shine for a moment in childhood, and then to be for ever a nonentity. The Russian Empire will desire to subjugate Europe, and will itself be subjugated. The Tartars, its subjects or neighbors, will become its masters and ours. This revolution appears to me inevitable. All the kings of Europe are working in concert to accelerate it.

CHAPTER IX

The People (continued)

As nature has set limits to the stature of a properly formed man, outside which it produces only giants and dwarfs; so likewise, with regard to the best constitution of a State, there are limits to its possible extent so that it may be neither too great to enable it to be well-governed, nor too small to enable it to maintain itself single-handed. There is in every body politic a maximum of force which it cannot exceed, and which is often diminished as the State is aggrandized. The more the social bond is extended, the more it is weakened; and, in general, a small State is proportionally stronger than a large one.

A thousand reasons demonstrate the truth of this maxim. In the first place, administration becomes more difficult at great distances, as a weight becomes heavier at the end of a longer lever. It also becomes more burdensome in proportion as its parts are multiplied; for every town has first its own administration, for which the people pay; every district has its administration, still paid for by the people; next, every province, then the superior governments, the satrapies, the vice-royalties, which must be paid for more dearly as we ascend, and always at the cost of the unfortunate people; lastly comes the supreme administration, which overwhelms everything. So many additional burdens perpetually exhaust the subjects; and far from being better governed by all these different orders, they are much worse governed than if they had but a single superior. Meanwhile, hardly any resources remain for cases of emergency; and when it is necessary to have recourse to them the State trembles on the brink of ruin.

Nor is this all; not only has the government less vigor and activity in enforcing observance of the laws, in putting a stop to vexations, in reforming abuses, and in forestalling seditious enterprises which may be entered upon in distant places; but the people have less affection for their chiefs whom they never see, for their country, which is in their eyes like the world, and for their fellow-citizens, most of whom are strangers to them. The same laws cannot be suitable to so many different provinces, which have different customs and different climates, and cannot tolerate the same form of government. Different laws beget only trouble and confusion among the nations which, living under the same chiefs and in constant communication, mingle or intermarry with one another, and, when subjected to other usages, never know whether their patrimony is really theirs. Talents are hidden, virtues ignored, vices unpunished, in that multitude of men, unknown to one another, whom the seat of the supreme administration gathers together in one place. The chiefs, overwhelmed with business, see nothing themselves; clerks rule the State. In a word, the measures that must be taken to maintain the general authority, which so many officers at a distance wish to evade or impose upon, absorb all the public attention; no regard for the welfare of the people remains, and scarcely any for their defense in time of need; and thus a body too huge for its constitution sinks and perishes, crushed by its own weight.

On the other hand, the State must secure a certain foundation, that it may possess stability and resist the shocks which it will infallibly experience, as well as sustain the efforts which it will be forced to make in order to maintain itself; for all nations have a kind of centrifugal force, by which they continually act one against another, and tend to aggrandize themselves at the expense of their neighbors, like the vortices of Descartes. Thus the weak are in danger of being quickly swallowed up, and none can preserve itself long except by putting itself in a kind of equilibrium with all, which renders the compression almost equal everywhere.

Hence we see that there are reasons for expansion and reasons for contraction; and it is not the least of a statesman's talents to find the proportion between the two which is most advantageous for the preservation of the State. We may say, in general, that the former, being only external and relative, ought to be subordinated to the others, which are internal and absolute. A healthy and strong constitution is the first thing to be sought; and we should rely more on the vigor that springs from a good government than on the resources furnished by an extensive territory.

States have, however, been constituted in such a way that the necessity of making conquests entered into their very constitution, and in order to maintain themselves they were forced to enlarge themselves continually. Perhaps they rejoiced greatly at this happy necessity, which nevertheless revealed to them, with the limit of their greatness, the inevitable moment of their fall.

CHAPTER X

The People (continued)

A BODY politic may be measured in two ways, viz., by the extent of its territory, and by the number of its people; and there is between these two modes of measurement a suitable relation according to which the State may be assigned its true dimensions. It is the men that constitute the State, and it is the soil that sustains the men; the due relation, then, is that the land should suffice for the maintenance of its inhabitants, and that there should be as many inhabitants as the land can sustain. In this proportion is found the maximum power of a given number of people; for if there is too much land, the care of it is burdensome, the cultivation inadequate, and the produce superfluous, and this is the proximate cause of defensive wars. If there is not enough land, the State is at the mercy of its neighbors for the additional quantity; and this is the proximate cause of offensive wars. Any nation which has, by its position, only the alternative between commerce and war is weak in itself; it is dependent on its neighbors and on events; it has only a short and precarious existence. It conquers and changes its situation, or it is conquered and reduced to nothing. It can preserve its freedom only by virtue of being small or great.

It is impossible to express numerically a fixed ratio between the extent of land and the number of men which are reciprocally sufficient, on account of the differences that are found in the quality of the soil, in its degree of fertility, in the nature of its products, and in the influence of climate, as well as on account of those which we observe in the constitutions of the inhabitants, of whom some consume little in a fertile country, while others consume much on an unfruitful soil. Further, attention must be paid to the greater or less fecundity of the women, to the conditions of the country, whether more or less favorable to population, and to the numbers which the legislator may hope to draw thither by his institutions; so that an opinion should be based not on what is seen, but on what is foreseen, while the actual state of the people should be less observed than that which it ought naturally to attain. In short, there are a thousand occasions on which the particular accidents of situation require or permit that more territory than appears necessary should be taken up. Thus men will spread out a good deal in a mountainous country, where the natural productions, viz., woods and pastures, require less labor, where experience teaches that women are more fecund than in the plains, and where with an extensive inclined surface there is only a small horizontal base, which alone should count for vegetation. On the other hand, people may inhabit a smaller space on the seashore, even among rocks and sands that are almost barren, because fishing can, in great measure, supply the deficiency in the productions of the earth, because men ought to be more concentrated in order to repel pirates, and because, further, it is easier to relieve the country, by means of colonies, of the inhabitants with which it is overburdened.

In order to establish a nation, it is necessary to add to these conditions one which cannot supply the place of any other, but without which they are all useless—it is that the people should enjoy abundance and peace; for the time of a State's formation is, like that of forming soldiers in a square, the time when the body is least capable of resistance and most easy to destroy. Resistance would be greater in a state of absolute disorder than at a moment of fermentation, when each is occupied with his own position and not with the common danger. Should a war, a famine, or a sedition supervene at this critical period, the State is inevitably overthrown.

Many governments, indeed, may be established during such storms, but then it is these very governments that destroy the State. Usurpers always bring about or select troublous times for passing, under cover of the public agitation, destructive laws which the people would never adopt when sober-minded. The choice of the moment for the establishment of a government is one of the surest marks for distinguishing the work of the legislator from that of the tyrant.

What nation, then, is adapted for legislation? That which is already united by some bond of interest, origin, or convention, but has not yet borne the real yoke of the laws; that which has neither customs nor superstitions firmly rooted; that which has no fear of being over-whelmed by a sudden invasion, but which, without entering into the disputes of its neighbors, can single-handed resist either of them, or aid one in repelling the other, that in which every member can be known by all, and in which there is no necessity to lay on a man a greater burden than a man can bear; that which can subsist without other nations, and without which every other nation can subsist,* that which is neither rich nor poor and is self-sufficing; lastly, that which combines the stability of an old nation with the docility of a new one. The work of legislation is rendered arduous not so much by what must be established as by what must be destroyed; and that which makes success so rare is the impossibility of finding the simplicity of nature conjoined with the necessities of society. All these conditions, it is true, are with difficulty combined; hence few well-constituted States are seen.

There is still one country in Europe capable of legislation; it is the island of Corsica. The courage and firmness which that brave nation has exhibited in recovering and defending its freedom would well deserve that some wise man should teach it how to preserve it. I have some presentiment that this small island will one day astonish Europe.

---

* If of two neighboring nations one could not subsist without the other, it would be a very hard situation for the first, and a very dangerous one for the second. Every wise nation in such a case will endeavor very quickly to free the other from this dependence. The republic of Thlascala, enclosed in the empire of Mexico, preferred to do without salt rather than buy it of the Mexicans or even accept it gratuitously. The wise Thlascalans saw a trap hidden beneath this generosity. They kept themselves free; and this small State, enclosed in that great empire, was at last the instrument of its downfall.

CHAPTER XI

The Different Systems of Legislation

IF we ask precisely wherein consists the greatest good of all, which ought to be the aim of every system of legislation, we shall find that it is summed up in two principal objects, *liberty* and *equality*—liberty, because any individual dependence is so much force withdrawn from the body of the State; equality, because liberty cannot subsist without it.

I have already said what civil liberty is. With regard to equality, we must not understand by this word that the degrees of power and wealth should be absolutely the same; but that, as to power, it should fall short of all violence, and never be exercised except by virtue of station and of the laws; while, as to wealth, no citizen should be rich enough to be able to buy another, and none poor enough to be forced to sell himself,* which supposes, on the part of the great, moderation in property and influence, and, on the part of ordinary citizens, repression of avarice and covetousness.

It is said that this equality is a chimera of speculation which cannot exist in practical affairs. But if the abuse is inevitable, does it follow that it is unnecessary even to

---

* If, then, you wish to give stability to the State, bring the two extremes as near together as possible; tolerate neither rich people nor beggars. These two conditions, naturally inseparable, are equally fatal to the general welfare; from the one class spring tyrants, from the other, the supporters of tyranny; it is always between these that the traffic in public liberty is carried on; the one buys and the other sells.

regulate it? It is precisely because the force of circumstances is ever tending to destroy equality that the force of legislation should always tend to maintain it.

But these general objects of every good institution ought to be modified in each country by the relations which arise both from the local situation and from the character of the inhabitants; and it is with reference to these relations that we must assign to each nation a particular system of institutions, which shall be the best, not perhaps in itself, but for the State for which it is designed. For instance, if the soil is unfruitful and barren, or the country too confined for its inhabitants, turn your attention to arts and manufactures, and exchange their products for the provisions that you require. On the other hand, if you occupy rich plains and fertile slopes, if, in a productive region, you are in need of inhabitants, bestow all your cares on agriculture, which multiplies men, and drive out the arts, which would only end in depopulating the country by gathering together in a few spots the few inhabitants that the land possesses.* If you occupy extensive and convenient coasts, cover the sea with vessels and foster commerce and navigation; you will have a short and brilliant existence. If the sea on your coasts bathes only rocks that are almost inaccessible, remain fish-eating barbarians; you will lead more peaceful, perhaps better, and certainly happier lives. In a word, besides the maxims common to all, each nation contains within itself some cause which influences it in a particular way, and renders its legislation suitable for it alone. Thus the Hebrews in ancient times, and the Arabs more recently, had religion as their chief object, the Athenians literature, Carthage and Tyre commerce, Rhodes navigation, Sparta war, Rome valor. The author of the *Spirit of the Laws*

---

* Any branch of foreign commerce, says the Marquis d'Argenson, diffuses merely a deceptive utility through the kingdom generally; it may enrich a few individuals, even a few towns, but the nation as a whole gains nothing, and the people are none the better for it.

has shown in a multitude of instances by what arts the legislator directs his institutions towards each of these objects.

What renders the constitution of a State really solid and durable is the observance of expediency in such a way that natural relations and the laws always coincide, the latter only serving, as it were, to secure, support, and rectify the former. But if the legislator, mistaken in his object, takes a principle different from that which springs from the nature of things; if the one tends to servitude, the other to liberty, the one to riches, the other to population, the one to peace, the other to conquests, we shall see the laws imperceptibly weakened and the constitution impaired; and the State will be ceaselessly agitated until it is destroyed or changed, and invincible nature has resumed her sway.

CHAPTER XII

Division of the Laws

IN order that everything may be duly regulated and the best possible form given to the commonwealth, there are various relations to be considered. First, the action of the whole body acting on itself, that is, the relation of the whole to the whole, or of the sovereign to the State; and this relation is composed of that of the intermediate terms, as we shall see hereafter.

The laws governing this relation bear the name of political laws, and are also called fundamental laws, not without some reason if they are wise ones; for, if in every State there is only one good method of regulating it, the people which has discovered it ought to adhere to it; but if the established order is bad, why should we regard as fundamental laws which prevent it from being good? Besides, in any case, a nation is always at liberty to change its laws, even the best; for if it likes to injure itself, who has a right to prevent it from doing so?

The second relation is that of the members with one another, or with the body as a whole, and this relation should, in respect of the first, be as small, and, in respect of the second, as great as possible; so that every citizen may be perfectly independent of all the rest, and in absolute dependence on the State. And this is always effected by the same means, for it is only the power of the State that secures the freedom of its members. It is from this second relation that civil laws arise.

We may consider a third kind of relation between the individual man and the law, viz., that of punishable disobedience; and this gives rise to the establishment of criminal laws, which at bottom are not so much a particular species of laws as the sanction of all the others.

To these three kinds of laws is added a fourth, the most important of all, which is graven neither on marble nor on brass, but in the hearts of the citizens; a law which creates the real constitution of the State, which acquires new strength daily, which, when other laws grow obsolete or pass away, revives them or supplies their place, preserves a people in the spirit of their institutions, and imperceptibly substitutes the force of habit for that of authority. I speak of manners, customs, and above all of opinion—a province unknown to our politicians, but one on which the success of all the rest depends; a province with which the great legislator is occupied in private, while he appears to confine himself to particular regulations, that are merely the arching of the cult, of which manners, slow to develop, form at length the immovable keystone.

Of these different classes, political laws, which constitute the form of government, alone relate to my subject.

BOOK III

BEFORE speaking of the different forms of government, let us try to fix the precise meaning of that word, which has not yet been very clearly explained.

CHAPTER I

Government in General

I WARN the reader that this chapter must be read carefully, and that I do not know the art of making myself intelligible to those that will not be attentive.

Every free action has two causes concurring to produce it; the one moral, viz., the will which determines the act; the other physical, viz., the power which executes it. When I walk towards an object, I must first will to go to it; in the second place, my feet must carry me to it. Should a paralytic wish to run, or an active man not wish to do so, both will remain where they are. The body politic has the same motive powers; in it, likewise, force and will are distinguished, the latter under the name of *legislative power,* the former under the name of *executive power*. Nothing is, or ought to be, done in it without their cooperation.

We have seen that the legislative power belongs to the people and can belong to it alone. On the other hand, it is easy to see from the principles already established, that the executive power cannot belong to the people generally as legislative or sovereign, because that power is exerted only in particular acts, which are not within the province of the law, nor consequently within that of the sovereign, all the acts of which must be laws.

The public force, then, requires a suitable agent to concentrate it and put it in action according to the directions of the general will, to serve as a means of communication between the State and the sovereign, to effect in some manner in the public person what the union of soul and body effects in a man. This is, in the State, the function of the government, improperly confounded with the sovereign of which it is only the minister.

What, then, is the government? An intermediate body established between the subjects and the sovereign for their mutual correspondence, charged with the execution of the laws and with the maintenance of liberty both civil and political.

The members of this body are called magistrates or *kings,* that is, *governors;* and the body as a whole bears the name *Prince.* Those therefore who maintain that the act by which a people submits to its chiefs is not a contract are quite right. It is absolutely nothing but a commission, an employment, in which, as simple officers of the sovereign, they exercise in its name the power of which it has made them depositaries, and which it can limit, modify, and resume when it pleases. The alienation of such a right, being incompatible with the nature of the social body, is contrary to the object of the association.

Consequently, I give the name *government* or supreme administration to the legitimate exercise of the executive power, and that of Prince or magistrate to the man or body charged with that administration.

It is in the government that are found the intermediate powers, the relations of which constitute the relation of the whole to the whole, or of the sovereign to the State. This last relation can be represented by that of the extremes of a continued proportion, of which the mean

---

* It is for this reason that at Venice the title of Most Serene Prince is given to the College, even when the Doge does not attend it.

proportional is the government. The government receives from the sovereign the commands which it gives to the people; and in order that the State may be in stable equilibrium it is necessary, everything being balanced, that there should be equality between the product or the power of the government taken by itself, and the product or power of the citizens, who are sovereign in the one aspect and subjects in the other.

Further, we could not alter any of the three terms without at once destroying the proportion. If the sovereign wishes to govern, or if the magistrate wishes to legislate, or if the subjects refuse to obey, disorder succeeds order, force and will no longer act in concert, and the State being dissolved falls into despotism or anarchy. Lastly, as there is but one mean proportional between each relation, there is only one good government possible in a State; but as a thousand events may change the relations of a people, not only may different governments be good for different peoples, but for the same people at different times.

To try and give an idea of the different relations that may exist between these two extremes, I will take for example the number of the people, as a relation most easy to express.

Let us suppose that the State is composed of ten thousand citizens. The sovereign can only be considered collectively and as a body; but every private person, in his capacity of subject, is considered as an individual; therefore the sovereign is to the subject as ten thousand is to one, that is, each member of the State has as his share only one ten-thousandth part of the sovereign authority, although he is entirely subjected to it.

If the nation consists of a hundred thousand men, the position of the subjects does not change, and each alike is subjected to the whole authority of the laws, while his vote, reduced to one hundred-thousandth, has ten times less influence in their enactment. The subject, then, always remaining a unit, the proportional power of the sovereign increases in the ratio of the number of the citizens. Whence it follows that the more the State is enlarged, the more does liberty diminish.

When I say that the proportional power increases, I mean that it is farther removed from equality. Therefore, the greater the ratio is in the geometrical sense, the less is the ratio in the common acceptation; in the former, the ratio, considered according to quantity, is measured by the exponent, and in the other, considered according to identity, it is estimated by the similarity.

Now, the less the particular wills correspond with the general will, that is, customs with laws, the more should the repressive power be increased. The government, then, in order to be effective, should be relatively stronger in proportion as the people are more numerous.

On the other hand, as the aggrandizement of the State gives the depositaries of the public authority more temptations and more opportunities to abuse their power, the more force should the government have to restrain the people, and the more should the sovereign have in its turn to restrain the government. I do not speak here of absolute force, but of the relative force of the different parts of the State.

It follows from this double ratio that the continued proportion between the sovereign, the Prince, and the people is not an arbitrary idea, but a necessary consequence of the nature of the body politic. It follows, further, that one of the extremes, viz., the people, as subject, being fixed and represented by unity, whenever the double ratio increases or diminishes, the single ratio increases or diminishes in like manner, and consequently the middle term is changed. This shows that there is no unique and absolute constitution of government, but that there may be as many governments different in nature as there are States different in size.

If, for the sake of turning this system to ridicule, it should be said that, in order to find this mean proportional and form the body of the government, it is, according to me, only necessary to take the square root of the number of the people, I should answer that I take

that number here only as an example; that the ratios of
which I speak are not measured only by the number of
men, but in general by the quantity of action, which
results from the combination of multitudes of causes;
that, moreover, if for the purpose of expressing myself in
fewer words, I borrow for a moment geometrical terms,
I am nevertheless aware that geometrical precision has
no place in moral quantities.

The government is on a small scale what the body
politic which includes it is on a large scale. It is a moral
person endowed with certain faculties, active like the
sovereign, passive like the State, and it can be resolved
into other similar relations; from which arises as a consequence a new proportion, and yet another within this,
according to the order of the magistracies, until we come
to an indivisible middle term, that is, to a single chief or
supreme magistrate, who may be represented, in the
middle of this progression, as unity between the series
of fractions and that of the whole numbers.

Without embarrassing ourselves with this multiplication of terms, let us be content to consider the government
as a new body in the State, distinct from the people and
from the sovereign, and intermediate between the two.

There is this essential difference between those two
bodies, that the State exists by itself, while the government exists only through the sovereign. Thus the dominant will of the Prince is, or ought to be, only the general
will, or the law; its force is only the public force concentrated in itself; so soon as it wishes to perform of itself
some absolute and independent act, the connexion of the
whole begins to be relaxed. If, lastly, the Prince should
chance to have a particular will more active than that
of the sovereign, and if, to enforce obedience to this
particular will, it should employ the public force which
is in its hands, in such a manner that there would be so
to speak two sovereigns, the one *de jure* and the other
de facto, the social union would immediately disappear,
and the body politic would be dissolved.

Further, in order that the body of the government may

have an existence, a real life, to distinguish it from the body of the State; in order that all its members may be able to act in concert and fulfill the object for which it is instituted, a particular personality is necessary to it, a feeling common to its members, a force, a will of its own tending to its preservation. This individual existence supposes assemblies, councils, a power of deliberating and resolving, rights, titles, and privileges which belong to the Prince exclusively, and which render the position of the magistrate more honorable in proportion as it is more arduous. The difficulty lies in the method of disposing, within the whole, this subordinate whole, in such a way that it may not weaken the general constitution in strengthening its own; that its particular force, intended for its own preservation, may always be kept distinct from the public force, designed for the preservation of the State; and, in a word, that it may always be ready to sacrifice the government to the people, and not the people to the government.

Moreover, although the artificial body of the government is the work of another artificial body, and has in some respects only a derivative and subordinate existence, that does not prevent it from acting with more or less vigor or celerity, from enjoying, so to speak, more or less robust health. Lastly, without directly departing from the object for which it was instituted, it may deviate from it more or less, according to the manner in which it is constituted.

From all these differences arise the different relations which the government must have with the body of the State, so as to accord with the accidental and particular relations by which the State itself is modified. For often the government that is best in itself will become the most vicious, unless its relations are changed so as to meet the defects of the body politic to which it belongs.

CHAPTER II

The Principle Which Constitutes the Different Forms of Government

To explain the general cause of these differences, I must here distinguish the Prince from the government, as I before distinguished the State from the sovereign.

The body of the magistracy may be composed of a greater or less number of members. We said that the ratio of the sovereign to the subjects was so much greater as the people were more numerous; and, by an evident analogy, we can say the same of the government with regard to the magistrates.

Now, the total force of the government, being always that of the State, does not vary; whence it follows that the more it employs this force on its own members, the less remains for operating upon the whole people.

Consequently, the more numerous the magistrates are, the weaker is the government. As this maxim is fundamental, let us endeavor to explain it more clearly.

We can distinguish in the person of the magistrate three wills essentially different: first, the will peculiar to the individual, which tends only to his personal advantage; secondly, the common will of the magistrates, which has reference solely to the advantage of the Prince, and which may be called the corporate will, being general in relation to the government, and particular in relation to the State of which the government forms part; in the third place, the will of the people, or the sovereign will, which is general both in relation to the State considered as the whole, and in relation to the government considered as part of the whole.

In a perfect system of legislation the particular or individual will should be inoperative; the corporate will proper to the government quite subordinate; and consequently the general or sovereign will always dominant, and the sole rule of all the rest.

On the other hand, according to the natural order, these different wills become more active in proportion as they are concentrated. Thus the general will is always the weakest, the corporate will has the second rank, and the particular will the first of all; so that in the government each member is, firstly, himself, next a magistrate, and then a citizen—a gradation directly opposed to that which the social order requires.

But suppose that the whole government is in the hands of a single man, then the particular will and the corporate will are perfectly united, and consequently the latter is in the highest possible degree of intensity. Now, as it is on the degree of will that the exertion of force depends, and as the absolute power of the government does not vary, it follows that the most active government is that of a single person.

On the other hand, let us unite the government with the legislative authority; let us make the sovereign the Prince, and all the citizens magistrates; then the corporate will, confounded with the general will, will have no more activity than the latter, and will leave the particular will in all its force. Thus the government, always with the same absolute force, will be at its minimum of relative force or activity.

These relations are incontestable, and other considerations serve still further to confirm them. We see, for example, that each magistrate is more active in his body than each citizen is in his, and that consequently the particular will has much more influence in the acts of government than in those of the sovereign; for every magistrate is almost always charged with some function of government, whereas each citizen, taken by himself, has no function of sovereignty. Besides, the more a State extends, the more is its real force increased, although it does not increase in proportion to its extent; but, while the State remains the same, it is useless to multiply magistrates, for the government acquires no greater real force, inasmuch as this force is that of the State, the quantity of which is always uniform. Thus the relative force or activity of the government diminishes without its absolute or real force being able to increase.

It is certain, moreover, that the dispatch of business is retarded in proportion as more people are charged with it; that, in laying too much stress on prudence, we leave too little to fortune; that opportunities are allowed to pass by, and that owing to excessive deliberation the fruits of deliberation are often lost.

I have just shown that the government is weakened in proportion to the multiplication of magistrates, and I have before demonstrated that the more numerous the people is, the more ought the repressive force to be increased. Whence it follows that the ratio between the magistrates and the government ought to be inversely as the ratio between the subjects and the sovereign; that is, the more the State is enlarged, the more should the government contract; so that the number of chiefs should diminish in proportion as the number of the people is increased.

But I speak here only of the relative force of the government, and not of its rectitude; for, on the other hand, the more numerous the magistracy is, the more does the corporate will approach the general will; whereas, under a single magistrate, this same corporate will is, as I have said, only a particular will. Thus, what is lost on one side can be gained on the other, and the art of the legislator consists in knowing how to fix the point where the force and will of the government, always in reciprocal proportion, are combined in the ratio most advantageous to the State.

CHAPTER III

Classification of Governments

WE have seen in the previous chapter why the different kinds or forms of government are distinguished by the number of members that compose them; it remains to be seen in the present chapter how this division is made.

The sovereign may, in the first place, commit the charge of the government to the whole people, or to the greater part of the people, in such a way that there may be more citizens who are magistrates than simple individual citizens. We call this form of government a *democracy*.

Or it may confine the government to a small number, so that there may be more ordinary citizens than magistrates; and this form bears the name of *aristocracy*.

Lastly, it may concentrate the whole government in the hands of a single magistrate from whom all the rest derive their power. This third form is the most common, and is called *monarchy*, or royal government.

We should remark that all these forms, or at least the first two, admit of degrees, and may indeed have a considerable range; for democracy may embrace the whole people, or be limited to a half. Aristocracy, in its turn, may restrict itself from a half of the people to the smallest number indeterminately. Royalty even is susceptible of some division. Sparta by its constitution always had two kings; and in the Roman Empire there were as many as eight Emperors at once without its being possible to say that the Empire was divided. Thus there is a point at which each form of government blends with the next; and we see that, under three denominations only, the government is really susceptible of as many different forms as the State has citizens.

What is more, this same government being in certain respects capable of subdivision into other parts, one administered in one way, another in another, there may result from combinations of these three forms a multitude of mixed forms, each of which can be multiplied by all the simple forms.

In all ages there has been much discussion about the best form of government, without consideration of the fact that each of them is the best in certain cases, and the worst in others.

If, in the different States, the number of the supreme magistrates should be in inverse ratio to that of the citizens, it follows that, in general, democratic government is suitable to small States, aristocracy to those of moderate size, and monarchy to large ones. This rule follows immediately from the principle. But how is it possible to estimate the multitude of circumstances which may furnish exceptions?

CHAPTER IV

Democracy

He that makes the law knows better than any one how it should be executed and interpreted. It would seem, then, that there could be no better constitution than one in which the executive power is united with the legislative; but it is that very circumstance which makes a democratic government inadequate in certain respects, because things which ought to be distinguished are not, and because the Prince and the sovereign, being the same person, only form as it were a government without government.

It is not expedient that he who makes the laws should execute them, nor that the body of the people should divert its attention from general considerations in order to bestow it on particular objects. Nothing is more dangerous than the influence of private interests on public affairs; and the abuse of the laws by the government is a lesser evil than the corruption of the legislator, which is the infallible result of the pursuit of private interests. For when the State is changed in its substance all reform becomes impossible. A people which would never abuse the government would likewise never abuse its independence; a people which always governed well would not need to be governed.

Taking the term in its strict sense, there never has existed, and never will exist, any true democracy. It is contrary to the natural order that the majority should govern and that the minority should be governed. It is impossible to imagine that the people should remain in perpetual assembly to attend to public affairs, and it is easily apparent that commissions could not be established for that purpose without the form of administration being changed.

In fact, I think I can lay down as a principle that when the functions of government are shared among several magistracies, the least numerous acquire, sooner or later, the greatest authority, if only on account of the facility in transacting business which naturally leads them on to that.

Moreover, how many things difficult to combine does not this government presuppose! First, a very small State, in which the people may be readily assembled, and in which every citizen can easily know all the rest; secondly, great simplicity of manners, which prevents a multiplicity of affairs and thorny discussions; next, considerable equality in rank and fortune, without which equality in rights and authority could not long subsist; lastly, little or no luxury, for luxury is either the effect of wealth or renders it necessary; it corrupts both the rich and the poor, the former by possession, the latter by covetousness; it betrays the country to effeminacy and vanity; it deprives the State of all its citizens in order to subject them one to another, and all to opinion.

That is why a famous author has assigned virtue as the principle of a republic, for all these conditions could not subsist without virtue; but, through not making the necessary distinctions, this brilliant genius has often lacked precision and sometimes clearness, and has not seen that the sovereign authority being everywhere the same, the same principle ought to have a place in every well-constituted State, in a greater or less degree, it is true, according to the form of government.

Let us add that there is no government so subject to civil wars and internal agitations as the democratic or popular, because there is none which tends so strongly and so constantly to change its form, none which demands more vigilance and courage to be maintained in its own form. It is especially in this constitution that the citizen should arm himself with strength and steadfastness, and say every day of his life from the bottom of his heart what a virtuous Palatine * said in the Diet of Poland: *Malo periculosam libertatem quam quietum servitium.*

If there were a nation of gods, it would be governed democratically. So perfect a government is unsuited to men.

---

* The Palatine of Posnania, father of the King of Poland, Duke of Lorraine.

CHAPTER V

Aristocracy

WE have here two moral persons quite distinct, viz., the government and the sovereign; and consequently two general wills, the one having reference to all the citizens, the other only to the members of the administration. Thus, although the government can regulate its internal policy as it pleases, it can never speak to the people except in the name of the sovereign, that is, in the name of the people themselves. This must never be forgotten.

The earliest societies were aristocratically governed. The heads of families deliberated among themselves about public affairs. The young men yielded readily to the authority of experience. Hence the names *priests, elders, senate, gerontes*. The savages of North America are still governed in this way at the present time, and are very well governed.

But in proportion as the inequality due to institutions prevailed over natural inequality, wealth or power* was preferred to age, and aristocracy became elective. Finally, the power transmitted with the father's property to the children, rendering the families patrician, made the government hereditary, and there were senators only twenty years old.

There are, then, three kinds of aristocracy—natural, elective, and hereditary. The first is only suitable for simple nations; the third is the worst of all governments. The second is the best; it is aristocracy properly so-called.

---

* It is clear that the word *optimates* among the ancients did not mean the best, but the most powerful.

Besides the advantage of the distinction between the two powers, aristocracy has that of the choice of its members; for in a popular government all the citizens are born magistrates; but this one limits them to a small number, and they become magistrates by election only;* a method by which probity, intelligence, experience, and all other grounds of preference and public esteem are so many fresh guarantees that men will be wisely governed.

Further, assemblies are more easily convoked; affairs are better discussed and are dispatched with greater order and diligence; while the credit of the State is better maintained abroad by venerable senators, than by an unknown or despised multitude.

In a word, it is the best and most natural order of things that the wisest should govern the multitude, when we are sure that they will govern it for its advantage and not for their own. We should not uselessly multiply means, nor do with twenty thousand men what a hundred chosen men can do still better. But we must observe that the corporate interest begins here to direct the public force in a less degree according to the rule of the general will, and that another inevitable propensity deprives the laws of a part of the executive power.

With regard to special expediencies, a State must not be so small, nor a people so simple and upright, that the execution of the laws should follow immediately upon the public will, as in a good democracy. Nor again must a nation be so large that the chief men, who are dispersed in order to govern it, can set up as sovereigns, each in his own province, and begin by making themselves independent so as at last to become masters.

---

* It is very important to regulate by law the form of election of magistrates; for, in leaving it to the will of the Prince, it is impossible to avoid falling into hereditary aristocracy, as happened in the republics of Venice and Berne. In consequence, the first has long been a decaying State, but the second is maintained by the extreme wisdom of its Senate; it is a very honorable and a very dangerous exception.

But if aristocracy requires a few virtues less than popular government, it requires also others that are peculiarly its own, such as moderation among the rich and contentment among the poor; for a rigorous equality would seem to be out of place in it, and was not even observed in Sparta.

Besides, if this form of government comports with a certain inequality of fortune, it is expedient in general that the administration of public affairs should be entrusted to those that are best able to devote their whole time to it, but not, as Aristotle maintains, that the rich should always be preferred. On the contrary, it is important that an opposite choice should sometimes teach the people that there are, in men's personal merits, reasons for preference more important than wealth.

CHAPTER VI

Monarchy

WE have hitherto considered the Prince as a moral and collective person united by the force of the laws, and as the depository of the executive power in the State. We have now to consider this power concentrated in the hands of a natural person, of a real man, who alone has a right to dispose of it according to the laws. He is what is called a monarch or a king.

Quite the reverse of the other forms of administration, in which a collective being represents an individual, in this one an individual represents a collective being; so that the moral unity that constitutes it is at the same time a physical unity in which all the powers that the law combines in the other with so much effort are combined naturally.

Thus the will of the people, the will of the Prince, the

public force of the State, and the particular force of the government, all obey the same motive power; all the springs of the machine are in the same hand, everything works for the same end; there are no opposite movements that counteract one another, and no kind of constitution can be imagined in which a more considerable action is produced with less effort. Archimedes, quietly seated on the shore, and launching without difficulty a large vessel, represents to me a skillful monarch, governing from his cabinet his vast States, and, while he appears motionless, setting everything in motion.

But if there is no government which has more vigor, there is none in which the particular will has more sway and more easily governs others. Everything works for the same end, it is true; but this end is not the public welfare, and the very power of the administration turns continually to the prejudice of the State.

Kings wish to be absolute, and from afar men cry to them that the best way to become so is to make themselves beloved by their people. This maxim is very fine, and also very true in certain respects; unfortunately it will always be ridiculed in courts. Power which springs from the affections of the people is doubtless the greatest, but it is precarious and conditional; princes will never be satisfied with it. The best kings wish to have the power of being wicked if they please, without ceasing to be masters. A political preacher will tell them in vain that, the strength of the people being their own, it is their greatest interest that the people should be flourishing, numerous, and formidable; they know very well that that is not true. Their personal interest is, in the first place, that the people should be weak and miserable, and should never be able to resist them. Supposing all the subjects always perfectly submissive, I admit that it would then be the Prince's interest that the people should be powerful, in order that this power, being his own, might render him formidable to his neighbors; but as this interest is only secondary and subordinate, and as the two suppositions are incompatible, it is natural that princes should always give preference to the maxim which is most immediately useful to them. It is this that Samuel strongly represented to the Hebrews; it is this that Machiavelli clearly demonstrated. While pretending to give lessons to kings, he gave great ones to peoples. The *Prince* of Machiavelli is the book of republicans.*

We have found, by general considerations, that monarchy is suited only to large States; and we shall find this again by examining monarchy itself. The more numerous the public administrative body is, the more does the ratio of the Prince to the subjects diminish and approach equality, so that this ratio is unity or equality even, in a democracy. This same ratio increases in proportion as the government contracts, and is at its maximum when the government is in the hands of a single person. Then the distance between the Prince and the people is too great, and the State lacks cohesion. In order to unify it, then, intermediate orders, princes, grandees, and nobles are required to fill them. Now, nothing at all of this kind is proper for a small State, which would be ruined by all these orders.

But if it is difficult for a great State to be well governed, it is much more so for it to be well governed by a single man; and every one knows what happens when the king appoints deputies.

One essential and inevitable defect, which will always render a monarchical government inferior to a republican one, is that in the latter the public voice hardly ever raises to the highest posts any but enlightened and capable

---

* Machiavelli was an honorable man and a good citizen; but, attached to the house of the Medici, he was forced, during the oppression of his country, to conceal his love for liberty. The mere choice of his execrable hero sufficiently manifests his secret intention; and the opposition between the maxims of his book the *Prince* and those of his *Discourses on Titus Livius* and his *History of Florence* shows that this profound politician has had hitherto only superficial or corrupt readers. The court of Rome has strictly prohibited his book; I certainly believe it, for it is that court which he most clearly depicts.

men, who fill them honorably; whereas those who succeed in monarchies are most frequently only petty mischief-makers, petty knaves, petty intriguers, whose petty talents, which enable them to attain high posts in courts, only serve to show the public their ineptitude as soon as they have attained them. The people are much less mistaken about their choice than the Prince is; and a man of real merit is almost as rare in a royal ministry as a fool at the head of a republican government. Therefore, when by some fortunate chance one of these born rulers takes the helm of affairs in a monarchy almost wrecked by such a fine set of ministers, it is quite astonishing what resources he finds, and his accession to power forms an epoch in a country.

In order that a monarchical State might be well-governed, it would be necessary that its greatness or extent should be proportioned to the abilities of him that governs. It is easier to conquer than to rule. With a sufficient lever, the world may be moved by a finger; but to support it the shoulders of Hercules are required. However small a State may be, the Prince is almost always too small for it. When, on the contrary, it happens that the State is too small for its chief, which is very rare, it is still badly governed, because the chief, always pursuing his own great designs, forgets the interests of the people, and renders them no less unhappy by the abuse of his transcendent abilities, than an inferior chief by his lack of talent. It would be necessary, so to speak, that a kingdom should be enlarged or contracted in every reign, according to the capacity of the Prince; whereas, the talents of a senate have more definite limits, the State may have permanent boundaries, and the administration prosper equally well.

The most obvious inconvenience of the government of a single person is the lack of that uninterrupted succession which forms in the two others a continuous connection. One king being dead, another is necessary; elections leave dangerous intervals; they are stormy; and unless the citizens are of a disinterestedness, an integrity, which this government hardly admits of, intrigue and corruption intermingle with it. It would be hard for a man to whom the State has been sold not to sell it in his turn, and indemnify himself out of the helpless for the money which the powerful have extorted from him. Sooner or later everything becomes venal under such an administration, and the peace which is then enjoyed under a king is worse than the disorder of an interregnum.

What has been done to prevent these evils? Crowns have been made hereditary in certain families; and an order of succession has been established which prevents any dispute on the demise of kings; that is to say, the inconvenience of regencies being substituted for that of elections, an appearance of tranquillity has been preferred to a wise administration, and men have preferred to risk having as their chiefs children, monsters, and imbeciles, rather than have a dispute about the choice of good kings. They have not considered that in thus exposing themselves to the risk of this alternative, they put almost all the chances against themselves. That was a very sensible answer of Dionysius the younger, to whom his father, in reproaching him with a dishonorable action, said: "Have I set you the example in this?" "Ah!" replied the son, "your father was not a king."

All things conspire to deprive of justice and reason a man brought up to govern others. Much trouble is taken, so it is said, to teach young princes the art of reigning; this education does not appear to profit them. It would be better to begin by teaching them the art of obeying. The greatest kings that history has celebrated were not trained to rule; that is a science which men are never less masters of than after excessive study of it, and it is better acquired by obeying than by ruling. *Nam utilissimus idem ac brevissimus bonarum malarumque rerum delectus, cogitare quid aut nolueris sub alio principe, aut volueris.*

A result of this want of cohesion is the instability of royal government, which, being regulated sometimes on one plan, sometimes on another, according to the character of the reigning Prince or that of the persons who reign for him, cannot long pursue a fixed aim or a consistent course of conduct, a variableness which always makes the State fluctuate between maxim and maxim, project and project, and which does not exist in other governments, where the Prince is always the same. So we see that, in general, if there is more cunning in a court, there is more wisdom in a senate, and that republics pursue their ends by more steadfast and regular methods; whereas every revolution in a royal ministry produces one in the State, the maxim common to all ministers, and to almost all kings, being to reverse in every respect the acts of their predecessors.

From this same want of cohesion is obtained the solution of a sophism very familiar to royal politicians; this is not only to compare civil government with domestic government, and the Prince with the father of a family, an error already refuted, but, further, to ascribe freely to this magistrate all the virtues which he might have occasion for, and always to suppose that the Prince is what he ought to be—on which supposition royal government is manifestly preferable to every other, because it is incontestably the strongest, and because it only lacks a corporate will more conformable to the general will to be also the best.

But if, according to Plato, a king by nature is so rare a personage, how many times will nature and fortune conspire to crown him? And if the royal education necessarily corrupts those who receive it, what should be expected from a succession of men trained to rule? It is, then, voluntary self-deception to confuse royal government with that of a good king. To see what this government is in itself, we must consider it under incapable or wicked princes; for such will come to the throne, or the throne will make them such.

These difficulties have not escaped our authors, but they have not been embarrassed by them. The remedy, they say, is to obey without murmuring; God gives bad kings in His wrath, and we must endure them as chastisements of heaven. Such talk is doubtless edifying, but I am inclined to think it would be more appropriate in a pulpit than in a book on politics. What should we say of a physician who promises miracles, and whose whole art consists in exhorting the sick man to be patient? We know well that when we have a bad government it must be endured; the question is to find a good one.

CHAPTER VII

Mixed Governments

PROPERLY speaking, there is no simple government. A single chief must have subordinate magistrates; a popular government must have a head. Thus, in the partition of the executive power, there is always a gradation from the greater number to the less, with this difference, that sometimes the majority depends on the minority, and sometimes the minority on the majority.

Sometimes there is an equal division, either when the constituent parts are in mutual dependence, as in the government of England; or when the authority of each part is independent, but imperfect, as in Poland. This latter form is bad, because there is no unity in the government, and the State lacks cohesion.

Is a simple or a mixed government the better? A question much debated among publicists, and one to which the same answer must be made that I have before made about every form of government.

The simple government is the better in itself, for the reason that it is simple. But when the executive power is not sufficiently dependent on the legislative, that is, when there is a greater proportion between the Prince and the sovereign than between the people and the Prince, this want of proportion must be remedied by dividing the government; for then all its parts have no less authority over the subjects, and their division renders them all together less strong against the sovereign.

The same inconvenience is also provided against by the establishment of intermediate magistrates, who, leaving the government in its entirety, only serve to balance the two powers and maintain their respective rights. Then the government is not mixed, but temperate.

The opposite inconvenience can be remedied by similar means, and, when the government is too lax, tribunals may be erected to concentrate it. That is customary in all democracies. In the first case the government is divided in order to weaken it, and in the second in order to strengthen it; for the maximum of strength and also of weakness is found in simple governments, while the mixed forms give a medium strength.

CHAPTER VIII

That Every Form of Government Is Not Fit for Every Country

LIBERTY, not being a fruit of all climates, is not within the reach of all peoples. The more we consider this principle established by Montesquieu, the more do we perceive its truth; the more it is contested, the greater opportunity is given to establish it by new proofs.

In all the governments of the world, the public person consumes, but produces nothing. Whence, then, comes the substance it consumes? From the labor of its members. It is the superfluity of individuals that supplies the necessaries of the public. Hence it follows that the civil

State can subsist only so long as men's labor produces more than they need.

Now this excess is not the same in all countries of the world. In several it is considerable, in others moderate, in others nothing, in others a minus quantity. This proportion depends on the fertility due to climate, on the kind of labor which the soil requires, on the nature of its products, on the physical strength of its inhabitants, on the greater or less consumption that is necessary to them, and on several other like proportions of which it is composed.

On the other hand, all governments are not of the same nature; there are some more or less wasteful; and the differences are based on this other principle, that the further the public contributions are removed from their source, the more burdensome they are. We must not measure this burden by the amount of the imposts, but by the distance they have to traverse in order to return to the hands from which they have come. When this circulation is prompt and well-established, it matters not whether little or much is paid; the people are always rich, and the finances are always prosperous. On the other hand, however little the people may contribute, if this little does not revert to them, they are soon exhausted by constantly giving; the State is never rich and the people are always in beggary.

It follows from this that the more the distance between the people and the government is increased, the more burdensome do the tributes become; therefore, in a democracy the people are least encumbered, in an aristocracy they are more so, and in a monarchy they bear the greatest weight. Monarchy, then, is suited only to wealthy nations; aristocracy, to States moderate both in wealth and size; democracy, to small and poor States.

Indeed, the more we reflect on it, the more do we find in this the difference between free and monarchical States. In the first, everything is used for the common advantage; in the others, public and private resources are reciprocal, and the former are increased by the diminution of the latter; lastly, instead of governing subjects in order to make them happy, despotism renders them miserable in order to govern them.

There are, then, in every climate natural causes by which we can assign the form of government which is adapted to the nature of the climate, and even say what kind of inhabitants the country should have.

Unfruitful and barren places, where the produce does not repay the labor, ought to remain uncultivated and deserted, or should only be peopled by savages; places where men's toil yields only bare necessaries ought to be inhabited by barbarous nations; in them any polity would be an impossibility. Places where the excess of the produce over the labor is moderate are suitable for free nations; those in which abundant and fertile soil yields much produce for little labor are willing to be governed monarchically, in order that the superfluity of the subjects may be consumed by the luxuries of the Prince; for it is better that this excess should be absorbed by the government than squandered by private persons. There are exceptions, I know; but these exceptions themselves confirm the rule, in that, sooner or later, they produce revolutions which restore things to their natural order.

We should always distinguish general laws from the particular causes which may modify their effects. If the whole south should be covered with republics, and the whole north with despotic States, it would not be less true that, through the influence of climate, despotism is suitable to warm countries, barbarism to cold countries, and a good polity to intermediate regions. I see, however, that while the principle is admitted, its application may be disputed; it will be said that some cold countries are very fertile, and some southern ones very unfruitful. But this is a difficulty only for those who do not examine the matter in all its relations. It is necessary, as I have already said, to reckon those connected with labor, resources, consumption, etc.

Let us suppose that the produce of two districts equal in area is in the ratio of five to ten. If the inhabitants of the former consume four and those of the latter nine parts, the surplus produce of the first will be one-fifth, and that of the second one-tenth. The ratio between these two surpluses being then inversely as that of the produce of each, the district which yields only five will give a surplus double that of the district which produces ten.

But it is not a question of double produce, and I do not think that any one dare, in general, place the fertility of cold countries even on an equality with that of warm countries. Let us, however, assume this equality; let us, if you will, put England in the scales with Sicily, and Poland with Egypt; more to the south we shall have Africa and India; more to the north we shall have nothing. For this equality in produce what a difference in the cultivation! In Sicily it is only necessary to scratch the soil; in England what care is needed to till it! But where more exertion is required to yield the same produce, the surplus must necessarily be very small.

Consider, besides this, that the same number of men consume much less in warm countries. The climate demands that people should be temperate in order to be healthy; Europeans who want to live as at home all die of dysentery and dyspepsia. "We are," says Chardin, "carnivorous beasts, wolves, in comparison with Asiatics. Some attribute the temperance of the Persians to the fact that their country is scantily cultivated; I believe, on the contrary, that their country is not very abundant in provisions because the inhabitants need very little. If their frugality," he continues, "resulted from the poverty of the country, it would be only the poor who would eat little, whereas it is the people generally; and more or less would be consumed in each province, according to the fertility of the country, whereas the same abstemiousness is found throughout the kingdom. They pride themselves greatly on their mode of living, saying that it is only necessary to look at their complexions, to see how much superior they are to those of Christians. Indeed, the complexions of the Persians are smooth; they have beautiful skins, delicate and clear; while the complexions of their subjects, the Armenians, who live in European fashion, are rough and blotched, and their bodies are coarse and heavy."

The nearer we approach to the Equator, the less do the people live upon. They eat scarcely any meat; rice, maize, *cuzcuz,* millet, cassava, are their ordinary foods. There are in India millions of men whose diet does not cost a half-penny a day. We see even in Europe palpable differences in appetite between northern and southern nations. A Spaniard will live for eight days on a German's dinner. In countries where men are most voracious luxury is directed to matters of consumption; in England it is displayed in a table loaded with meats; in Italy you are regaled with sugar and flowers.

Again, luxury in dress presents similar differences. In climates where the changes of the seasons are sudden and violent, garments are better and simpler; in those where people dress only for ornament, splendor is more sought after than utility, for clothes themselves are a luxury. At Naples you will see men every day walking to Posilippo with gold-embroidered coats, and no stockings. It is the same with regard to buildings; everything is sacrificed to magnificence when there is nothing to fear from injury by the atmosphere. In Paris and in London people must be warmly and comfortably housed; in Madrid they have superb drawing-rooms, but no windows that shut, while they sleep in mere closets.

The foods are much more substantial and nutritious in warm countries; this is a third difference which cannot fail to influence the second. Why do people eat so many vegetables in Italy? Because they are good, nourishing, and of excellent flavor. In France, where they are grown only on water, they are not nourishing and count almost for nothing on the table; they do not, however, occupy less ground, and they cost at least as much labor to cultivate. It is found by experience that the wheats of Barbary, inferior in other respects to those of France, yield much more flour, and that those of France, in their turn, yield more than the wheats of the north. Whence we may infer that a similar gradation is observable generally, in the same direction, from the Equator to the Pole. Now is it not a manifest disadvantage to have in an equal quantity of produce a smaller quantity of nutriment?

To all these different considerations I may add one which springs from, and strengthens, them; it is that warm countries have less need of inhabitants than cold countries, but would be able to maintain a greater number; hence a double surplus is produced, always to the advantage of despotism. The greater the surface occupied by the same number of inhabitants, the more difficult do rebellions become, because measures cannot be concerted promptly and secretly, and because it is always easy for the government to discover the plans and cut off communications. But the more closely packed a numerous population is, the less power has a government to usurp the sovereignty; the chiefs deliberate as securely in their cabinets as the Prince in his council, and the multitude assemble in the squares as quickly as the troops in their quarters. The advantage, then, of a tyrannical government lies in this, that it acts at great distances. By help of the points of support which it procures, its power increases with the distance, like that of levers.* That of the people, on the other hand, acts only when concentrated; it evaporates and disappears as it extends, like the effect of powder scattered on the ground, which takes fire only grain by grain. The least populous countries are thus the best adapted for tyranny; wild beasts reign only in deserts.

---

* This does not contradict what I said before (Book II, chapter ix) on the inconveniences of large States; for there it was a question of the authority of the government over its members, and here it is a question of its power against its subjects. Its scattered members serve as points of support to it for operating at a distance upon the people, but it has no point of support for acting on its members themselves. Thus, the length of the lever is the cause of its weakness in the one case, and of its strength in the other.

CHAPTER IX

The Marks of a Good Government

WHEN, then, it is asked absolutely which is the best government, an insoluble and likewise indeterminate question is propounded; or, if you will, it has as many correct solutions as there are possible combinations in the absolute and relative positions of the nations.

But if it were asked by what sign it can be known whether a given people is well or ill governed, that would be a different matter, and the question of fact might be determined.

It is, however, not settled, because every one wishes to decide it in his own way. Subjects extol the public tranquillity, citizens the liberty of individuals; the former prefer security of possessions, the latter, that of persons; the former are of opinion that the best government is the most severe, the latter maintain that it is the mildest; the one party wish that crimes should be punished and the other that they should be prevented; the one party think it well to be feared by their neighbors, the other party prefer to be unacquainted with them; the one party are satisfied when money circulates, the other party demand that the people should have bread. Even though there should be agreement on these and other similar points, would further progress be made? Since moral quantities lack a precise mode of measurement, even if people were in accord about the sign, how could they be so about the valuation of it?

For my part, I am always astonished that people fail to recognize a sign so simple, or that they should have the insincerity not to agree about it. What is the object of political association? It is the preservation and prosperity of its members. And what is the surest sign that they are preserved and prosperous? It is their number and population. Do not, then, go and seek elsewhere for this sign so much discussed. All other things being equal, the government under which, without external aids, without naturalizations, and without colonies, the citizens increase and multiply most, is infallibly the best. That under which a people diminishes and decays is the worst. Statisticians, it is now your business; reckon, measure, compare.*

---

* On the same principle must be judged the centuries which deserve preference in respect of the prosperity of the human race. Those in which literature and art were seen to flourish have been too much admired, without the secret object of their cultivation being penetrated, without their fatal consequences being considered: *Idque apud imperitos humanitas vocabatur, quum pars servitutis esset.* Shall we never detect in the maxims of books the gross self-interest which makes the authors speak? No, whatever they may say, when, notwithstanding its brilliancy, a country is being depopulated, it is untrue that all goes well, and it is not enough that a poet should have an income of 100,000 livres for his epoch to be the best of all. The apparent repose and tranquillity of the chief men must be regarded less than the welfare of nations as a whole, and especially that of the most populous States. Hail lays waste a few cantons, but it rarely causes scarcity. Riots and civil wars greatly startle the chief men; but they do not produce the real misfortunes of nations, which may even be abated, while it is being disputed who shall tyrannize over them. It is from their permanent condition that their real prosperity or calamities spring; when all is left crushed under the yoke, it is then that everything perishes; it is then that the chief men, destroying them at their leisure, *ubi solitudinem faciunt, pacem appellant.* When the broils of the great agitated the kingdom of France, and the coadjutor of Paris carried a poniard in his pocket to the *Parlement,* that did not prevent the French nation from living happily and harmoniously in free and honorable ease. Greece of old flourished in the midst of the most cruel wars; blood flowed there in streams, and the whole country was covered with men. It seemed, said Machiavelli, that amid murders, proscriptions, and civil wars, our republic became more powerful; the virtues of its citizens, their manners, their independence, were more effectual in strengthening it than all its dissensions had been in weakening it. A little agitation gives energy to men's minds, and what makes the race truly prosperous is not so much peace as liberty.

CHAPTER X

The Abuse of the Government and Its Tendency to Degenerate

As the particular will acts incessantly against the general will, so the government makes a continual effort against the sovereignty. The more this effort is increased, the more is the constitution altered; and as there is here no other corporate will which, by resisting that of the Prince, may produce equilibrium with it, it must happen sooner or later that the Prince at length oppresses the sovereign and violates the social treaty. Therein is the inherent and inevitable vice which, from the birth of the body politic, tends without intermission to destroy it, just as old age and death at length destroy the human body.

There are two general ways by which a government degenerates, viz., when it contracts, or when the State is dissolved.

The government contracts when it passes from the majority to the minority, that is, from democracy to aristocracy, and from aristocracy to royalty. That is its natural tendency.* If it retrograded from the minority

---

* The slow formation and the progress of Venice in her lagoons present a notable example of this succession; it is indeed astonishing that, after more than twelve hundred years, the Venetians seem to be still only in the second stage, which began with the *Serrar di Consiglio* in 1198. As for the ancient Doges,

to the majority, it might be said to relax; but this inverse progress is impossible.

In reality, the government never changes its form except when its exhausted energy leaves it too weak to preserve itself; and if it becomes still more relaxed as it extends, its force will be annihilated, and it will no longer subsist. We must therefore concentrate the energy as it dwindles; otherwise the State which it sustains will fall into ruin.

The dissolution of the State may occur in two ways.

Firstly, when the Prince no longer administers the State in accordance with the laws; and, secondly, when he usurps the sovereign power. Then a remarkable change takes place—the State, and not the government, contracts; I mean that the State dissolves, and that another is formed within it, which is composed only of the members of the government, and which is to the rest of the people nothing more than their master and their tyrant. So that as soon as the government usurps the sovereignty, the social compact is broken, and all the

---

with whom they are reproached, whatever the *Squittinio della libertà veneta* may say, it is proved that they were not their sovereigns.

People will not fail to bring forward as an objection to my views the Roman Republic, which followed, it will be said, a course quite contrary, passing from monarchy to aristocracy, and from aristocracy to democracy. I am very far from regarding it in this way.

The first institution of Romulus was a mixed government, which speedily degenerated into despotism. From peculiar causes the State perished before its time, as we see a newborn babe die before attaining manhood. The expulsion of the Tarquins was the real epoch of the birth of the Republic. But it did not at first assume a regular form, because, through not abolishing the patrician order, only a half of the work was done. For, in this way, the hereditary aristocracy, which is the worst of legitimate administrations, remaining in conflict with the democracy, the form of the government, always uncertain and fluctuating, was fixed, as Machiavelli has shown, only on the institution of the

ordinary citizens, rightfully regaining their natural liberty, are forced, but not morally bound, to obey.

The same thing occurs also when the members of the government usurp separately the power which they ought to exercise only collectively; which is no less a violation of the laws, and occasions still greater disorder. Then there are, so to speak, as many Princes as magistrates; and the State, not less divided than the government, perishes or changes its form.

When the State is broken up, the abuse of the government, whatever it may be, takes the common name of *anarchy*. To distinguish, democracy degenerates into *ochlocracy*, aristocracy into *oligarchy*; I should add that royalty degenerates into *tyranny*; but this last word is equivocal and requires explanation.

In the vulgar sense a tyrant is a king who governs with violence and without regard to justice and the laws.

---

tribunes; not till then was there a real government and a true democracy. Indeed, the people then were not only sovereign, but also magistrates and judges; the Senate was only a subordinate tribunal for moderating and concentrating the government; and the consuls themselves, although patricians, although chief magistrates, although generals with absolute authority in war, were in Rome only the presidents of the people.

From that time, moreover, the government seemed to follow its natural inclination, and tend strongly to aristocracy. The patriciate abolishing itself as it were, the aristocracy was no longer in the body of patricians as it is at Venice and Genoa, but in the body of the Senate, composed of patricians and plebeians, and also in the body of tribunes when they began to usurp an active power; for words make no difference in things, and when a nation has chiefs to govern for them, whatever name those chiefs bear, they always form an aristocracy.

From the abuses of aristocracy sprang the civil wars and the triumvirate. Sylla, Julius Cæsar, Augustus, became in fact real monarchs; and at length, under the despotism of Tiberius, the State was broken up. Roman history, then, does not belie my principle, but confirms it.

In the strict sense, a tyrant is a private person who arrogates to himself the royal authority without having a right to it. It is in this sense that the Greeks understood the word tyrant; they bestowed it indifferently on good and bad Princes whose authority was not legitimate.* Thus *tyrant* and *usurper* are two words perfectly synonymous.

To give different names to different things, I call the usurper of royal authority a *tyrant,* and the usurper of sovereign power a *despot.* The tyrant is he who, contrary to the laws, takes upon himself to govern according to the laws; the despot is he who sets himself above the laws themselves. Thus the tyrant cannot be a despot, but the despot is always a tyrant.

---

* *Omnes enim et habentur et dicuntur tyranni, qui potestate utuntur perpetua in ea civitate quae libertate usa est.* (Corn. Nep., *in Miltiad.,* cap. viii) It is true that Aristotle *(Mor. Nicom.,* Book VIII, cap. x) distinguishes the tyrant from the king, by the circumstance that the former governs for his own benefit, and the latter only for the benefit of his subjects; but besides the fact that, in general, all the Greek authors have taken the word *tyrant* in a different sense, as appears especially from Xenophon's *Hiero,* it would follow from Aristotle's distinction that, since the beginning of the world, not a single king has yet existed.

CHAPTER XI

The Dissolution of the Body Politic

Such is the natural and inevitable tendency of the best constituted governments. If Sparta and Rome have perished, what State can hope to endure for ever? If we wish to form a durable constitution, let us, then, not dream of making it eternal. In order to succeed we must not attempt the impossible, nor flatter ourselves that we are giving to the work of men a stability which human things do not admit of.

The body politic, as well as the human body, begins to die from its birth, and bears in itself the causes of its own destruction. But both may have a constitution more or less robust, and fitted to preserve them a longer or shorter time. The constitution of man is the work of nature; that of the State is the work of art. It does not rest with men to prolong their lives; it does rest with them to prolong that of the State as far as possible, by giving it the best constitution practicable. The best constituted will come to an end, but not so soon as another, unless some unforeseen accident brings about its premature destruction.

The principle of political life is in the sovereign authority. The legislative power is the heart of the State; the executive power is its brain, giving movement to all the parts. The brain may be paralyzed and yet the individual may live. A man remains an imbecile and lives; but so soon as the heart ceases its functions, the animal dies.

It is not by laws that the State subsists, but by the legislative power. The law of yesterday is not binding today; but tacit consent is presumed from silence, and the sovereign is supposed to confirm continually the laws which it does not abrogate when able to do so. Whatever it has once declared that it wills, it wills always, unless the declaration is revoked.

Why, then, do people show so much respect for ancient laws? It is on account of their antiquity. We must believe that it is only the excellence of the ancient laws which has enabled them to be so long preserved; unless the sovereign had recognized them as constantly salutary, it would have revoked them a thousand times. That is why, far from being weakened, the laws are ever acquiring fresh vigor in every well-constituted State; the prejudice in favor of antiquity renders them more venerable every day; while, wherever laws are weakened as they grow old, this fact proves that there is no longer any legislative power, and that the State no longer lives.

CHAPTER XII

How the Sovereign Authority Is Maintained

THE sovereign, having no other force than the legislative power, acts only through the laws; and the laws being nothing but authentic acts of the general will, the sovereign can act only when the people are assembled. The people assembled, it will be said; what a chimera! It is a chimera today; but it was not so two thousand years ago. Have men changed their nature?

The limits of the possible in moral things are less narrow than we think; it is our weaknesses, our vices, our prejudices, that contract them. Sordid souls do not believe in great men; vile slaves smile with a mocking air at the word *liberty*.

From what has been done let us consider what can be done. I shall not speak of the ancient republics of Greece; but the Roman Republic was, it seems to me, a great State, and the city of Rome a great city. The last census in Rome showed that there were 400,000 citizens bearing arms, and the last enumeration of the Empire showed more than 4,000,000 citizens, without reckoning subjects, foreigners, women, children, and slaves.

What a difficulty, we might suppose, there would be in assembling frequently the enormous population of the capital and its environs. Yet few weeks passed without the Roman people being assembled, even several times. Not only did they exercise the rights of sovereignty, but a part of the functions of government. They discussed certain affairs and judged certain causes, and in the public assembly the whole people were almost as often magistrates as citizens.

By going back to the early times of nations, we should find that the majority of the ancient governments, even monarchical ones, like those of the Macedonians and the Franks, had similar councils. Be that as it may, this single incontestable fact solves all difficulties; inference from the actual to the possible appears to me sound.

CHAPTER XIII

How the Sovereign Authority Is Maintained (continued)

IT is not sufficient that the assembled people should have once fixed the constitution of the State by giving their sanction to a body of laws; it is not sufficient that they should have established a perpetual government, or that they should have once for all provided for the election of magistrates. Besides the extraordinary assemblies which unforeseen events may require, it is necessary that there should be fixed and periodical ones which nothing can abolish or prorogue; so that, on the appointed day, the people are rightfully convoked by the law, without needing for that purpose any formal summons.

But, excepting these assemblies which are lawful by their date alone, every assembly of the people that has not been convoked by the magistrates appointed for that duty and according to the prescribed forms, ought to be regarded as unlawful and all that is done in it as invalid, because even the order to assemble ought to emanate from the law.

As for the more or less frequent meetings of the lawful assemblies, they depend on so many considerations that no precise rules can be given about them. Only it may be said generally that the more force a government has, the more frequently should the sovereign display itself.

This, I shall be told, may be good for a single city; but what is to be done when the State comprises many cities? Will the sovereign authority be divided? Or must it be concentrated in a single city and render subject all the rest?

I answer that neither alternative is necessary. In the first place, the sovereign authority is simple and undivided, and we cannot divide it without destroying it. In the second place, a city, no more than a nation, can be lawfully subject to another, because the essence of the body politic consists in the union of obedience and liberty, and these words, *subject* and *sovereign,* are correlatives, the notion underlying them being expressed in the one word citizen

I answer, further, that it is always an evil to combine several towns into a single State, and, in desiring to effect such a union, we must not flatter ourselves that we shall avoid the natural inconveniences of it. The abuses of great States cannot be brought as an objection against a man who only desires small ones. But how can small States be endowed with sufficient force to resist great ones? Just in the same way as when the Greek towns of old resisted the Great King, and as more recently Holland and Switzerland have resisted the House of Austria.

If, however, the State cannot be reduced to proper limits, one resource still remains; it is not to allow any capital, but to make the government sit alternately in each town, and also to assemble in them by turns the estates of the country.

People the territory uniformly, extend the same rights everywhere, spread everywhere abundance and life; in this way the State will become at once the strongest and the best governed that may be possible. Remember that the walls of the towns are formed solely of the remains of houses in the country. For every palace that I see rising in the capital, I seem to see a whole rural district laid in ruins.

CHAPTER XIV

How the Sovereign Authority Is Maintained (continued)

So soon as the people are lawfully assembled as a sovereign body, the whole jurisdiction of the government ceases, the executive power is suspended, and the person of the meanest citizen is as sacred and inviolable as that of the first magistrate, because where the represented are, there is no longer any representative. Most of the tumults that arose in Rome in the *comitia* proceeded from ignorance or neglect of this rule. The consuls were then only presidents of the people and the tribunes simple orators; * the Senate had no power at all.

These intervals of suspension, in which the Prince recognizes or ought to recognize the presence of a superior, have always been dreaded by that power; and these assemblies of the people, which are the shield of the body politic and the curb of the government, have in all ages been the terror of the chief men; hence such men are never wanting in solicitude, objections, obstacles, and promises, in the endeavor to make the citizens disgusted with the assemblies. When the latter are avaricious, cowardly, pusillanimous, and more desirous of

* Almost in the sense given to this term in the Parliament of England. The resemblance between their offices would have set the consuls and tribunes in conflict, even if all jurisdiction had been suspended.

repose than of freedom, they do not long hold out against the repeated efforts of the government; and thus, as the resisting force constantly increases, the sovereign authority at last disappears, and most of the States decay and perish before their time.

But between the sovereign authority and an arbitrary government there is sometimes introduced an intermediate power of which I must speak.

CHAPTER XV

Deputies or Representatives

So soon as the service of the State ceases to be the principal business of the citizens, and they prefer to render aid with their purses rather than their persons, the State is already on the brink of ruin. Is it necessary to march to battle, they pay troops and remain at home; is it necessary to go to the council, they elect deputies and remain at home. As a result of indolence and wealth, they at length have soldiers to enslave their country and representatives to sell it.

It is the bustle of commerce and of the arts, it is the greedy pursuit of gain, it is effeminacy and love of comforts, that commute personal services for money. Men sacrifice a portion of their profit in order to increase it at their ease. Give money and soon you will have chains. That word *finance* is a slave's word; it is unknown among citizens. In a country that is really free, the citizens do everything with their hands and nothing with money; far from paying for exemption from their duties, they would pay to perform them themselves. I am far removed from ordinary ideas; I believe that statute-labor (*les corvées*) is less repugnant to liberty than taxation is.

The better constituted a State is, the more do public affairs outweigh private ones in the minds of the citizens. There is, indeed, a much smaller number of private affairs, because the amount of the general prosperity furnishes a more considerable portion to that of each individual, and less remains to be sought by individual exertions. In a well-conducted city-state every one hastens to the assemblies; while under a bad government no one cares to move a step in order to attend them, because no one takes an interest in the proceedings, since it is foreseen that the general will will not prevail; and so at last private concerns become all-absorbing. Good laws pave the way for better ones; bad laws lead to worse ones. As soon as any one says of the affairs of the State, "Of what importance are they to me?" we must consider that the State is lost.

The decline of patriotism, the active pursuit of private interests, the vast size of States, conquests, and the abuses of government have suggested the plan of deputies or representatives of the people in the assemblies of the nation. It is this which in certain countries they dare to call the third estate. Thus the private interest of two orders is put in the first and second rank, the public interest only in the third.

Sovereignty cannot be represented for the same reason that it cannot be alienated; it consists essentially in the general will, and the will cannot be represented; it is the same or it is different; there is no medium. The deputies of the people, then, are not and cannot be its representatives; they are only its commissioners and can conclude nothing definitely. Every law which the people in person have not ratified is invalid; it is not a law. The English nation thinks that it is free, but is greatly mistaken, for it is so only during the election of members of Parliament; as soon as they are elected, it is enslaved and counts for nothing. The use which it makes of the brief moments of freedom renders the loss of liberty well-deserved.

The idea of representatives is modern; it comes to us from feudal government, that absurd and iniquitous government, under which mankind is degraded and the name of man dishonored. In the republics, and even in the monarchies, of antiquity, the people never had representatives; they did not know the word. It is very singular that in Rome, where the tribunes were so sacred, it was not even imagined that they could usurp the functions of the people, and in the midst of so great a multitude, they never attempted to pass of their own accord a single *plebiscitum*. We may judge, however, of the embarrassment which the crowd sometimes caused from what occurred in the time of the Gracchi, when a part of the citizens gave their votes on the housetops. But where right and liberty are all in all, inconveniences are nothing. In that wise nation everything was estimated at a true value; it allowed the lictors to do what the tribunes had not dared to do, and was not afraid that the lictors would want to represent it.

To explain, however, in what manner the tribunes sometimes represented it, it is sufficient to understand how the government represents the sovereign. The law being nothing but the declaration of the general will, it is clear that in their legislative capacity the people cannot be represented; but they can and should be represented in the executive power, which is only force applied to law. This shows that very few nations would, upon careful examination, be found to have laws. Be that as it may, it is certain that the tribunes, having no share in the executive power, could never represent the Roman people by right of their office, but only by encroaching on the rights of the Senate.

Among the Greeks, whatever the people had to do, they did themselves; they were constantly assembled in the public place. They lived in a mild climate and they were not avaricious; slaves performed the manual labor; the people's great business was liberty. Not having the same advantages, how are you to preserve the same rights? Your more rigorous climates give you more wants; * for six months in a year the public place is untenable, and your hoarse voices cannot be heard in the open air. You care more for gain than for liberty, and you fear slavery far less than you do misery.

What! is liberty maintained only with the help of slavery? Perhaps; extremes meet. Everything which is not according to nature has its inconveniences, and civil society more than all the rest. There are circumstances so unfortunate that people can preserve their freedom only at the expense of that of others, and the citizen cannot be completely free except when the slave is enslaved to the utmost. Such was the position of Sparta. As for you, modern nations, you have no slaves, but you are slaves; you pay for their freedom with your own. In vain do you boast of this preference; I find in it more of cowardice than of humanity.

I do not mean by all this that slaves are necessary and that the right of slavery is lawful, since I have proved the contrary; I only mention the reasons why modern nations who believe themselves free have representatives, and why ancient nations had none. Be that as it may, as soon as a nation appoints representatives, it is no longer free; it no longer exists.

After very careful consideration I do not see that it is possible henceforward for the sovereign to preserve among us the exercise of its rights unless the State is very small. But if it is very small, will it not be subjugated? No; I shall show hereafter † how the external power of a great nation can be combined with the convenient polity and good order of a small State.

---

* To adopt in cold countries the effeminacy and luxuriousness of Orientals is to be willing to assume their chains, and to submit to them even more necessarily than they do.

† It is this which I had intended to do in the sequel to this work, when, in treating of external relations, I came to confederations—a wholly new subject, the principles of which have yet to be established.

CHAPTER XVI

That the Institution of the Government Is Not a Contract

THE legislative power being once well established, the question is to establish also the executive power; for this latter, which operates only by particular acts, not being of the essence of the other, is naturally separated from it. If it were possible that the sovereign, considered as such, should have the executive power, law and fact would be so confounded that it could no longer be known what is law and what is not; and the body politic, thus perverted, would soon become a prey to the violence against which it was instituted.

The citizens being all equal by the social contract, all can prescribe what all ought to do, while no one has a right to demand that another should do what he will not do himself. Now, it is properly this right, indispensable to make the body politic live and move, which the sovereign gives to the Prince in establishing the government.

Several have pretended that the instrument in this establishment is a contract between the people and the chiefs whom they set over themselves—a contract by which it is stipulated between the two parties on what conditions the one binds itself to rule, the other to obey. It will be agreed, I am sure, that this is a strange method of contracting. But let us see whether such a position is tenable.

First, the supreme authority can no more be modified than alienated; to limit it is to destroy it. It is absurd and contradictory that the sovereign should acknowledge a superior; to bind itself to obey a master is to regain full liberty.

Further, it is evident that this contract of the people with such or such persons is a particular act; whence it follows that the contract cannot be a law nor an act of sovereignty, and that consequently it is unlawful.

Moreover, we see that the contracting parties themselves would be under the law of nature alone, and without any security for the performance of their reciprocal engagements, which is in every way repugnant to the civil state. He who possesses the power being always capable of executing it, we might as well give the name contract to the act of a man who should say to another: "I give you all my property, on condition that you restore me what you please."

There is but one contract in the State—that of association; and this of itself excludes any other. No public contract can be conceived which would not be a violation of the first.

CHAPTER XVII

The Institution of the Government

UNDER what general notion, then, must be included the act by which the government is instituted? I shall observe first that this act is complex, or composed of two others, viz., the establishment of the law and the execution of the law.

By the first, the sovereign determines that there shall be a governing body established in such or such a form; and it is clear that this act is a law.

By the second, the people nominate the chiefs who will be entrusted with the government when established.

Now, this nomination, being a particular act, is not a second law, but only a consequence of the first, and a function of the government.

The difficulty is to understand how there can be an act of government before the government exists, and how the people, who are only sovereign or subjects, can, in certain circumstances, become the Prince or the magistrates.

Here, however, is disclosed one of those astonishing properties of the body politic, by which it reconciles operations apparently contradictory; for this is effected by a sudden conversion of sovereignty into democracy in such a manner that, without any perceptible change, and merely by a new relation of all to all, the citizens, having become magistrates, pass from general acts to particular acts, and from the law to the execution of it.

This change of relation is not a subtlety of speculation without example in practice; it occurs every day in the Parliament of England, in which the Lower House on certain occasions resolves itself into Grand Committee in order to discuss business better, and thus becomes a simple commission instead of the sovereign court that it was the moment before. In this way it afterwards reports to itself, as the House of Commons, what it has just decided in Grand Committee.

Such is the advantage peculiar to a democratic government, that it can be established in fact by a simple act of the general will; and after this, the provisional government remains in power, should that be the form adopted, or establishes in the name of the sovereign the government prescribed by the law; and thus everything is according to rule. It is impossible to institute the government in any other way that is legitimate without renouncing the principles heretofore established.

CHAPTER XVIII

Means of Preventing Usurpations of the Government

FROM these explanations it follows, in confirmation of chapter XVI, that the act which institutes the government is not a contract, but a law; that the depositaries of the executive power are not the masters of the people, but its officers; that the people can appoint them and dismiss them at pleasure; that for them it is not a question of contracting, but of obeying; and that in undertaking the functions which the State imposes on them, they simply fulfill their duty as citizens, without having in any way a right to discuss the conditions.

When, therefore, it happens that the people institute a hereditary government, whether monarchical in a family or aristocratic in one order of citizens, it is not an engagement that they make, but a provisional form which they give to the administration, until they please to regulate it differently.

It is true that such changes are always dangerous, and that the established government must never be touched except when it becomes incompatible with the public good; but this circumspection is a maxim of policy, not a rule of right; and the State is no more bound to leave the civil authority to its chief men than the military authority to its generals.

Moreover, it is true that in such a case all the formalities requisite to distinguish a regular and lawful act from a seditious tumult, and the will of a whole people from the clamors of a faction, cannot be too carefully observed. It is especially in this case that only such concessions should be made as cannot in strict justice be refused; and from this obligation also the Prince derives a great advantage in preserving its power in spite of the people, without their being able to say that it has usurped the power; for while appearing to exercise nothing but its rights, it may very easily extend them, and, under pretext of maintaining the public peace, obstruct the assemblies designed to reestablish good order; so that it takes advantage of a silence which it prevents from being broken, or of irregularities which it causes to be committed, so as to assume in its favor the approbation of those whom fear renders silent and punish those that dare to speak. It is in this way that the Decemvirs, having at first been elected for one year, and then kept in office for another year, attempted to retain their power in perpetuity by no longer permitting the *comitia* to assemble; and it is by this easy method that all the governments in the world, when once invested with the public force, usurp sooner or later the sovereign authority.

The periodical assemblies of which I have spoken before are fitted to prevent or postpone this evil, especially when they need no formal convocation; for then the Prince cannot interfere with them, without openly proclaiming itself a violator of the laws and an enemy of the State.

These assemblies, which have as their object the maintenance of the social treaty, ought always to be opened with two propositions, which no one should be able to suppress, and which should pass separately by vote.

The first: "Whether it pleases the sovereign to maintain the present form of government."

The second: "Whether it pleases the people to leave the administration to those at present entrusted with it."

I presuppose here what I believe that I have proved, viz., that there is in the State no fundamental law which cannot be revoked, not even the social compact; for if all the citizens assembled in order to break this compact by a solemn agreement, no one can doubt that it would be quite legitimately broken. Grotius even thinks that each man can renounce the State of which he is a member, and regain his natural freedom and his property by quitting the country.* Now it would be absurd if all the citizens combined should be unable to do what each of them can do separately.

---

* It must be clearly understood that no one should leave in order to evade his duty and relieve himself from serving his country at a moment when it needs him. Flight in that case would be criminal and punishable; it would no longer be retirement, but desertion.

BOOK IV

CHAPTER I

That the General Will Is Indestructible

So long as a number of men in combination are considered as a single body, they have but one will, which relates to the common preservation and to the general well-being. In such a case all the forces of the State are vigorous and simple, and its principles are clear and luminous; it has no confused and conflicting interests; the common good is everywhere plainly manifest and only good sense is required to perceive it. Peace, union, and equality are foes to political subtleties. Upright and simpleminded men are hard to deceive because of their simplicity; allurements and refined pretexts do not impose upon them; they are not even cunning enough to be dupes. When, in the happiest nation in the world, we see troops of peasants regulating the affairs of the State under an oak and always acting wisely, can we refrain from despising the refinements of other nations, who make themselves illustrious and wretched with so much art and mystery?

A State thus governed needs very few laws; and in so far as it becomes necessary to promulgate new ones, this necessity is universally recognized. The first man to propose them only gives expression to what all have previously felt, and neither factions nor eloquence will be needed to pass into law what every one has already resolved to do, so soon as he is sure that the rest will act as he does.

What deceives reasoners is that, seeing only States that are ill-constituted from the beginning, they are impressed with the impossibility of maintaining such a policy in those States; they laugh to think of all the follies to which a cunning knave, an insinuating speaker, can persuade the people of Paris or London. They know not that Cromwell would have been put in irons by the people of Berne, and the Duke of Beaufort imprisoned by the Genevese.

But when the social bond begins to be relaxed and the State weakened, when private interests begin to make themselves felt and small associations to exercise influence on the State, the common interest is injuriously affected and finds adversaries; unanimity no longer reigns in the voting; the general will is no longer the will of all; opposition and disputes arise, and the best counsel does not pass uncontested.

Lastly, when the State, on the verge of ruin, no longer subsists except in a vain and illusory form, when the social bond is broken in all hearts, when the basest interest shelters itself impudently under the sacred name of the public welfare, the general will becomes dumb; all, under the guidance of secret motives, no more express their opinions as citizens than if the State had never existed; and, under the name of laws, they deceitfully pass unjust decrees which have only private interest as their end.

Does it follow from this that the general will is destroyed or corrupted? No; it is always constant, unalterable, and pure; but it is subordinated to others which get the better of it. Each, detaching his own interest from the common interest, sees clearly that he cannot completely separate it; but his share in the injury done to the State appears to him as nothing in comparison with the exclusive advantage which he aims at appropriating to himself. This particular advantage being excepted, he desires the general welfare for his own interests quite as strongly as any other. Even in selling his vote for money, he does not extinguish in himself the general will, but eludes it. The fault that he commits is to change the state of the question, and to answer something different from what he was asked; so that, instead of saying by a vote: "It is beneficial to the State," he says: "It is beneficial to a certain man or a certain party that such or such a motion should pass." Thus the law of public order in assemblies is not so much to maintain in them the general will as to ensure that it shall always be consulted and always respond.

I might in this place make many reflections on the simple right of voting in every act of sovereignty—a right which nothing can take away from the citizens—and on that of speaking, proposing, dividing, and discussing, which the government is always very careful to leave to its members only; but this important matter would require a separate treatise, and I cannot say everything in this one.

CHAPTER II

Voting

WE see from the previous chapter that the manner in which public affairs are managed may give a sufficiently trustworthy indication of the character and health of the body politic. The more that harmony reigns in the assemblies, that is, the more the voting approaches unanimity, the more also is the general will predominant; but long discussions, dissensions, and uproar proclaim the ascendancy of private interests and the decline of the State.

This is not so clearly apparent when two or more orders enter into its constitution, as, in Rome, the patricians and plebeians, whose quarrels often disturbed the *comitia,* even in the palmiest days of the Republic; but this exception is more apparent than real, for, at that time, by a vice inherent in the body politic, there were, so to speak, two States in one; what is not true of the two together is true of each separately. And, indeed, even in the most stormy times, the *plebiscita* of the people, when the Senate did not interfere with them, always passed peaceably and by a large majority of votes; the citizens having but one interest, the people had but one will.

At the other extremity of the circle unanimity returns; that is, when the citizens, fallen into slavery, have no longer either liberty or will. Then fear and flattery change votes into acclamations; men no longer deliberate, but adore or curse. Such was the disgraceful mode of speaking in the Senate under the Emperors. Sometimes it was done with ridiculous precautions. Tacitus observes that under Otho the senators, in overwhelming Vitellius with execrations, affected to make at the same time a frightful noise, in order that, if he happened to become master, he might not know what each of them had said.

From these different considerations are deduced the principles by which we should regulate the method of counting votes and of comparing opinions, according as the general will is more or less easy to ascertain and the State more or less degenerate.

There is but one law which by its nature requires unanimous consent, that is, the social compact; for civil association is the most voluntary act in the world; every man being born free and master of himself, no one can, under any pretext whatever, enslave him without his assent. To decide that the son of a slave is born a slave is to decide that he is not born a man.

If, then, at the time of the social compact, there are opponents of it, their opposition does not invalidate the contract, but only prevents them from being included in it; they are foreigners among citizens. When the State is established, consent lies in residence; to dwell in the territory is to submit to the sovereignty.*

Excepting this original contract, the vote of the majority always binds all the rest, this being a result of the contract itself. But it will be asked how a man can be free and yet forced to conform to wills which are not his own. How are opponents free and yet subject to laws they have not consented to?

I reply that the question is wrongly put. The citizen consents to all the laws, even to those which are passed in spite of him, and even to those which punish him when he dares to violate any of them. The unvarying will of all the members of the State is the general will; it is through that that they are citizens and free.† When a law is proposed in the assembly of the people, what is asked of them is not exactly whether they approve the proposition or reject it, but whether it is conformable or not to the general will, which is their own; each one in giving his vote expresses his opinion thereupon; and from the counting of the votes is obtained the declaration of the general will. When, therefore, the opinion opposed to my own prevails, that simply shows that I was mistaken, and that what I considered to be the general will was not so. Had my private opinion prevailed, I should have done something other than I wished; and in that case I should not have been free.

This supposes, it is true, that all the marks of the

---

* This must always be understood to relate to a free State; for otherwise family, property, want of an asylum, necessity, or violence, may detain an inhabitant in a country against his will; and then his residence alone no longer supposes his consent to the contract or to the violation of it.

† At Genoa we read in front of the prisons and on the fetters of the galley slaves the word, *Libertas*. This employment of the device is becoming and just. In reality, it is only the malefactors in all States who prevent the citizen from being free. In a country where all such people are in the galleys the most perfect liberty will be enjoyed.

general will are still in the majority; when they cease to be so, whatever side we take, there is no longer any liberty.

In showing before how particular wills were substituted for general wills in public resolutions, I have sufficiently indicated the means practicable for preventing this abuse; I will speak of it again hereafter. With regard to the proportional number of votes for declaring this will, I have also laid down the principles according to which it may be determined. The difference of a single vote destroys unanimity; but between unanimity and equality there are many unequal divisions, at each of which this number can be fixed according to the condition and requirements of the body politic.

Two general principles may serve to regulate these proportions: the one, that the more important and weighty the resolutions, the nearer should the opinion which prevails approach unanimity; the other, that the greater the dispatch requisite in the matter under discussion, the more should we restrict the prescribed difference in the division of opinions; in resolutions which must be come to immediately, the majority of a single vote should suffice. The first of these principles appears more suitable to laws, the second to affairs. Be that as it may, it is by their combination that are established the best proportions which can be assigned for the decision of a majority.

CHAPTER III

Elections

WITH regard to the elections of the Prince and the magistrates, which are, as I have said, complex acts, there are two modes of procedure, viz., choice and lot. Both have been employed in different republics, and a very complicated mixture of the two is seen even now in the election of the Doge of Venice.

"Election by lot," says Montesquieu, "is of the nature of democracy." I agree, but how is it so? "The lot," he continues, "is a mode of election which mortifies no one; it leaves every citizen a reasonable hope of serving his country." But these are not the reasons.

If we are mindful that the election of the chiefs is a function of government and not of sovereignty, we shall see why the method of election by lot is more in the nature of democracy, in which the administration is by so much the better as its acts are less multiplied.

In every true democracy, the magistracy is not a boon but an onerous charge, which cannot fairly be imposed on one individual rather than on another. The law alone can impose this burden on the person upon whom the lot falls. For then, the conditions being equal for all, and the choice not being dependent on any human will, there is no particular application to alter the universality of the law.

In an aristocracy the Prince chooses the Prince, the government is maintained by itself, and voting is rightly established.

The instance of the election of the Doge of Venice, far from destroying this distinction, confirms it; this composite form is suitable in a mixed government. For it is an error to take the government of Venice as a true aristocracy. If the people have no share in the government, the nobles themselves are numerous. A multitude of poor *Barnabotes* never come near any magistracy, and have for their nobility only the empty title of Excellency and the right to attend the Great Council. This Great Council being as numerous as our General Council at Geneva, its illustrious members have no more privileges than our simple citizens (*citoyens*). It is certain that, setting aside the extreme disparity of the two Republics, the burgesses (*la bourgeoisie*) of Geneva exactly correspond to the Venetian order of patricians; our natives (*natifs*) and residents (*habitants*) represent the citizens and people of Venice; our peasants (*paysans*) represent the subjects of the mainland; in short, in whatever way we consider this Republic apart from its size, its government is no more aristocratic than ours. The whole difference is that, having no chief for life, we have not the same need for election by lot.

Elections by lot would have few drawbacks in a true democracy, in which, all being equal as well in character and ability as in sentiments and fortune, the choice would become almost indifferent. But I have already said that there is no true democracy.

When choice and lot are combined, the first should be employed to fill the posts that require peculiar talents, such as military appointments; the other is suitable for those in which good sense, justice, and integrity are sufficient, such as judicial offices, because, in a well-constituted State, these qualities are common to all the citizens.

Neither lot nor voting has any place in a monarchical government. The monarch being by right sole Prince and sole magistrate, the choice of his lieutenants belongs to him alone. When the Abbé de Saint-Pierre proposed to multiply the councils of the King of France and to elect the members of them by ballot, he did not see that he was proposing to change the form of government.

It would remain for me to speak of the method for

recording and collecting votes in the assembly of the people; but perhaps the history of the Roman policy in that respect will explain more clearly all the principles which I might be able to establish. It is not unworthy of a judicious reader to see in some detail how public and private affairs were dealt with in a council of 200,000 men.

CHAPTER IV

The Roman Comitia

WE have no very trustworthy records of the early times of Rome; there is even great probability that most of the things which have been handed down are fables,* and, in general, the most instructive part of the annals of nations, which is the history of their institution, is the most defective. Experience every day teaches us from what causes spring the revolutions of empires; but, as nations are no longer in process of formation, we have scarcely anything but conjectures to explain how they have been formed.

The customs which are found established at least testify that these customs had a beginning. Of the traditions that go back to these origins, those which the greatest authorities countenance, and which the strongest reasons confirm, ought to pass as the most undoubted. These are the principles which I have tried to follow in inquiring

* The name of *Rome*, which is alleged to be derived from *Romulus*, is Greek and means *force*; the name of *Numa* is also Greek and means *law*. What likelihood is there that the first two kings of that city should have borne at the outset names so clearly related to what they did?

how the freest and most powerful nation in the world exercised its supreme power.

After the foundation of Rome, the growing republic, that is, the army of the founder, composed of Albans, Sabines, and foreigners, was divided into three classes, which, from this division, took the name of *tribes*. Each of these tribes was subdivided into ten *curiæ*, and each *curia* into *decuriæ*, at the head of which were placed *curiones* and *decuriones*.

Besides this, a body of one hundred horsemen or knights, called a *centuria*, was drawn from each tribe, whence we see that these divisions, not very necessary in a town, were at first only military. But it seems that an instinct of greatness induced the little town of Rome from the first to adopt a policy suitable to the capital of the world.

From this first division an inconvenience soon resulted; the tribe of the Albans * and that of the Sabines † remaining always in the same condition, while that of the foreigners ‡ increased continually through perpetual accessions, the last soon outnumbered the two others. The remedy which Servius found for this dangerous abuse was to change the mode of division, and for the division by races, which he abolished, to substitute another derived from the districts of the city occupied by each tribe. Instead of three tribes he made four, each of which occupied one of the hills of Rome and bore its name. Thus, in remedying the existing inequality, he also prevented it for the future; and in order that this might be a division, not only of localities, but of men, he prohibited the inhabitants of one quarter from removing into another, which prevented the races from being mingled.

He also doubled the three old *centuriæ* of cavalry and added twelve others to them, but still under the old names—a simple and judicious means by which he ef-

* Ramnenses.

† Tatientes.

‡ Luceres.

fected a distinction between the body of knights and that of the people, without making the latter murmur.

To these four urban tribes Servius added fifteen others, called rural tribes, because they were formed of inhabitants of the country, divided into so many cantons. Afterwards as many new ones were formed; and the Roman people were at length divided into thirty-five tribes, a number which remained fixed until the close of the Republic.

From this distinction between the urban and the rural tribes resulted an effect worthy of notice, because there is no other instance of it, and because Rome owed to it both the preservation of her manners and the growth of her empire. It might be supposed that the urban tribes soon arrogated to themselves the power and the honors, and were ready to disparage the rural tribes. It was quite the reverse. We know the taste of the old Romans for a country life. This taste they derived from their wise founder, who united with liberty rural and military works, and relegated, so to speak, to the towns arts, trades, intrigue, wealth, and slavery.

Thus every eminent man that Rome had being a dweller in the fields and a tiller of the soil, it was customary to seek in the country only for the defenders of the Republic. This condition, being that of the worthiest patricians, was honored by everyone; the simple and laborious life of villagers was preferred to the lax and indolent life of the burgesses of Rome; and many who would have been only wretched proletarians in the city became, as laborers in the fields, respected citizens. It is not without reason, said Varro, that our high-minded ancestors established in the village the nursery of those hardy and valiant men who defended them in time of war and sustained them in time of peace. Pliny says positively that the rural tribes were honored because of the men that composed them, while the worthless whom it was desired to disgrace were transferred as a mark of ignominy into the urban tribes. The Sabine Appius Claudius, having come to settle in Rome, was there loaded with honors and enrolled in a rural tribe, which afterwards took the name of his family. Lastly, all the freedmen entered the urban tribes, never the rural; and during the whole of the Republic there is not a single example of any of these freedmen attaining a magistracy, although they had become citizens.

This maxim was excellent, but was pushed so far that at length a change, and certainly an abuse, in government, resulted from it.

First, the censors, after having long arrogated the right of transferring citizens arbitrarily from one tribe to another, allowed the majority to be enrolled in whichever they pleased—a permission which certainly was in no way advantageous, and took away one of the great resources of the censorship. Further, since the great and powerful all enrolled themselves in the rural tribes, while the freedmen who had become citizens remained with the populace in the urban ones, the tribes in general had no longer any district or territory, but all were so intermingled that it was impossible to distinguish the members of each except by the registers; so that the idea of the word *tribe* passed thus from the real to the personal, or rather became almost a chimera.

Moreover, it came about that the urban tribes, being close at hand, were often the most powerful in the *comitia*, and sold the State to those who stooped to buy the votes of the mob of which they were composed.

With regard to the *curiæ*, the founder having formed ten in each tribe, the whole Roman people, at that time enclosed in the walls of the city, consisted of thirty *curiæ*, each of which had its temples, its gods, its officers, its priests, and its festivals called *compitalia*, resembling the *paganalia* which the rural tribes had afterwards.

In the new division of Servius, the number thirty being incapable of equal distribution into four tribes, he was unwilling to touch them; and the *curiæ*, being independent of the tribes, became another division of the inhabitants of Rome. But there was no question of *curiæ* either in the rural tribes or in the people composing them, because the tribes having become a purely civil institution, and another mode of levying troops having been introduced, the military divisions of Romulus were found superfluous. Thus, although every citizen was enrolled in a tribe, it was far from being the case that each was enrolled in a *curia*.

Servius made yet a third division, which had no relation to the two preceding, but became by its effects the most important of all. He distributed the whole Roman people into six classes, which he distinguished, not by the place of residence, nor by the men, but by property; so that the first classes were filled with rich men, the last with poor men, and the intermediate ones with those who enjoyed a moderate fortune. These six classes were subdivided into one hundred and ninety-three other bodies called *centuriæ*, and these bodies were so distributed that the first class alone comprised more than a half, and the last formed only one. It thus happened that the class least numerous in men had most *centuriæ*, and that the last entire class was counted as only one subdivision, although it alone contained more than a half of the inhabitants of Rome.

In order that the people might not so clearly discern the consequences of this last form, Servius affected to give it a military aspect. He introduced in the second class two *centuriæ* of armorers, and two of makers of instruments of war in the fourth; in each class, except the last, he distinguished the young and the old, that is to say, those who were obliged to bear arms, and those who were exempted by law on account of age—a distinction which, more than that of property, gave rise to the necessity of frequently repeating the *census* or enumeration; finally, he required that the assembly should be held in the *Campus Martius*, and that all who were qualified for service by age should gather there with their arms.

The reason why he did not follow in the last class this same division into seniors and juniors is, that the honor of bearing arms for their country was not granted to the populace of which it was composed; it was necessary to have homes in order to obtain the right of defending them; and out of those innumerable troops of beggars with which the armies of kings nowadays glitter, there is perhaps not one but would have been driven with scorn from a Roman cohort when soldiers were defenders of liberty.

Yet again, there was in the last class a distinction between the *proletarii* and those who were called *capite censi*. The former, not altogether destitute, at least supplied citizens to the State, sometimes even soldiers in pressing need. As for those who had nothing at all and could only be counted by heads, they were regarded as altogether unimportant, and Marius was the first who condescended to enroll them.

Without deciding here whether this third enumeration was good or bad in itself, I think I may affirm that nothing but the simple manners of the early Romans—their disinterestedness, their taste for agriculture, their contempt for commerce and for the ardent pursuit of gain— could have rendered it practicable. In what modern nation would rapacious greed, restlessness of spirit, intrigue, continual changes of residence, and the perpetual revolutions of fortune have allowed such an institution to endure for twenty years without the whole State being subverted? It is, indeed, necessary to observe carefully that morality and the censorship, more powerful than this institution, corrected its imperfections in Rome, and that many a rich man was relegated to the class of the poor for making too much display of his wealth.

From all this we may easily understand why mention is scarcely ever made of more than five classes, although there were really six. The sixth, which furnished neither soldiers to the army, nor voters to the *Campus Martius* *

---

* I say, "to the *Campus Martius*," because it was there that the *comitia centuriata* assembled; in the two other forms the people assembled in the *Forum* or elsewhere; and then the *capite censi* had as much influence and authority as the chief citizens.

and which was almost useless in the Republic, rarely counted as anything.

Such were the different divisions of the Roman people. Let us see now what effect they produced in the assemblies. These assemblies, lawfully convened, were called *comitia*; they were usually held in the *Forum* of Rome or in the *Campus Martius*, and were distinguished as *comitia curiata, comitia centuriata,* and *comitia tributa,* in accordance with that one of the three forms by which they were regulated. The *comitia curiata* were founded by Romulus, the *comitia centuriata* by Servius, and the *comitia tributa* by the tribunes of the people. No law received sanction, no magistrate was elected, except in the *comitia*; and as there was no citizen who was not enrolled in a *curia*, in a *centuria*, or in a tribe, it follows that no citizen was excluded from the right of voting, and that the Roman people were truly sovereign *de jure* and *de facto*.

In order that the *comitia* might be lawfully assembled, and that what was done in them might have the force of law, three conditions were necessary: the first, that the body or magistrate which convoked them should be invested with the necessary authority for that purpose; the second, that the assembly should be held on one of the days permitted by law; the third, that the auguries should be favorable.

The reason for the first regulation need not be explained; the second is a matter of police; thus it was not permitted to hold the *comitia* on feast days and market days, when the country people, coming to Rome on business, had no leisure to pass the day in the place of assembly. By the third, the Senate kept in check a proud and turbulent people, and seasonably tempered the ardor of seditious tribunes; but the latter found more than one means of freeing themselves from this constraint.

Laws and the election of chiefs were not the only points submitted for the decision of the *comitia*; the Roman people having usurped the most important functions of government, the fate of Europe may be said to have been determined in their assemblies. This variety of subjects gave scope for the different forms which these assemblies took according to the matters which had to be decided.

To judge of these different forms, it is sufficient to compare them. Romulus, in instituting the *curiæ*, desired to restrain the Senate by means of the people, and the people by means of the Senate, while ruling equally over all. He therefore gave the people by this form all the authority of numbers in order to balance that of power and wealth, which he left to the patricians. But, according to the spirit of a monarchy, he left still more advantage to the patricians through the influence of their clients in securing a plurality of votes. This admirable institution of patrons and clients was a masterpiece of policy and humanity, without which the patrician order, so opposed to the spirit of a republic, could not have subsisted. Rome alone has had the honor of giving to the world such a fine institution, from which there never resulted any abuse, and which notwithstanding has never been followed.

Since the form of the assembly of the *curiæ* subsisted under the kings down to Servius, and since the reign of the last Tarquin is not considered legitimate, the royal laws were on this account generally distinguished by the name of *leges curiatæ*.

Under the Republic the assembly of the *curiæ*, always limited to the four urban tribes, and containing only the Roman populace, did not correspond either with the Senate, which was at the head of the patricians, or with the tribunes, who, although plebeians, were at the head of the middle-class citizens. It therefore fell into disrepute; and its degradation was such that its thirty assembled lictors did what the *comitia curiata* ought to have done.

The *comitia centuriata* was so favorable to the aristocracy that we do not at first see why the Senate did not always prevail in the *comitia* which bore that name, and by which the consuls, censors, and other curule magistrates were elected. Indeed, of the one hundred and ninety-three *centuriæ* which formed the six classes of the whole Roman people, the first class comprising ninety-eight, and the votes being counted only by *centuriæ*, this first class alone outnumbered in votes all the others. When all these *centuriæ* were in agreement, the recording of votes was even discontinued; what the minority had decided passed for a decision of the multitude; and we may say that in the *comitia centuriata* affairs were regulated rather by the majority of crowns (*écus*) than of votes.

But this excessive power was moderated in two ways: first, the tribunes usually, and a great number of plebeians always, being in the class of the rich, balanced the influence of the patricians in this first class. The second means consisted in this, that instead of making the *centuriæ* vote according to their order, which would have caused the first class to begin always, one of them * was drawn by lot and proceeded alone to the election; after which all the *centuriæ*, being summoned on another day according to their rank, renewed the election and usually confirmed it. Thus the power of example was taken away from rank to be given to lot, according to the principle of democracy.

From this practice resulted yet another advantage; the citizens from the country had time, between the two elections, to gain information about the merits of the candidate provisionally chosen, and so record their votes with knowledge of the case. But, under pretense of dispatch, this practice came to be abolished and the two elections took place on the same day.

The *comitia tributa* were properly the council of the Roman people. They were convoked only by the tribunes; in them the tribunes were elected and passed their *plebiscita*. Not only had the Senate no status in them—it had not even a right to attend; and, being compelled

---

* This *centuria*, thus chosen by lot, was called *prærogativa*, because its suffrage was demanded first; hence came the word *prerogative*.

to obey laws on which they could not vote, the senators were, in this respect, less free than the meanest citizens. This injustice was altogether impolitic, and alone sufficed to invalidate the decrees of a body to which all the citizens were not admitted. If all the patricians had taken part in these *comitia* according to the rights which they had as citizens, having become in that case simple individuals, they would have scarcely influenced a form in which votes were counted by the head, and in which the meanest proletarian had as much power as the Chief of the Senate.

We see, then, that besides the order which resulted from these different divisions for the collection of the votes of so great a people, these divisions were not reduced to forms immaterial in themselves, but that each had results corresponding with the purposes for which it was chosen.

Without entering upon this in greater detail, it follows from the preceding explanations that the *comitia tributa* were more favorable to popular government, and the *comitia centuriata* to aristocracy. With regard to the *comitia curiata*, in which the Roman populace alone formed the majority, as they served only to favor tyranny and evil designs, they deserved to fall into discredit, the seditious themselves refraining from a means which would too plainly reveal their projects. It is certain that the full majesty of the Roman people was found only in the *comitia centuriata*, which were alone complete, seeing that the rural tribes were absent from the *comitia curiata* and the Senate and the patricians from the *comitia tributa*.

The mode of collecting the votes among the early Romans was as simple as their manners, although still less simple than in Sparta. Each gave his vote with a loud voice, and a recording officer duly registered it; a majority of votes in each tribe determined the suffrage of the tribe; a majority of votes among the tribes determined the suffrage of the people; and so with the *curiæ* and *centuriæ*. This was a good practice so long as probity prevailed among the citizens and every one was ashamed to record his vote publicly for an unjust measure or an unworthy man; but when the people were corrupted and votes were bought, it was expedient that they should be given secretly in order to restrain purchasers by distrust and give knaves an opportunity of not being traitors.

I know that Cicero blames this change and attributes to it in part the fall of the Republic. But although I feel the weight which Cicero's authority ought to have in this matter, I cannot adopt his opinion; on the contrary, I think that through not making sufficient changes of this kind, the downfall of the State was hastened. As the regimen of healthy persons is unfit for invalids, so we should not desire to govern a corrupt people by the laws which suit a good nation. Nothing supports this maxim better than the duration of the republic of Venice, only the semblance of which now exists, solely because its laws are suitable to none but worthless men.

Tablets, therefore, were distributed to the citizens by means of which each could vote without his decision being known; new formalities were also established for the collection of tablets, the counting of votes, the comparison of numbers, etc.; but this did not prevent suspicions as to the fidelity of the officers * charged with these duties. At length edicts were framed, the multitude of which proves their uselessness.

Towards the closing years, they were often compelled to resort to extraordinary expedients in order to supply the defects of the laws. Sometimes prodigies were feigned; but this method, which might impose on the people, did not impose on those who governed them. Sometimes an assembly was hastily summoned before the candidates had had time to canvass. Sometimes a whole sitting was consumed in talking when it was seen that the people having been won over were ready to pass a bad resolution. But at last ambition evaded everything; and it seems incredible that in the midst of so many

---

* *Custodes, diribitores, rogatores, suffragiorum.*

abuses, this great nation, by favor of its ancient institutions, did not cease to elect magistrates, to pass laws, to judge causes, and to dispatch public and private affairs with almost as much facility as the Senate itself could have done.

CHAPTER V

The Tribuneship

WHEN an exact relation cannot be established among the constituent parts of the State, or when indestructible causes are incessantly changing their relations, a special magistracy is instituted, which is not incorporated with the others, but which replaces each term in its true relation, forming a connection or middle term either between the Prince and the people, or between the Prince and the sovereign, or if necessary between both at once.

This body, which I shall call the *tribuneship*, is the guardian of the laws and of the legislative power. It sometimes serves to protect the sovereign against the government, as the tribunes of the people did in Rome; sometimes to support the government against the people, as the Council of Ten now does in Venice; and sometimes to maintain an equilibrium among all parts, as the ephors did in Sparta.

The tribuneship is not a constituent part of the State, and should have no share in the legislative or in the executive power; but it is in this very circumstance that its own power is greatest; for, while unable to do anything, it can prevent everything. It is more sacred and more venerated, as defender of the laws, than the Prince that executes them and the sovereign that enacts them. This was very clearly seen in Rome, when those proud patricians, who always despised the people as a whole, were forced to bow before a simple officer of the people, who had neither auspices nor jurisdiction.

The tribuneship, wisely moderated, is the strongest support of a good constitution; but if its power be ever so little in excess, it overthrows everything. Weakness is not natural to it; and provided it has some power, it is never less than it should be.

It degenerates into tyranny when it usurps the executive power, of which it is only the moderator, and when it wishes to make the laws which it should only defend. The enormous power of the ephors, which was without danger so long as Sparta preserved her morality, accelerated the corruption when it had begun. The blood of Agis, slain by these tyrants, was avenged by his successor; but the crime and the punishment of the ephors alike hastened the fall of the republic, and, after Cleomenes, Sparta was no longer of any account. Rome, again, perished in the same way; and the excessive power of the tribunes, usurped by degrees, served at last, with the aid of laws framed on behalf of liberty, as a shield for the emperors who destroyed her. As for the Council of Ten in Venice, it is a tribunal of blood, horrible both to the patricians and to the people; and, far from resolutely defending the laws, it has only served since their degradation for striking secret blows which men dare not remark.

The tribuneship, like the government, is weakened by the multiplication of its members. When the tribunes of the Roman people, at first two in number and afterwards five, wished to double this number, the Senate allowed them to do so, being quite sure of controlling some by means of others, which did not fail to happen.

The best means of preventing the usurpations of such a formidable body, a means of which no government has hitherto availed itself, would be, not to make this body permanent, but to fix intervals during which it should remain suspended. These intervals, which should not be long enough to allow abuses time to become established, can be fixed by law in such a manner that it may be easy to shorten them in case of need by means of extraordinary commissions.

This method appears to me free from objection, because, as I have said, the tribuneship, forming no part of the constitution, can be removed without detriment; and it seems to me efficacious, because a magistrate newly established does not start with the power that his predecessor had, but with that which the law gives him.

CHAPTER VI

The Dictatorship

THE inflexibility of the laws, which prevents them from being adapted to emergencies, may in certain cases render them pernicious, and thereby cause the ruin of the State in a time of crisis. The order and tardiness of the forms require a space of time which circumstances sometimes do not allow. A thousand cases may arise for which the legislator has not provided, and to perceive that everything cannot be foreseen is a very needful kind of foresight.

We must therefore not desire to establish political institutions so firmly as to take away the power of suspending their effects. Even Sparta allowed her laws to sleep.

But only the greatest dangers can outweigh that of changing the public order, and the sacred power of the laws should never be interfered with except when the safety of the country is at stake. In these rare and obvious cases, the public security is provided for by a special act, which entrusts the care of it to the most worthy man.

This commission can be conferred in two ways, according to the nature of the danger.

If an increase in the activity of the government suffices to remedy this evil, we may concentrate it in one or two of its members; in that case it is not the authority of the laws which is changed but only the form of their administration. But if the danger is such that the formal process of law is an obstacle to our security, a supreme head is nominated, who may silence all the laws and suspend for a moment the sovereign authority. In such a case the general will is not doubtful, and it is clear that the primary intention of the people is that the State should not perish. In this way the suspension of the legislative power does not involve its abolition; the magistrate who silences it can make it speak; he dominates it without having power to represent it; he can do everything but make laws.

The first method was employed by the Roman Senate when it charged the consuls, by a consecrated formula, to provide for the safety of the Republic. The second was adopted when one of the two consuls nominated a dictator,* a usage of which Alba had furnished the precedent to Rome.

At the beginning of the Republic they very often had recourse to the dictatorship, because the State had not yet a sufficiently firm foundation to be able to maintain itself by the vigor of its constitution alone.

Public morality rendering superfluous at that time many precautions that would have been necessary at another time, there was no fear either that a dictator would abuse his authority or that he would attempt to retain it beyond the term. On the contrary, it seemed that so great a power must be a burden to him who was invested with it, such haste did he make to divest himself of it, as if to take the place of the laws were an office too arduous and too dangerous.

* This nomination was made by night and in secret as if they were ashamed to set a man above the laws.

Therefore it is the danger, not of its abuse, but of its degradation, that makes me blame the indiscreet use of this supreme magistracy in early times; for while it was freely used at elections, at dedications, and in purely formal matters, there was reason to fear that it would become less formidable in case of need, and that the people would grow accustomed to regard as an empty title that which was only employed in empty ceremonies.

Towards the close of the Republic, the Romans, having become more circumspect, used the dictatorship sparingly with as little reason as they had formerly been prodigal of it. It was easy to see that their fear was ill-founded; that the weakness of the capital then constituted its security against the magistrates whom it had within it; that a dictator could, in certain cases, defend the public liberty without ever being able to assail it; and that the chains of Rome would not be forged in Rome itself, but in her armies. The slight resistance which Marius made against Sylla, and Pompey against Cæsar, showed clearly what might be looked for from the authority within against the force without.

This error caused them to commit great mistakes; such, for example, was that of not appointing a dictator in the Catiline affair; for as it was only a question of the interior of the city, or at most of some province of Italy, a dictator, with the unlimited authority that the laws gave him, would have easily broken up the conspiracy, which was suppressed only by a combination of happy accidents such as human prudence could not have foreseen.

Instead of that, the Senate was content to entrust all its power to the consuls; whence it happened that Cicero, in order to act effectively, was constrained to exceed his authority in a material point, and that, although the first transports of joy caused his conduct to be approved, he was afterwards justly called to account for the blood of citizens shed contrary to the laws, a reproach which could not have been brought against a dictator. But the consul's eloquence won over everybody; and he himself, although a Roman, preferred his own glory to his country's good, and sought not so much the most certain and legitimate means of saving the State as the way to secure the whole credit of this affair.* Therefore he was justly honored as the liberator of Rome and justly punished as a violator of the laws. However brilliant his recall may have been, it was certainly a pardon.

Moreover, in whatever way this important commission may be conferred, it is important to fix its duration at a very short term which can never be prolonged. In the crises which cause it to be established, the State is soon destroyed or saved; and, the urgent need having passed away, the dictatorship becomes tyrannical or useless. In Rome the dictators held office for six months only, and the majority abdicated before the end of this term. Had the term been longer, they would perhaps have been tempted to prolong it still further, as the Decemvirs did their term of one year. The dictator only had time to provide for the necessity which had led to his election; he had no time to think of other projects.

---

* He could not be satisfied about this in proposing a dictator; he dared not nominate himself, and could not feel sure that his colleague would nominate him.

CHAPTER VII

The Censorship

JUST as the declaration of the general will is made by the law, the declaration of public opinion is made by the censorship. Public opinion is a kind of law of which the censor is minister, and which he only applies to particular cases in the manner of the Prince.

The censorial tribunal, then, far from being the arbiter of the opinion of the people, only declares it, and so soon as it departs from this position, its decisions are fruitless and ineffectual.

It is useless to distinguish the character of a nation from the objects of its esteem, for all these things depend on the same principle and are necessarily intermixed. In all the nations of the world it is not nature but opinion which decides the choice of their pleasures. Reform men's opinions and their manners will be purified of themselves. People always like what is becoming or what they judge to be so; but it is in this judgment that they make mistakes; the question, then, is to guide their judgment. He who judges of manners judges of honor; and he who judges of honor takes his law from opinion.

The opinions of a nation spring from its constitution. Although the law does not regulate morality, it is legislation that gives it birth, and when legislation becomes impaired, morality degenerates; but then the judgment of the censors will not do what the power of the laws has failed to do.

It follows from this that the censorship may be useful to preserve morality, never to restore it. Institute censors while the laws are vigorous; so soon as they have lost their power all is over. Nothing that is lawful has any force when the laws cease to have any.

The censorship supports morality by preventing opinions from being corrupted, by preserving their integrity through wise applications, sometimes even by fixing them when they are still uncertain. The use of seconds in duels, carried to a mad extreme in the kingdom of France, was abolished by these simple words in an edict of the king: "As for those who have the cowardice to appoint seconds." This judgment, anticipating that of the public, immediately decided it. But when the same edicts wanted to declare that it was also cowardice to fight a duel, which is very true, but contrary to common opinion, the public ridiculed this decision, on which its judgment was already formed.

I have said elsewhere * that as public opinion is not subject to constraint, there should be no vestige of this in the tribunal established to represent it. We cannot admire too much the art with which this force, wholly lost among the moderns, was set in operation among the Romans and still better among the Lacedæmonians.

A man of bad character having brought forward a good measure in the Council of Sparta, the ephors, without regarding him, caused the same measure to be proposed by a virtuous citizen. What an honor for the one, what a stigma for the other, without praise or blame being given to either! Certain drunkards from Samos † defiled the tribunal of the ephors; on the morrow a public edict granted permission to the Samians to be filthy. A real punishment would have been less severe than such impunity. When Sparta pronounced what was or was not honorable, Greece made no appeal from her decisions.

---

* I merely indicate in this chapter what I have treated at greater length in the *Letter to M. d'Alembert*.

† They were from another island, which the delicacy of our language forbids us to name on this occasion.

CHAPTER VIII

Civil Religion

MEN had at first no kings except the gods and no government but a theocracy. They reasoned like Caligula, and at that time they reasoned rightly. A long period is needed to change men's sentiments and ideas in order that they may resolve to take a fellowman as a master and flatter themselves that all will be well.

From the single circumstance that a god was placed at the head of every political society, it followed that there were as many gods as nations. Two nations foreign to each other, and almost always hostile, could not long acknowledge the same master; two armies engaged in battle with each other could not obey the same leader. Thus from national divisions resulted polytheism, and, from this, theological and civil intolerance, which are by nature the same, as will be shown hereafter.

The fancy of the Greeks that they recognized their own gods among barbarous nations arose from their regarding themselves as the natural sovereigns of those nations. But in our days that is a very ridiculous kind of erudition which turns on the identity of the gods of different nations, as if Moloch, Saturn, and Chronos could be the same god! As if the Baal of the Phœnicians, the Zeus of the Greeks, and the Jupiter of the Latins could be the same! As if there could be anything in common among imaginary beings bearing different names!

But if it is asked why under paganism, when every State had its worship and its gods, there were no wars of religion, I answer that it was for the same reason that each State, having its peculiar form of worship as well

as its own government, did not distinguish its gods from
its laws. Political warfare was also religious; the departments of the gods were, so to speak, fixed by the limits
of the nations. The god of one nation had no right over
other nations. The gods of the pagans were not jealous
gods; they shared among them the empire of the world;
even Moses and the Hebrew nation sometimes counte-
nanced this idea by speaking of the god of Israel. It is
true that they regarded as nought the gods of the Canaan-
ites, proscribed nations, devoted to destruction, whose
country they were to occupy; but see how they spoke
of the divinities of the neighboring nations whom they
were forbidden to attack: "The possession of what
belongs to Chamos your god," said Jephthah to the
Ammonites, "is it not lawfully your due? By the same
title we possess the lands which our conquering god has
acquired." * In this, it seems to me, there was a well-
recognized parity between the rights of Chamos and
those of the god of Israel.

But when the Jews, subjected to the kings of Babylon,
and afterwards to the kings of Syria, obstinately refused
to acknowledge any other god than their own, this refusal,
being regarded as a rebellion against the conqueror, drew
upon them the persecutions which we read of in their
history, and of which no other instance appears before
Christianity.†

Every religion, then, being exclusively attached to the
laws of the State which prescribed it, there was no other

---

* "Nonne ea quae possidet Chamos deus tuus tibi jure deben-
tur?" (Judges xi: 24). Such is the text of the Vulgate. Père de
Carrières has translated it thus: "Do you not believe that you
have a right to possess what belongs to Chamos your god?" I am
ignorant of the force of the Hebrew text, but I see that in the
Vulgate Jephthah positively acknowledges the right of the god
Chamos, and that the French translator weakens this acknowl-
edgment by an "according to you" which is not in the Latin.

† There is the strongest evidence that the war of the Phoc-
æans, called a sacred war, was not a war of religion. Its object
was to punish sacrilege, and not to subdue unbelievers.

way of converting a nation than to subdue it, and no other missionaries than conquerors; and the obligation to change their form of worship being the law imposed on the vanquished, it was necessary to begin by conquering before speaking of conversions. Far from men fighting for the gods, it was, as in Homer, the gods who fought for men; each sued for victory from his own god and paid for it with new altars. The Romans, before attacking a place, summoned its gods to abandon it; and when they left to the Tarentines their exasperated gods, it was because they then regarded these gods as subjected to their own and forced to pay them homage. They left the vanquished their gods as they left them their laws. A crown for the Capitoline Jupiter was often the only tribute that they imposed.

At last, the Romans having extended their worship and their laws with their empire, and having themselves often adopted those of the vanquished, the nations of this vast empire, since the right of citizenship was granted to all, found insensibly that they had multitudes of gods and religions, almost the same everywhere; and this is why paganism was at length known in the world as only a single religion.

It was in these circumstances that Jesus came to establish on earth a spiritual kingdom, which, separating the religious from the political system, destroyed the unity of the State, and caused the intestine divisions which have never ceased to agitate Christian nations. Now this new idea of a kingdom in the other world having never been able to enter the minds of the pagans, they always regarded Christians as actual rebels, who, under cover of a hypocritical submission, only sought an opportunity to make themselves independent and supreme, and to usurp by cunning the authority which, in their weakness, they pretended to respect. This was the cause of persecutions.

What the pagans had feared came to pass. Then everything changed its aspect; the humble Christians altered their tone, and soon this pretended kingdom of the other world became, under a visible chief, the most violent despotism in this world.

As, however, there have always been a Prince and civil laws, a perpetual conflict of jurisdiction has resulted from this double power, which has rendered any good polity impossible in Christian States; and no one has ever succeeded in understanding whether he was bound to obey the ruler or the priest.

Many nations, however, even in Europe or on its outskirts, wished to preserve or to reestablish the ancient system, but without success; the spirit of Christianity prevailed over everything. The sacred worship always retained or regained its independence of the sovereign, and without any necessary connection with the body of the State. Muhammad had very sound views; he thoroughly unified his political system; and so long as his form of government subsisted under his successors, the caliphs, the government was quite undivided and in that respect good. But the Arabs having become flourishing, learned, polished, effeminate, and indolent, were subjugated by the barbarians, and then the division between the two powers began again. Although it may be less apparent among the Muhammadans than among the Christians, the division nevertheless exists, especially in the sect of Ali; and there are States, such as Persia, in which it is still seen.

Among us, the kings of England have established themselves as heads of the church, and the Tsars have done the same; but by means of this title they have made themselves its ministers rather than its rulers; they have acquired not so much the right of changing it as the power of maintaining it; they are not its legislators but only its princes. Wherever the clergy form a corporation,*

---

* It must, indeed, be remarked that it is not so much the formal assemblies, like those in France, that bind the clergy into one body, as the communion of churches. Communion and excommunication are the social pact of the clergy, a pact by means of which they will always be the masters of nations and kings. All priests who are of the same communion are fellow citizens,

they are masters and legislators in their own country. There are, then, two powers, two sovereigns, in England and in Russia, just as elsewhere.

Of all Christian authors, the philosopher Hobbes is the only one who has clearly seen the evil and its remedy, and who has dared to propose a reunion of the heads of the eagle and the complete restoration of political unity, without which no State or government will ever be well constituted. But he ought to have seen that the domineering spirit of Christianity was incompatible with his system, and that the interest of the priest would always be stronger than that of the State. It is not so much what is horrible and false in his political theory as what is just and true that has rendered it odious.*

I believe that by developing historical facts from this point of view, the opposite opinions of Bayle and Warburton might easily be refuted. The former of these maintains that no religion is useful to the body politic; the latter, on the other hand, asserts that Christianity is its strongest support. To the first it might be proved that no State was ever founded without religion serving as its basis, and to the second, that the Christian law is more injurious than useful to a firm constitution of the State. In order to succeed in making myself understood, I need only give a little more precision to the exceedingly vague ideas about religion in its relation to my subject.

Religion, considered with reference to society, which is either general or particular, may also be divided into two kinds, viz., the religion of the man and that of the

---

though they are as far asunder as the poles. This invention is a masterpiece of policy. There was nothing similar among pagan priests; therefore they never formed a body of clergy.

* See, among others, in a letter from Grotius to his brother of the 11th April, 1643, what that learned man approves and what he blames in the book *De Cive*. It is true that, inclined to indulgence, he appears to pardon the author for the good for the sake of the evil, but everyone is not so merciful.

citizen. The first, without temples, without altars, without rites, limited to the purely internal worship of the supreme God and to the eternal duties of morality, is the pure and simple religion of the Gospel, the true theism, and what may be called the natural divine law. The other, inscribed in a single country, gives to it its gods, its peculiar and tutelary patrons. It has its dogmas, its rites, its external worship prescribed by the laws; outside the single nation which observes it, everything is for it infidel, foreign, and barbarous; it extends the duties and rights of men only as far as its altars. Such were all the religions of early nations, to which may be given the name of divine law, civil or positive.

There is a third and more extravagant kind of religion, which, giving to men two sets of laws, two chiefs, two countries, imposes on them contradictory duties, and prevents them from being at once devout men and citizens. Such is the religion of the Lamas, such is that of the Japanese, such is Roman Christianity. This may be called the religion of the priest. There results from it a kind of mixed and unsocial law which has no name.

Considered politically, these three kinds of religion all have their defects. The third is so evidently bad that it would be a waste of time to stop and prove this. Whatever destroys social unity is good for nothing; all institutions which put a man in contradiction with himself are worthless.

The second is good so far as it combines divine worship with love for the laws, and, by making their country the object of the citizens' adoration, teaches them that to serve the State is to serve the guardian deity. It is a kind of theocracy, in which there ought to be no pontiff but the Prince, no other priests than the magistrates. Then to die for one's country is to suffer martyrdom, to violate the laws is to be impious, and to subject a guilty man to public execration is to devote him to the wrath of the gods: *Sacer esto.*

But it is evil in so far as being based on error and falsehood, it deceives men, renders them credulous and superstitious, and obscures the true worship of the Deity with vain ceremonial. It is evil, again, when, becoming exclusive and tyrannical, it makes a nation sanguinary and intolerant, so that it thirsts after nothing but murder and massacre, and believes that it is performing a holy action in killing whosoever does not acknowledge its gods. This puts such a nation in a natural state of war with all others, which is very prejudicial to its own safety.

There remains, then, the religion of man or Christianity, not that of today, but that of the Gospel, which is quite different. By this holy, sublime, and pure religion, men, children of the same God, all recognize one another as brethren, and the social bond which unites them is not dissolved even at death.

But this religion, having no particular relation with the body politic, leaves to the laws only the force that they derive from themselves, without adding to them any other; and thereby one of the great bonds of the particular society remains ineffective. What is more, far from attaching the hearts of citizens to the State, it detaches them from it and from all earthly things. I know of nothing more contrary to the social spirit.

We are told that a nation of true Christians would form the most perfect society conceivable. In this supposition I see only one great difficulty—that a society of true Christians would be no longer a society of men.

I say even that this supposed society, with all its perfection, would be neither the strongest nor the most durable; by virtue of its perfection it would lack cohesion; its perfection, indeed, would be its destroying vice.

Each man would perform his duty; the people would be obedient to the laws, the chief men would be just and moderate, and the magistrates upright and incorruptible; the soldiers would despise death; there would be neither vanity nor luxury. All this is very good; but let us look further.

Christianity is an entirely spiritual religion, concerned solely with heavenly things; the Christian's country is not of this world. He does his duty, it is true; but he does it with a profound indifference as to the good or ill success of his endeavors. Provided that he has nothing to reproach himself with, it matters little to him whether all goes well or ill here below. If the State is flourishing, he scarcely dares to enjoy the public felicity; he fears to take a pride in the glory of his country. If the State declines, he blesses the hand of God which lies heavy on his people.

In order that the society might be peaceable and harmony maintained, it would be necessary for all citizens without exception to be equally good Christians; but if unfortunately there happens to be in it a single ambitious man, a single hypocrite, a Catiline or a Cromwell, for example, such a man will certainly obtain an advantage over his pious compatriots. Christian charity does not suffer men readily to think ill of their neighbors. As soon as a man has found by cunning the art of imposing on them and securing to himself a share in the public authority, he is invested with dignity; God wills that he should be reverenced. Soon he exercises dominion; God wills that he should be obeyed. The depositary of this power abuses it; this is the rod with which God punishes His children. They would have scruples about driving out the usurper; it would be necessary to disturb the public peace, to employ violence, to shed blood; all this ill accords with the meekness of the Christian, and, after all, does it matter whether they are free or enslaved in this vale of woes? The essential thing is to reach paradise, and resignation is but one means the more towards that.

Some foreign war comes on; the citizens march to battle without anxiety; none of them think of flight. They do their duty, but without an ardent desire for victory; they know better how to die than to conquer. What matters it whether they are the victors or the vanquished? Does not Providence know better than they what is needful for them? Conceive what an advantage a bold, impetuous, enthusiastic enemy can derive from this stoical indifference! Set against them those noble peoples who are consumed with a burning love of glory and of country. Suppose your Christian republic opposed to Sparta or Rome; the pious Christians will be beaten, crushed, destroyed, before they have time to collect themselves, or they will owe their safety only to the contempt which the enemy may conceive for them. To my mind that was a noble oath of the soldiers of Fabius; they did not swear to die or to conquer, they swore to return as conquerors, and kept their oath. Never would Christians have done such a thing; they would have believed that they were tempting God.

But I am mistaken in speaking of a Christian republic; each of these two words excludes the other. Christianity preaches only servitude and dependence. Its spirit is too favorable to tyranny for the latter not to profit by it always. True Christians are made to be slaves; they know it and are hardly aroused by it. This short life has too little value in their eyes.

Christian troops are excellent, we are told. I deny it; let them show me any that are such. For my part, I know of no Christian troops. The crusades will be cited. Without disputing the valor of the crusaders, I shall observe that, far from being Christians, they were soldiers of the priest, citizens of the Church; they fought for their spiritual country, which the Church had somehow rendered temporal. Properly regarded, this brings us back to paganism; as the Gospel does not establish a national religion, any sacred war is impossible among Christians.

Under the pagan emperors Christian soldiers were brave; all Christian authors affirm it, and I believe it. There was a rivalry of honor against the pagan troops. As soon as the emperors became Christians, this rivalry no longer subsisted; and when the cross had driven out the eagle, all the Roman valor disappeared.

But, setting aside political considerations, let us return to the subject of right and determine principles on this important point. The right which the social pact gives to the sovereign over its subjects does not, as I have said, pass the limits of public utility.* Subjects, then, owe no account of their opinions to the sovereign except so far as those opinions are of moment to the community. Now it is very important for the State that every citizen should have a religion which may make him delight in his duties; but the dogmas of this religion concern neither the State nor its members, except so far as they affect morality and the duties which he who professes it is bound to perform towards others. Each may have, in addition, such opinions as he pleases, without its being the business of the sovereign to know them; for, as he has no jurisdiction in the other world, the destiny of his subjects in the life to come, whatever it may be, is not his affair, provided they are good citizens in this life.

There is, however, a purely civil profession of faith, the articles of which it is the duty of the sovereign to determine, not exactly as dogmas of religion, but as sentiments of sociability, without which it is impossible to be a good citizen or a faithful subject.† Without having power to compel any one to believe them, the sovereign may banish from the State whoever does not believe them; it may banish him not as impious, but as unsociable, as incapable of sincerely loving law and justice and of sacrificing at need his life to his duty. But if any one, after publicly acknowledging these dogmas, behaves like an

---

* "In the commonwealth," says the Marquis d'Argenson, "each is perfectly free in what does not injure others." That is the unalterable limit; it cannot be more accurately placed. I could not deny myself the pleasure of sometimes quoting this manuscript, although it is not known to the public, in order to do honor to the memory of an illustrious and honorable man, who preserved even in office the heart of a true citizen, and just and sound opinions about the government of his country.

† Cæsar, in pleading for Catiline, tried to establish the dogma of the mortality of the soul; Cato and Cicero, to confute him, did not waste time in philosophizing; they were content to show that Cæsar spoke as a bad citizen and put forward a doctrine pernicious to the State. Indeed, it was that which the Roman Senate had to decide, and not a theological question.

unbeliever in them, he should be punished with death; he has committed the greatest of crimes, he has lied before the laws.

The dogmas of civil religion ought to be simple, few in number, stated with precision, and without explanations or commentaries. The existence of the Deity, powerful, wise, beneficent, prescient, and bountiful, the life to come, the happiness of the just, the punishment of the wicked, the sanctity of the social contract and of the laws; these are the positive dogmas. As for the negative dogmas, I limit them to one only, that is, intolerance; it belongs to the creeds which we have excluded.

Those who distinguish civil intolerance from theological intolerance are, in my opinion, mistaken. These two kinds of intolerance are inseparable. It is impossible to live at peace with people whom we believe to be damned; to love them would be to hate God who punishes them. It is absolutely necessary to reclaim them or to punish them. Wherever theological intolerance is allowed, it cannot but have some effect in civil life; * and as soon as it has any, the sovereign is no longer sovereign even in secular affairs; from that time the priests are the real masters; the kings are only their officers.

Now that there is, and can be, no longer any exclusive national religion, we should tolerate all those which tolerate others, so far as their dogmas have nothing contrary to the duties of a citizen. But whosoever dares to

---

* Marriage, for example, being a civil contract, has civil consequences, without which it is even impossible for society to subsist. Let us, then, suppose that a clergy should succeed in arrogating to itself the sole right to perform this act, a right which it must necessarily usurp in every intolerant religion; then, is it not clear that in taking the opportunity to strengthen the Church's authority, it will render ineffectual that of the Prince, which will no longer have any subjects except those which the clergy are pleased to give it? Having the option of marrying or not marrying people, according as they hold or do not hold such or such a doctrine, according as they admit or reject such or such a

say: "Outside the Church no salvation," ought to be driven from the State, unless the State be the Church and the Prince be the pontiff. Such a dogma is proper only in a theocratic government; in any other it is pernicious. The reason for which Henry IV is said to have embraced the Romish religion ought to have made any honorable man renounce it, and especially any prince who knew how to reason.

CHAPTER IX

Conclusion

AFTER laying down the principles of political right and attempting to establish the State on its foundations, it would remain to strengthen it in its external relations; which would comprise the law of nations, commerce, the right of war and conquests, public rights, alliances, negotiations, treaties, etc. But all this forms a new subject too vast for my limited scope. I ought always to have confined myself to a narrower sphere.

formulary, according as they are more or less devoted to it, is it not clear that by behaving prudently and keeping firm, the Church alone will dispose of inheritances, offices, citizens, and the State itself, which cannot subsist when only composed of bastards? But, it will be said, men will appeal as against abuses; they will summon, issue decrees, and seize on the temporalities. What a pity! The clergy, however little they may have, I do not say of courage, but of good sense, will let this be done and go their way; they will quietly permit appealing, adjourning, decreeing, seizing, and will end by remaining masters. It is not, it seems to me, a great sacrifice to abandon a part, when one is sure of getting possession of the whole.

DISCOURSE
on the
Origin and Foundation
of
Inequality Among Mankind

*Non in depravatis, sed in his quae bene secundum naturam se habent, considerandum est quid sit naturale.** ARISTOTLE, *Politics*, 1, 2.

---

* "We should consider what is natural not in things which are depraved, but in those which are rightly ordered according to nature."

Notice Regarding the Notes

I have appended a few notes to this work, following my indolent custom of working by fits and starts. These notes sometimes digress too far from the subject to be read with the text. Therefore I have placed them at the end of the Discourse, in which I have tried my best to follow a straight path. Those who have the courage to continue may enjoy beating the bushes a second time and try to go through the notes. As to the others, it is no great matter if they do not read them at all.

DEDICATION
to the
Republic of Geneva

MOST HONORABLE, MAGNIFICENT, AND SOVEREIGN LORDS,

CONVINCED that it belongs only to a virtuous citizen to present his country those acknowledgments it may become her to receive, I have been for thirty years past, endeavoring to render myself worthy to offer you some public homage. In the meantime, this fortunate occasion replacing in some degree the insufficiency of my efforts, I have presumed rather to follow the dictates of zeal, than to wait till I should be authorized by merit. Having had the good fortune to be born a subject of Geneva, how could I reflect on the natural equality of mankind, and that inequality which they have introduced, without admiring the profound wisdom by which both the one and the other are happily combined in this State, and contribute, in a manner the most conformable to the law of nature, and the most favorable to community, to the security of public order and the happiness of individuals? In my researches after the best and most sensible maxims, which might be laid down for the constitution of government, I was surprised to find them all united in yours; so that had I not been a fellow-citizen, I should have thought it indispensable in me to present such a picture of human society to that people, who of all others, seem to be possessed of its greatest advantages, and to have best guarded against its abuses.

If I had had to choose the place of my birth, I should have preferred a community proportioned in its extent to the limits of the human faculties; that is to the possibility of being well governed: in which every person being capable of his employment, no one should be obliged to commit to others the trust he ought to discharge himself: a State in which its individuals might be so well known to each other, that neither the secret machinations of vice, nor the modesty of virtue should be able to escape the notice and judgment of the public; and in which the agreeable custom of seeing and knowing each other, should occasion the love of their country to be rather an affection for its inhabitants than for its soil.

I should have chosen for my birthplace a country in which the interest of the sovereign could not be separated from that of the subject; to the end that all the motions of the machine of government might ever tend to the general happiness. And as this could not be the case, unless where the sovereignty is lodged in the people, it follows that I should have preferred a prudently tempered democracy.

I should have been desirous to live and die free: that is, so far subject to the laws that neither I, nor any other body else, should have it in our power to cast off their honorable yoke: that agreeable and salutary yoke to which the haughtiest necks bend with the greater docility, as they are formed to bear no other.

I should have desired, therefore, that no person within the State should be able to say he was above the laws; nor that any person without, should be able to dictate such as the State should be obliged to obey. For, whatever the constitution of a government, if there be a single member of it who is not subject to the laws, all the rest are necessarily at his discretion. And if there be a national chief within, and a foreign chief without, however they may divide their authority, it is impossible that both should be duly obeyed and the State well governed.

I should not have chosen to live in a republic of recent institution, however excellent its laws, for fear the government being otherwise framed than circumstances might require, it might either disagree with the new subjects, or the subjects disagree with the new government; in which case the State might be shaken to pieces and destroyed almost as soon as founded.

For it is with liberty as it is with solid and succulent foods, or with rich wines, proper to nourish and fortify robust constitutions accustomed to them, but pernicious, destructive and intoxicating to weak and delicate temperaments, to which they are not adapted. A people once accustomed to masters are not able to live without them. If they attempt at any time to shake off their yoke, they lose still more freedom; for, by mistaking licentiousness for liberty, to which it is diametrically opposed, they generally become greater slaves to some impostor, who loads them with fresh chains. The Romans themselves, an example for every succeeding free people, were incapable of governing themselves on their expulsion of the Tarquins. Debased by slavery, and the ignominious tasks imposed on them, they were at first no better than a stupid mob, which it was requisite to manage and govern with the greatest wisdom; so that, being accustomed by degrees to breathe the salutary air of liberty, their minds which had been enervated or rather brutalized under the burden of slavery, might gradually acquire that severity of manners and spirit of fortitude which rendered them at length the most respectable nation upon earth.

I should have searched out for my country, therefore, some peaceful and happy republic, whose antiquity lost itself, as it were, in the obscurity of time: one that had experienced only such salutary shocks as served to display and confirm the courage and patriotism of its subjects; and whose citizens, long accustomed to a prudent independence, were not only free, but worthy of their freedom.

I should have made choice of a country, diverted, by a fortunate impotence, from the brutal love of conquest; and secured, by a still more fortunate situation, from becoming itself the conquest of other states: a free city situated between several nations, none of which should find it their interest to attack it, yet all think themselves interested in preventing its being attacked by others: a republic, in short, which should present nothing to tempt the ambition of its neighbors; but might reasonably depend on their assistance in case of need. It would follow that a republican State so happily situated as I have supposed, could have nothing to fear but from itself; and that, if its members accustomed themselves to the exercise of arms, it must be to keep alive that military ardor and courage, which is so suitable to free men, and tends to keep up their taste for liberty, rather than through the necessity of providing for their own defense.

I should have sought a country, in which the legislative power should be vested in all its citizens: for who can better judge than themselves of the propriety of the terms, on which they mutually agree to live together in the same community? Not that I should have approved of plebiscites, like those among the Romans, in which the leaders of the State, and those most interested in its preservation, were excluded from those deliberations on which its security frequently depended; and in which, by the most absurd inconsistency, the magistrates were deprived of privileges enjoyed by the lowest citizens.

On the contrary, I should have desired that, in order to prevent self-interested and ill-designed projects, with any of those dangerous innovations which at length ruined the Athenians, no person should be at liberty to propose new laws at pleasure: but that this should be the exclusive privilege of the magistrates; and that even these should use it with so much caution, that the people on their part should be so reserved in giving their consent to such laws; and that the promulgation of theirs should be attended with so much solemnity, that before the constitution could be affected by them, there might be time enough given for all to be convinced, that it is the great antiquity of the laws which principally contributes to render them sacred and venerable, that the people soon learn to despise those which they see daily altered, and that States, by accustoming themselves to neglect their ancient customs under pretense of improvement, frequently introduce greater evils than those they endeavor to remove.

I should have particularly avoided a republic, as one that must of course be ill-governed, in which the people, imagining themselves capable of subsisting without magistrates, or at least without investing them with anything more than a precarious authority, should imprudently reserve to themselves the administration of civil affairs and the execution of their own laws. Such must have been the rude constitution of the primitive governments, directly emerging from the state of nature; and this was another of the vices that contributed to the dissolution of the republic of Athens.

But I should have chosen a republic, the individuals of which, contented with the privileges of giving sanction to their laws, and of deciding in a body, according to the recommendations of the leaders, the most important public affairs, should have established respectable tribunals; carefully distinguished their several departments; and electing annually some of their fellow-citizens, of the greatest capacity and integrity, to administer justice and govern the State; a community, in short, in which the virtue of the magistrates thus bearing testimony to the wisdom of the people, they would mutually honor each other. So that if ever any fatal misunderstandings should arise to disturb the public peace, even these intervals of confusion and error should bear the marks of moderation, reciprocal esteem, and of a mutual respect for the laws; certain signs and pledges of a reconciliation as lasting as sincere. Such are the advantages, most honorable, magnificent and sovereign Lords, which I should have sought in the country I had chosen.

And if providence had added to all these, a delightful situation, a temperate clime, a fertile soil, and the most charming views that present themselves under heaven, I should desire only, to complete my felicity, the peaceful enjoyment of all these blessings, in the bosom of this happy country; living in agreeable society with my fellow-citizens, and exercising towards them from their own example, the duties of friendship, humanity, and every other virtue, that I might leave behind me the honorable memory of a worthy man, and an incorruptible and virtuous patriot.

But, if less fortunate or too late grown wise, I saw myself reduced to end an infirm and languishing life in other climates, vainly regretting that peaceful repose which I forfeited in the imprudence of my youth, I would at least have entertained the same sentiments within myself, though denied the opportunity of avowing and indulging them in my native country. Affected with a tender and disinterested love for my distant fellow-citizens, I should have addressed them from my heart, in about the following terms.

"My dear countrymen, or rather my brethren, since the ties of blood unite most of us, as well as the laws, it gives me pleasure that I cannot think of you, without thinking, at the same time, of all the blessings you enjoy, the value of which none of you, perhaps, are so aware as I to whom they are lost. The more I reflect on your situation, both civil and political, the less can I conceive that the present state of human nature will admit of a better. In all other governments, even when it is a question of securing the greatest welfare of the State, they are always confined to ideal projects, or at least to bare possibilities. But as for you, your happiness is complete. You have nothing to do but enjoy it; you require nothing more to be made perfectly happy, than to know how to be satisfied with being so. Your sovereignty, acquired or recovered by the sword, and maintained for two centuries past by your valor and wisdom, is at length fully and universally acknowledged. Your boundaries are fixed, your rights confirmed and your repose secured by honorable treaties. Your constitution is excellent, dictated by the profoundest wisdom, and guaranteed by friendly and respectable powers. Your State enjoys perfect tranquillity; you have nothing to fear either from wars or conquerors: you have no other master than the wise laws you have yourselves made; and which are administered by upright magistrates of your own choosing. You are neither so wealthy as to be enervated by softness, and so to lose, in the pursuit of frivolous pleasures, a taste for real happiness and solid virtue; nor yet are you so poor as to require more assistance from strangers than your own industry is sufficient to procure you. In the meantime that precious liberty, which is maintained in great States only by exorbitant taxation, costs you hardly anything for its preservation.

"May a republic, so wisely and happily constituted, last forever, as well for an example to other nations, as for the felicity of its own subjects! This is the only wish you have left to make; the only subject of your solicitude. It depends, for the future, on yourselves alone, not to make you happy, your ancestors have saved you that trouble, but to render that happiness lasting, by your prudence in its enjoyment. It is on your constant unanimity, your obedience to the laws, and your respect for the magistrates, that your preservation depends. If there remain among you the smallest seeds of enmity or distrust, hasten to root them up, as an accursed leaven from which sooner or later will result your misfortunes and the destruction of the State. I conjure you all to examine the bottom of your hearts, and to hearken to the secret voice of your own consciences. Is there any among you who can find, throughout the universe, a more upright, more enlightened and more respectable body than that of your own magistracy? Do not all its members set you an example of moderation, of simplicity of manners, of respect for the laws, and of the most sincere reconciliation? Place, therefore, without reservations that salutary confidence in such wise leaders, which reason ever owes to virtue. Consider they are the objects of your own choice; that they justify that choice; and that the honors, due to those whom you have exalted to dignity, are necessarily reflected back on yourselves. Is there any among you so ignorant, as not to know that, when the laws lose their force, and the magistrates their authority, neither the persons nor properties of individuals are any longer secure? Why, therefore, should you hesitate to do that cheerfully and confidently, which your true interest, your duty and even common prudence will ever require?

"Let not a culpable and fatal indifference to the support of the constitution, ever induce you to neglect, in case of need, the prudent advice of the most enlightened and zealous of your fellow-citizens: but let equity, moderation and firmness of resolution continue to regulate all your proceedings; exhibiting you to the whole universe as an example of a valiant and modest people, equally jealous of their honor and their liberty. Beware particularly, this is the last advice I shall give you, of sinister interpretations and calumniating reports, the secret motives of which are often more dangerous than the actions at which they are levelled. The whole house will be awake and take the first alarm, given by a trusty and watchful mastiff, who barks only at the approach of thieves; but we ever abominate the impertinent yelping of those noisy curs, who are perpetually disturbing the public repose, and whose continual and ill-timed warnings prevent our attending to them when they may be needed."

And you, most honorable and magnificent Lords, you, the worthy and respectable magistrates of a free people, permit me to offer you in particular my duty and homage. If there be in the world a station capable of conferring honor on the persons who fill it, it is undoubtedly that which virtue and talents combine to bestow; that of which you have rendered yourselves worthy, and to which you have been promoted by your fellow-citizens. Their worth adds a new luster to yours; since men who are capable of governing others have chosen you to govern them, I cannot help esteeming you as superior to all other magistrates, as a free people, and particularly that over which you have the honor to preside, is by its wisdom and knowledge superior to the populace of other States.

May I be permitted to cite an example of which there ought to have existed better remains; an example which will be ever near and dear to my heart. I cannot recall to mind, without the most agreeable emotions, the person and manners of that virtuous citizen, to whom I owe my being, and by whom I was instructed, in my infancy, in the respect which is due to you. I see him still, subsisting on his manual labor, and improving his mind by the study of the sublimest truths. I see, lying before him, the works of Tacitus, Plutarch and Grotius, intermixed with the tools of his trade. At his side stands his darling son, receiving, alas with too little profit, the tender instructions of the best of fathers. But, though the follies of a wild youth caused me a while to forget his prudent lessons, I have at length the happiness to experience that, whatever propensity one may have to vice, it is not easy for an education, thus affectionately bestowed, to be ever entirely thrown away.

Such, my most honorable and magnificent lords, are the citizens, and even the common inhabitants of the country under your government; such are those intelligent and sensible men, of which, under the name of mechanics and tradespeople, it is usual, in other nations to entertain a false and contemptible idea. My father, I own it with pleasure, was in no wise distinguished from his fellow-citizens. He was only such as they are all: and yet, such as he was, there is no country in which his acquaintance would not have been coveted, and cultivated even with advantage by men of the first distinction. It would not become me, nor is it, thank heaven, at all necessary for me to remind you of the regard which such men have a right to expect of their magistrates, to whom they are equal both by birth and education, and inferior only by that preference which they voluntarily pay to your merit, and in so doing lay claim on their part to some sort of gratitude.

It is with a lively satisfaction I learn with how much gentleness and condescendence you temper that gravity which becomes the ministers of the law; and that you so well repay them, by your esteem and attentions, that respect and obedience which they justly pay to you. This conduct is not only just but prudent, as it wisely tends to obliterate many unhappy events, which ought to be buried in eternal oblivion; * it is also by so much the more prudential, as this generous and equitable people find a pleasure in their duty; as they are naturally inclined to doing you honor, as those who are the most zealous to maintain their own rights and privileges are at the same time the best disposed to respect yours.

It ought not to be thought surprising that the leaders of a civil society should have its welfare and glory at heart: but it is uncommonly fortunate for them, when those persons who look upon themselves as the magistrates, or rather the masters of a more holy and sublime country, demonstrate their affection for the earthly spot which maintains them. I am happy in having it in my power to make so singular an exception in favor of my own country; and to rank, in the number of its best citizens, those zealous depositaries of the sacred articles of our established faith; those venerable pastors whose powerful and captivating eloquence is so much the better calculated to enforce the maxims of the gospel, as they are themselves the first to put them in practice.

The whole world is informed of the great success with which the oratory of the pulpit is cultivated at Geneva; but, being too much used to hear divines preach one thing, and see them practice another, few people have an opportunity to know how far the true spirit of Christianity, holiness of manners, severity with regard to themselves and indulgence to their neighbors, prevail throughout the whole body of our ministers. It is, perhaps, in

---

* Rousseau is referring to uprisings by a large part of the population which was oppressed by the ruling oligarchy. The description of the government of Geneva is largely false, and an example of Rousseau's frequent tactics of duplicity. He is trying to win the favor of the Genevan authorities.

the power of the city of Geneva alone to produce an edifying example of so perfect an union subsisting between its clergy and men of letters. And it is in great degree, on their wisdom, their known moderation, and on their zeal for the prosperity of the State that I build my hopes of its constant and perpetual tranquillity.

At the same time, I remark, with a pleasure mixed with surprise and veneration, how much they detest the horrid maxims of those holy and barbarous men, of whom history furnishes us with more than one example; who, in order to support the pretended prerogative of the deity, that is to say their own interest, have been so much the less sparing of human blood, as they were more assured that their own should be always respected.

I must not here forget that precious half of the republic, which makes the happiness of the other; and whose tenderness and prudence preserve its tranquillity and virtue. Amiable and virtuous daughters of Geneva, it will be always the lot of your sex to govern ours. Happy, so long as your chaste influence, solely exercised within the limits of conjugal union, is exerted only for the glory of the State and the happiness of the public. It is thus the female sex commanded at Sparta; and thus that you deserve to command at Geneva.

What man can be such a barbarian as to resist the voice of honor and reason, breathing from the lips of an affectionate wife? Who would not despise the tawdry charms of luxury, on beholding the simplicity and modesty of an attire, which, from the luster it derives from you, seems to be the most favorable to beauty? It is your task to perpetuate, by the insinuating spirit of your manners, by your innocent and amiable influence, a respect for the laws of the State, and harmony among individuals. It is yours to reunite divided families by happy marriages; and, above all things, to correct, by the persuasive mildness of your lessons and the modest graces of your discourse, those extravagances which our young people pick up in other countries; from whence, instead of many useful things that come within the reach of their observation and practice, they bring home hardly anything but a puerile air and ridiculous manner, acquired among loose women, and the admiration of I know not what pretended grandeur, a paltry indemnification for slavery and unworthy of the real greatness of true liberty.

Continue, therefore, always to be what you are, the chaste guardians of our manners, and the gentle links of our peace; exerting on every occasion the privileges of the heart and of nature to the advantage of moral obligation and the interests of virtue.

I flatter myself no sinister event will ever prove me to have been mistaken, in building on such a foundation my hopes of the felicity of my fellow-citizens and the glory of the republic. It must be confessed, however, that with all these advantages, it will not shine with that exterior luster, by which the eyes of the generality of mankind are affected, a puerile and fatal taste for which is the most mortal enemy to the happiness and liberty of a State.

Let dissolute youth seek elsewhere those transient pleasures which are followed by long repentance. Let pretenders to taste elsewhere admire the grandeur of palaces, the beauty of equipages, the sumptuousness of furniture, the pomp of public entertainments, with all the refinements of luxury and effeminacy. Geneva boasts nothing but men; such a sight has nevertheless its value, and those who have a taste for it are at least as good as the admirers of the other things.

Deign, most honorable, magnificent and sovereign lords, all and each, to receive, and with equal goodness, this respectful testimony of the interest I take in your common prosperity. And, if I have been so unhappy as to be guilty of any indiscreet transport, in this glowing effusion of my heart, I beseech you to pardon, and impute it to the tender affection of a real patriot, and to the ardent and lawful zeal of a man, who places his own greatest felicity in the prospect of seeing you happy.

I am, with the most profound respect, most honorable, magnificent and sovereign lords,

Chambéry, June 12, 1754

Your most humble, and most obedient servant and fellow-citizen.
JEAN-JACQUES ROUSSEAU

PREFACE

THE most useful and least perfected of all human studies is, in my opinion, that of man, and I dare say that the inscription on the Temple of Delphi did alone contain a more important and difficult precept than all the huge volumes of the moralists.* I therefore consider the subject of this discourse as one of the most interesting questions philosophy can propose, and, unhappily for us, one of the most knotty philosophers can labor to solve: For how is it possible to know the source of the inequality among men, without knowing men themselves? And how shall man be able to see himself, such as nature formed him, in spite of all the alterations which a long succession of years and events must have produced in his original constitution, and how shall he be able to distinguish what is of his own essence, from what the circumstances he has been in and the progress he has made have added to, or changed in, his primitive condition? The human soul, like the statue of Glaucus which time, the sea and storms had so much disfigured that it resembled a wild beast more than a god, the human soul, I say, altered in society by the perpetual succession of a thousand causes, by the acquisition of numberless discoveries and errors, by the changes that have happened in the constitution of the body, by the perpetual jarring of the passions, has in a manner so changed in appearance as to be scarcely distinguishable; and by now we

* The inscription read, "Know thyself," and "Nothing in excess."

perceive in it, instead of a being always acting from certain and invariable principles, instead of that heavenly and majestic simplicity which its author had impressed upon it, nothing but the shocking contrast of passion that thinks it reasons, and an understanding grown delirious.

But what is still more cruel, as every advance made by the human species serves only to remove it still further from its primitive condition, the more we accumulate new knowledge, the more we deprive ourselves of the means of acquiring the most important of all; and it is, in a manner, by the mere dint of studying man that we have lost the power of knowing him.

It is easy to perceive that it is in these successive alterations of the human constitution that we must look for the first origin of those differences that distinguish men, who, it is universally allowed, are naturally as equal among themselves as were the animals of every species before various physical causes had introduced those varieties we now observe among some of them. In fact, it is not possible to conceive how these first changes, whatever causes may have produced them, could have altered, all at once and in the same manner, all the individuals of the species. It seems obvious that while some improved or impaired their condition, or acquired divers good or bad qualities not inherent in their nature, the rest continued a longer time in their primitive state; and such was among men the first source of inequality, which it is much easier thus to point out in general, than to trace back with precision to its true causes.

Let not then my readers imagine that I dare flatter myself with having seen what I think is so difficult to discover. I have opened some arguments; I have risked some conjectures; but not so much from any hopes of being able to solve the question, as with a view of throwing upon it some light, and giving a true statement of it. Others may with great facility penetrate further in the same road, but none will find it an easy matter to get to the end of it. For it is no such easy task to distinguish between what is natural and what is artificial in the present constitution of man, and to make oneself well acquainted with a state which, if ever it did, does not now, and in all probability never will exist, and of which, notwithstanding, it is absolutely necessary to have just notions to judge properly of our present state. A man must be even more a philosopher than most people think, to take upon himself to determine exactly what precautions are requisite to make solid observations upon this subject; and, in my opinion, a good solution of the following problem would not be unworthy of the Aristotles and Plinys of our age: What experiments are requisite to know man as constituted by nature, and which are the best methods of making these experiments in the midst of society? For my own part, I am so far from pretending to solve this problem, that I think I have sufficiently reflected on the subject of it to dare answer beforehand, that the wisest philosophers would not be too wise to direct such experiments, nor the most powerful sovereigns too powerful to make them; a concurrence of circumstances which there is hardly any reason to expect, and especially with that perseverance, or rather that succession of knowledge, penetration, and good will requisite on both sides to insure success.

These investigations, so difficult to make and which hitherto have been so little thought of, are however the only means left us to remove a thousand difficulties which prevent our seeing the true foundations of human society. It is this ignorance of the nature of man that casts so much uncertainty and obscurity on the genuine definition of natural right: for the idea of right, as Monsieur Burlamaqui * says, and still more that of natural right, are ideas evidently relative to the nature of man. It is therefore from this very nature of man, he continues, from his constitution and his state, that we are to deduce the principles of this science.

It is impossible to observe, without both surprise and

---

* Author of *Principes du droit naturel* (Geneva, 1747).

scandal, the little agreement there is to be found on this important subject between the different authors that have treated of it. Among the gravest writers, you will scarce find two of the same opinion. Not to speak of the ancient philosophers, who, one would imagine, had set out to contradict each other in regard to the most fundamental principles, the Roman jurisconsults make man and all other animals, without distinction, subject to the same natural law, because they consider under this name, rather that law which nature imposes upon herself than that which she prescribes; or, more probably, on account of the particular acceptation of the word, law, among these jurisconsults, who, on this occasion, seem to have understood nothing more by it than the general relations established by nature between all animated beings for the sake of their common preservation. The moderns, by not admitting anything under the word law but a rule prescribed to a moral being, that is to say, a being intelligent, free, and considered with a view to his relations to other beings, must of course confine to the only animal endowed with reason, that is, to man, the competency of the natural law; but then, by defining this law, every one of them his own way, they establish it on such metaphysical principles, that so far from being able to find out these principles by themselves, there are very few persons among us capable of so much as understanding them. Thus, therefore, all the definitions of these learned men, definitions in everything else so constantly at variance, agree only in this, that it is impossible to understand the law of nature, and consequently to obey it, without being a very subtle reasoner and a very profound metaphysician. This is no more nor less than saying that men must have employed for the establishment of society a fund of knowledge, which it is a very difficult matter, nay absolutely impossible, for most persons to develop, even in a state of society.

As men, therefore, are so little acquainted with nature, and agree so ill about the meaning of the word *law*, it would be very difficult for them to agree on a good definition of natural law. Accordingly, all those we meet with in books, besides lacking uniformity, err by being derived from several kinds of knowledge which men do not naturally enjoy, and from advantages they can have no notion of, as long as they remain in a state of nature. The writers of these books set out by examining what rules it would be proper for men to agree to among themselves for their common interest; and then they proceed to give the name of natural law to a collection of these rules, without any other proof than the advantage they find would result from a universal compliance with it. This is, no doubt, a very easy method of striking out definitions, and of explaining the nature of things by an almost arbitrary fitness.

But as long as we remain unacquainted with the constitution of natural man, it will be in vain for us to attempt to determine what law he received, or what law suits him best. All we can plainly distinguish in regard to that law is that for it to be law, not only the will of him whom it obliges must be able to submit to it knowingly, but also that, for it to be natural, it must speak immediately by the voice of nature.

Laying aside therefore all the scientific treatises, which teach us merely to consider men such as they have made themselves, and confining myself to the first and most simple operations of the human soul, I think I can distinguish in it two principles prior to reason; one of them interests us deeply in our own preservation and welfare, the other inspires us with a natural aversion to seeing any other being, but especially any being like ourselves, suffer or perish. It is from the concurrence and the combination our mind is capable of forming between these two principles, without there being the least necessity for adding to them that of sociability, that, in my opinion, flow all the rules of natural right; rules, which reason is afterwards obliged to reestablish upon other foundations, when by its successive developments, it has at last stifled nature itself.

By proceeding in this manner, we shall not be obliged

to make man a philosopher before he is a man. His obligations are not dictated to him merely by the slow voice of wisdom; and as long as he does not resist the internal impulses of compassion, he never will do any harm to another man, nor even to any sentient being, except in those lawful cases where his own preservation happens to come in question, and it is of course his duty to give himself the preference. By this means too we may put an end to the ancient disputes concerning the participation of other animals in the law of nature; for it is plain that, as they want both reason and free will, they cannot be acquainted with that law; however, as they partake in some measure of our nature in virtue of that sensibility with which they are endowed, we may well imagine they ought likewise to partake of the benefit of the natural law, and that man owes them a certain kind of duty.* In fact, it seems that, if I am obliged not to injure any being like myself, it is not so much because he is a reasonable being, as because he is a sensible being; and this quality, by being common to men and beasts, ought to exempt the latter from any unnecessary injuries the former might be able to do them.

This same study of original man, of his real needs, and of the fundamental principles of his duties, is likewise the only good method we can take, to surmount an infinite number of difficulties concerning the origin of moral inequality, the true foundations of political bodies, the reciprocal rights of their members, and a thousand other similar questions that are as important as they are ill-understood.

If we consider human society with a calm and disinterested eye, it seems at first sight to show us nothing but the violence of the powerful and the oppression of the weak; the mind is shocked at the cruelty of the one, and equally grieved at the blindness of the other; and as nothing is less stable in human life than those exterior

---

* Descartes had maintained that animals are merely machines, without conscious feeling.

relations, which chance produces oftener than wisdom, and which are called weakness or power, poverty or riches, human establishments appear at the first glance like so many castles built upon quicksand; it is only by taking a nearer survey of them, and by removing the dust and the sand which surround and disguise the edifice, that we can perceive the unshakable basis upon which it stands, and learn to respect its foundations. Now, without a serious study of man, his natural faculties and their successive developments, we shall never succeed in making these distinctions, and in separating, in the present constitution of things, what comes from the divine will from what human contrivance has aspired to do. The political and moral reflections, to which the important question I examine gives rise, are therefore useful in many ways; and the hypothetical history of governments is, in regard to man, an instructive lesson in every respect. By considering what we should have become, had we been left to ourselves, we ought to learn to bless him, whose gracious hand, correcting our institutions, and giving them an unshakable foundation, has thereby prevented the disorders which they otherwise must have produced, and made our happiness flow from means, which seemed bound to complete our misery.

> *Quem te Deus esse*
> *Jussit, et humana qua parte locatus es in re, Disce.* *

---

* "Learn whom God has ordered you to be and in what part in human affairs you have been placed." (Persius, *Satires*, III, 71.)

DISCOURSE
on the
Origin and the Foundation
of
Inequality Among Mankind

〰〰〰〰〰〰

It is of man I am to speak; and the question into which I am inquiring informs me that it is to men that I am going to speak; for to those alone, who are not afraid of honoring truth, it belongs to propose discussions of this kind. I shall therefore defend with confidence the cause of mankind before the sages, who invite me to stand up in its defense; and I shall think myself happy, if I can but behave in a manner not unworthy of my subject and of my judges.

I conceive two species of inequality among men; one which I call natural, or physical inequality, because it is established by nature, and consists in the difference of age, health, bodily strength, and the qualities of the mind, or of the soul; the other which may be termed moral, or political inequality, because it depends on a kind of convention, and is established, or at least authorized by the common consent of mankind. This species of inequality consists in the different privileges, which some men enjoy, to the prejudice of others, such as that of being richer, more honored, more powerful, and even that of exacting obedience from them.

It were absurd to ask, what is the cause of natural inequality, seeing the bare definition of natural inequality answers the question: it would be more absurd still to inquire, if there might not be some essential connection between the two species of inequality, as it would be asking, in other words, if those who command are necessarily better men than those who obey; and if strength of body or of mind, wisdom or virtue are always to be found in individuals, in the same proportion with power, or riches: a question, fit perhaps to be discussed by slaves in the hearing of their masters, but unbecoming free and reasonable beings in quest of truth.

What therefore is precisely the subject of this discourse? It is to point out, in the progress of things, that moment, when, right taking place of violence, nature became subject to law; to unfold that chain of amazing events, in consequence of which the strong submitted to serve the weak, and the people to purchase imaginary ease, at the expense of real happiness.

The philosophers, who have examined the foundations of society, have all perceived the necessity of tracing it back to a state of nature, but not one of them has ever got there. Some of them have not scrupled to attribute to man in that state the ideas of justice and injustice, without troubling themselves to prove that he really must have had such ideas, or even that such ideas were useful to him: others have spoken of the natural right of every man to keep what belongs to him, without letting us know what they meant by the word *belong*; others, without further ceremony ascribing to the strongest an authority over the weakest, have immediately brought government into being, without thinking of the time requisite for men to form any notion of the things signified by the words authority and government. All of them, in fine, constantly harping on wants, avidity, oppression, desires and pride, have transferred to the state of nature ideas picked up in the bosom of society. In speaking of savages they described citizens. Nay, few of our own writers seem to have so much as doubted, that a state of nature did once actually exist; though it plainly appears by sacred history, that even the first man, immediately furnished as he was by God himself with both instructions and precepts, never lived in that state, and that, if we give to the Books of Moses that credit which every Christian philosopher ought to give to them, we must deny that, even before the Deluge, such a state ever existed among men, unless they fell into it by some extraordinary event: a paradox very difficult to maintain, and altogether impossible to prove.

Let us begin, therefore, by laying aside facts, for they do not affect the question. The researches, in which we may engage on this occasion, are not to be taken for historical truths, but merely as hypothetical and conditional reasonings, fitter to illustrate the nature of things, than to show their true origin, like those systems, which our naturalists daily make of the formation of the world. Religion commands us to believe that men, having been drawn by God himself out of a state of nature, are unequal, because it is His pleasure they should be so; but religion does not forbid us to draw conjectures solely from the nature of man, considered in itself, and from that of the beings which surround him, concerning the fate of mankind, had they been left to themselves. This is then the question I am to answer, the question I propose to examine in the present discourse. As mankind in general has an interest in my subject, I shall endeavor to use a language suitable to all nations; or rather, forgetting the circumstances of time and place in order to think of nothing but the men I speak to, I shall suppose myself in the Lyceum of Athens, repeating the lessons of my masters before the Platos and the Xenocrates of that famous seat of philosophy as my judges, and in presence of the whole human species as my audience.

O man, of whatever country you are, whatever your opinions may be, attend to my words; here is your history such as I think I have read it, not in books composed by your fellowmen, for they are liars, but in the book of nature which never lies. All that comes from her will be true, nor will there be anything false, but where I may happen, without intending it, to introduce something of my own. The times I am going to speak of are very remote. How much are you changed from what you once were! It is in a manner the life of your species that I am going to write, from the qualities which you have received, and which your education and your habits have succeeded in depraving, but could not destroy. There is, I feel, an age at which every individual would choose to stop; and you will look for the age at which, had you your wish, your species had stopped. Discontented with your present condition for reasons which threaten your unhappy posterity with still greater vexations, you will perhaps wish it were in your power to go back; and this sentiment ought to be considered a panegyric of your first ancestors, a criticism of your contemporaries, and a source of terror to those who may have the misfortune of coming after you.

FIRST PART

HOWEVER important it may be, in order to form a proper judgment of the natural state of man, to consider him from his origin, and to examine him, as it were, in the first embryo of the species, I shall not attempt to trace his organization through its successive developments: I shall not stop to examine in the animal system what he may have been in the beginning, in order to have become at last what he actually is. I shall not inquire, whether, as Aristotle thinks, his extended nails were no better at first than crooked talons; whether his whole body was not, bear-like, thickly covered with hair; and whether, walking upon all fours, his looks directed to the earth, and confined to a horizon of a few paces extent, did not at once point out the nature and limits of his ideas. I could only form vague, and almost imaginary, conjectures on this subject. Comparative anatomy has not as yet made sufficient progress; and the observations of natural philosophy are too uncertain, to establish upon such foundations the basis of any solid reasoning. For this reason, without having recourse to the supernatural information with which we have been favored on this head, or paying any attention to the changes, that must have happened in the internal, as well as external conformation of man, in proportion as he applied his limbs to new purposes, and took to new foods, I shall suppose his conformation to have always been, what we now behold it; that he always walked on two feet, made the same use of his hands that we do of ours, extended his looks over the whole face of nature, and measured with his eyes the vast extent of the heavens.*

If I strip this being, thus constituted, of all the supernatural gifts which he may have received, and of all the artificial faculties, which he could not have acquired but by slow degrees; if I consider him, in a word, such as he must have issued from the hands of nature; I see an animal less strong than some, and less agile than others, but, upon the whole, the most advantageously organized of any: I see him satisfying his hunger under an oak, and his thirst at the first brook; I see him laying himself down to sleep at the foot of the same tree that afforded him his meal; and there are all his wants completely supplied.

The earth, left to its own natural fertility, and covered with immense woods that no hatchet ever disfigured, offers at every step food and shelter to every species of animals. Men, dispersed among them, observe and imitate their industry, and thus rise as high as the instinct of beasts; with this advantage, that, whereas every species of beasts is confined to one peculiar instinct, man, who perhaps has not any that particularly belongs to him, appropriates to himself those of all other animals, and lives equally upon most of the different foods, which

* Rousseau was well acquainted with the theory of evolution that had been sketched by his friend, Diderot, in his *Pensées sur l'interprétation de la nature* (1753).

they only divide among themselves; a circumstance which qualifies him to find his subsistence more easily than any of them.

Accustomed from their infancy to the inclemency of the weather, and to the rigor of the different seasons; inured to fatigue, and obliged to defend, naked and without arms, their life and their prey against the other wild inhabitants of the forest, or at least to avoid their fury by flight, men acquire a robust and almost unalterable constitution. The children, bringing with them into the world the excellent constitution of their parents, and strengthening it by the same exercises that first produced it, attain by this means all the vigor that the human frame is capable of. Nature treats them exactly in the same manner that Sparta treated the children of her citizens; those who come well formed into the world she renders strong and robust, and destroys all the rest; differing in this respect from our societies, in which the State, by permitting children to become burdensome to their parents, murders them without distinction in the wombs of their mothers.

The body being the only instrument that savage man is acquainted with, he employs it to different uses, of which ours, for want of practice, are incapable; and we may thank our industry for the loss of that strength and agility, which necessity obliges him to acquire. Had he a hatchet, would his hand so easily snap off from an oak so stout a branch? Had he a sling, would it hurl a stone to so great a distance? Had he a ladder, would he climb so nimbly up a tree? Had he a horse, would he run with such swiftness? Give civilized man but time to gather about him all his machines, and no doubt he will outmatch the savage: but if you have a mind to see a contest still more unequal, place them naked and unarmed one opposite to the other; and you will soon discover the advantage there is in perpetually having all our forces constantly at our disposal, in being constantly prepared against all events, and in always carrying ourselves, as it were, whole and entire about us.

Hobbes would have it that man is naturally void of fear, and intent only upon attacking and fighting. An illustrious philosopher * thinks on the contrary, and Cumberland and Pufendorf likewise affirm it, that nothing is more timid than man in a state of nature, that he is always in a tremble, and ready to fly at the first motion he perceives, at the first noise that strikes his ears. This, indeed, may be very true in regard to objects with which he is not acquainted; and I make no doubt of his being terrified at every new sight that presents itself, whenever he cannot distinguish the physical good and evil which he may expect from it, nor compare his strength with the dangers he has to encounter; circumstances that seldom occur in a state of nature, where all things proceed in so uniform a manner, and the face of the earth is not liable to those sudden and continual changes occasioned in it by the passions and inconstancies of men living in bodies. But savage man living dispersed among other animals and finding himself early under a necessity of measuring his strength with theirs, soon makes a comparison between both, and finding that he surpasses them more in address, than they surpass him in strength, he learns not to be any longer in dread of them. Turn out a bear or a wolf against a sturdy, active, resolute savage (and this they all are), provided with stones and a good stick, and you will soon find that the danger is at least equal on both sides, and that after several trials of this kind, wild beasts, who are not fond of attacking each other, will not be very disposed to attack man, whom they have found every whit as wild as themselves. As to animals who have really more strength than man has address, he is, in regard to them, what other weaker species are, who find means to subsist notwithstanding; he has even this great advantage over such weaker species, that being equally fleet with them, and finding on every tree an almost inviolable asylum, he is always at liberty to accept or to refuse the encounter,

* Montesquieu, in the *Esprit des lois,* I, ii.

to fight or to fly. Let us add that it appears that no animal naturally makes war on man, except in the case of self-defense or extreme hunger; nor ever expresses against him any of these violent antipathies, which seem to indicate that one species is intended by nature for the food of another.

But there are other more formidable enemies, and against which man is not provided with the same means of defense; I mean natural infirmities, infancy, old age, and sickness of every kind; melancholy proofs of our weakness, whereof the two first are common to all animals, and the last chiefly attends man living in a state of society. It is even observable in regard to infancy, that the mother being able to carry her child about with her, wherever she goes, can perform the duty of a nurse with a great deal less trouble than the females of many other animals, who are obliged to be constantly going and coming with no small labor and fatigue, one way to look out for their own subsistence, and another to suckle and feed their young ones. True it is that, if the woman happens to perish, her child is exposed to the greatest danger of perishing with her; but this danger is common to a hundred other species, whose young ones require a great deal of time to be able to provide for themselves; and if our infancy is longer than theirs, our life is longer likewise; so that, in this respect too, all things are in a manner equal; not but that there are other rules concerning the duration of the first age of life, and the number of the young of man and other animals, but they do not belong to my subject. With old men, who stir and perspire but little, the demand for food diminishes with their abilities to provide it; and as a savage life would exempt them from the gout and the rheumatism, and old age is of all ills that which human assistance is least capable of alleviating, they would at last go off, without its being perceived by others that they ceased to exist, and almost without perceiving it themselves.

In regard to sickness, I shall not repeat the vain and false declamations made use of to discredit medicine by most men, while they enjoy their health; I shall only ask if there are any solid observations from which we may conclude that in those countries, where the healing art is most neglected, the mean duration of man's life is shorter than in those where it is most cultivated? And how is it possible this should be the case, if we inflict more diseases upon ourselves than medicine can supply us with remedies! The extreme inequalities in the manner of living of the several classes of mankind, the excess of idleness in some, and of labor in others, the facility of irritating and satisfying our sensuality and our appetites, the too exquisite and out of the way foods of the rich, which fill them with fiery juices, and bring on indigestions, the unwholesome food of the poor, of which even, bad as it is, they very often fall short, and the want of which tempts them, every opportunity that offers, to eat greedily and overload their stomachs; late nights, excesses of every kind, immoderate transports of all the passions, fatigues, mental exhaustion, in a word, the numberless pains and anxieties annexed to every condition, and which the mind of man is constantly a prey to; these are the fatal proofs that most of our ills are of our own making, and that we might have avoided them all by adhering to the simple, uniform and solitary way of life prescribed to us by nature. Allowing that nature intended we should always enjoy good health, I dare almost affirm that a state of reflection is a state against nature, and that the man who meditates is a degenerate animal. We need only call to mind the good constitution of savages, of those at least whom we have not destroyed by our strong liquors; we need only reflect, that they are strangers to almost every disease, except those occasioned by wounds and old age, to be in a manner convinced that the history of human diseases might be easily written by pursuing that of civil societies. Such at least was the opinion of Plato, who concluded from certain remedies made use of or approved by Podalirius and Machaon at the Siege of Troy, that several disorders, which these remedies were found to bring on in his days, were not known among men at that remote period; and Celsus relates that dieting, so necessary nowadays, was first invented by Hippocrates.

Man therefore, in a state of nature where there are so few sources of sickness, can have no great occasion for physic, and still less for physicians; neither is the human species more to be pitied in this respect, than any other species of animals. Ask those who make hunting their recreation or business, if in their excursions they meet with many sick or feeble animals. They meet with many carrying the marks of considerable wounds, that have been perfectly well healed and closed up; with many, whose bones formerly broken, and whose limbs almost torn off, have completely knit and united, without any other surgeon but time, any other regimen but their usual way of living, and whose cures were not the less perfect for their not having been tortured with incisions, poisoned with drugs, or worn out by fasting. In a word, however useful medicine well administered may be to us who live in a state of society, it is still past doubt, that if, on the one hand, the sick savage, destitute of help, has nothing to hope for except from nature, on the other, he has nothing to fear but from its ills; a circumstance which often renders his situation preferable to ours.

Let us therefore beware of confusing savage man with the men with whom we associate. Nature behaves towards all animals left to her care with a predilection that seems to prove how jealous she is of that prerogative. The horse, the cat, the bull, nay the ass itself, have generally a higher stature, and always a more robust constitution, more vigor, more strength and courage in their forests than in our houses; they lose half these advantages by becoming domestic animals; it looks as if all our attention to treat them kindly, and to feed them well, served only to bastardize them. It is thus with man himself. In proportion as he becomes sociable and a slave to others, he becomes weak, fearful, mean-spirited, and his soft and effeminate way of living at once completes the enervation of his strength and of his courage. We may add, that there must be still a wider difference between man and man in a savage and domestic condition, than between beast and beast; for as men and beasts have been treated alike by nature, all the comforts with which men indulge themselves, still more than they do the beasts tamed by them, are so many particular causes which make them degenerate more markedly.

Nakedness, therefore, the want of houses, and of all these superfluities, which we consider as so very necessary, are not such mighty evils in respect to these primitive men, and much less still any obstacle to their preservation. Their skins, it is true, are destitute of hair; but then they have no occasion for any such covering in warm climates; and in cold climates they soon learn to apply to that use those of the animals they have conquered; they have only two feet to run with, but they have two hands to defend themselves with, and provide for all their wants; their children, perhaps, learn to walk later and with difficulty, but their mothers carry them with ease; an advantage not granted to other species of animals, with whom the mother, when pursued, is obliged to abandon her young ones, or regulate her step by theirs. In short, unless we admit those singular and fortuitous concurrences of circumstances, which I shall speak of hereafter, and which, it is very possible, may never have existed, it is evident, in any case, that the man who first made himself clothes and built himself a cabin supplied himself with things which he did not much need, since he had lived without them till then; and why should he not have been able to support, in his riper years, the same kind of life, which he had supported from his infancy?

Alone, idle, and always surrounded with danger, savage man must be fond of sleep, and sleep lightly like other animals, who think but little, and may, in a manner, be said to sleep all the time they do not think: self-preservation being almost his only concern, he must exercise those faculties most which are most serviceable in attacking and in defending, whether to subdue his prey, or to prevent his becoming that of other animals: those organs, on the contrary, which softness and sensuality can alone improve, must remain in a state of rudeness, utterly incompatible with all manner of delicacy; and as his senses are divided on this point, his touch and his taste must be extremely coarse and blunt; his sight, his hearing, and his smelling equally subtle: such is the animal state in general, and accordingly, if we may believe travelers, it is that of most savage nations. We must not therefore be surprised, that the Hottentots of the Cape of Good Hope distinguish with their naked eyes ships on the ocean, at as great a distance as the Dutch can discern them with their glasses; nor that the savages of America should have tracked the Spaniards with their smell, to as great a degree of exactness, as the best dogs could have done; nor that all these barbarous nations support nakedness without pain, use such large quantities of pimento to give their food a relish, and drink like water the strongest liquors of Europe.

As yet I have considered man merely in his physical capacity; let us now endeavor to examine him in a metaphysical and moral light.

I can discover nothing in any animal but an ingenious machine, to which nature has given senses to wind itself up, and guard, to a certain degree, against everything that might destroy or disorder it. I perceive the very same things in the human machine, with this difference, that nature alone operates in all the operations of the beast, whereas man, as a free agent, has a share in his. One chooses by instinct; the other by an act of liberty; for which reason the beast cannot deviate from the rules that have been prescribed to it, even in cases where such deviation might be useful, and man often deviates from the rules laid down for him to his prejudice. Thus a pigeon would starve near a dish of the best meat, and a cat on a heap of fruit or corn, though both might very well support life with the food which they thus disdain, did they but bethink themselves to make a trial of it.

It is in this manner that dissolute men run into excesses, which bring on fevers and death itself; because the mind depraves the senses, and when nature ceases to speak, the will still continues to dictate.

All animals have ideas, since all animals have senses; they even combine their ideas to a certain degree, and, in this respect, it is only the difference of such degree that constitutes the difference between man and beast: some philosophers have even advanced, that there is a greater difference between some men and some others, than between some men and some beasts; it is not therefore so much the understanding that constitutes, among animals, the specific distinction of man, as his quality of a free agent. Nature speaks to all animals, and beasts obey her voice. Man feels the same impulse, but he at the same time perceives that he is free to resist or to acquiesce; and it is in the consciousness of this liberty, that the spirituality of his soul chiefly appears: for natural philosophy explains, in some measure, the mechanism of the senses and the formation of ideas; but in the power of willing, or rather of choosing, and in the consciousness of this power, nothing can be discovered but acts, that are purely spiritual, and cannot be accounted for by the laws of mechanics.

But even if the difficulties, in which all these questions are involved, should leave some room to dispute on this difference between man and beast, there is another very specific quality that distinguishes them, and a quality which will admit of no dispute; this is the faculty of improvement; * a faculty which, as circumstances offer, successively unfolds all the other faculties, and resides among us not only in the species, but in the individuals that compose it; whereas a beast is, at the end of some months, all he ever will be during the rest of his life; and his species, at the end of a thousand years, precisely what it was the first year of that thousand. Why is

* Rousseau uses the word *perfectibilité*, which means the capacity to make progress.

man alone subject to dotage? Is it not, because he thus returns to his primitive condition? And because, while the beast, which has acquired nothing and has likewise nothing to lose, continues always in possession of his instinct, man, losing by old age, or by accidents, all the acquisitions he had made in consequence of his *perfectibility*, thus falls back even lower than beasts themselves? It would be a melancholy necessity for us to be obliged to allow that this distinctive and almost unlimited faculty is the source of all man's misfortunes; that it is this faculty, which, though by slow degrees, draws him out of his original condition, in which his days would slide away insensibly in peace and innocence; that it is this faculty, which, in a succession of ages, produces his discoveries and mistakes, his virtues and his vices, and, in the long run, renders him both his own and nature's tyrant. (i) It would be shocking to be obliged to commend, as a beneficent being, whoever he was that first suggested to the Orinoco Indians the use of those boards which they bind on the temples of their children, and which secure to them the enjoyment of some part at least of their natural imbecility and happiness.

Savage man, abandoned by nature to pure instinct, or rather indemnified for the instinct which has perhaps been denied to him by faculties capable of immediately supplying its place, and of raising him afterwards a great deal higher, would therefore begin with purely animal functions: to see and to feel would be his first condition, which he would enjoy in common with other animals. To will and not to will, to wish and to fear, would be the first, and in a manner, the only operations of his soul, until new circumstances occasioned new developments.

Let moralists say what they will, the human understanding is greatly indebted to the passions, which, on their side, are likewise universally allowed to be greatly indebted to the human understanding. It is by the activity of our passions, that our reason improves; we covet knowledge merely because we covet enjoyment, and it is impossible to conceive, why a man exempt from fears and desires should take the trouble to reason. The passions, in their turn, owe their origin to our needs, and their increase to our progress in science; for we cannot desire or fear anything, but in consequence of the ideas we have of it, or of the simple impulses of nature; and savage man, destitute of every species of knowledge, experiences no passions but those of this last kind; his desires never extend beyond his physical wants; (k) He knows no goods but food, a female, and rest; he fears no evils but pain, and hunger; I say pain, and not death; for no animal, merely as such, will ever know what it is to die, and the knowledge of death, and of its terrors, is one of the first acquisitions made by man, in consequence of his deviating from the animal state.

I could easily, were it necessary, cite facts in support of this opinion, and show that the progress of the mind has everywhere kept pace exactly with the wants to which nature had left the inhabitants exposed, or to which circumstances had subjected them, and consequently to the passions, which inclined them to provide for these wants. I could exhibit in Egypt the arts starting up, and extending themselves with the inundations of the Nile; I could pursue them in their progress among the Greeks, where they were seen to bud, grow, and rise to the heavens, in the midst of the sands and rocks of Attica, without being able to take root on the fertile banks of the Europus; I would observe, that, in general, the inhabitants of the north are more industrious than those of the south, because they can less do without industry; as if nature thus meant to make all things equal, by giving to the mind that fertility she has denied to the soil.

But leaving aside the uncertain testimony of history, who does not perceive that everything seems to remove from savage man the temptation and the means of altering his condition? His imagination paints nothing to him; his heart asks nothing from him. His moderate wants are so easily supplied with what he everywhere finds ready to his hand, and he stands at such a distance from the degree of knowledge requisite to covet more, that he can neither have foresight nor curiosity. The spectacle of nature, by growing quite familiar to him, becomes at last equally indifferent. It is constantly the same order, constantly the same revolutions; he has not sense enough to feel surprise at the sight of the greatest wonders; and it is not in his mind we must look for that philosophy, which man must have to know how to observe once, what he has every day seen. His soul, which nothing disturbs, gives itself up entirely to the consciousness of its present existence, without any thought of even the nearest futurity; and his projects, equally confined with his views, scarce extend to the end of the day. Such is, even at present, the degree of foresight in the Caribbean: he sells his cotton bed in the morning, and comes in the evening, with tears in his eyes, to buy it back, not having foreseen that he should want it again the next night.

The more we meditate on this subject, the wider does the distance between mere sensation and the most simple knowledge become in our eyes; and it is impossible to conceive how man, by his own powers alone, without the assistance of communication, and the spur of necessity, could have got over so great an interval. How many ages perhaps revolved, before man beheld any other fire but that of the heavens? How many different accidents must have concurred to make them acquainted with the most common uses of this element? How often have they let it go out, before they knew the art of reproducing it? And how often perhaps has not every one of these secrets perished with the discoverer? What shall we say of agriculture, an art which requires so much labor and foresight; which depends upon other arts; which, it is very evident, can be practiced only in a society which had at least begun, and which does not so much serve to draw from the earth food which it would yield them without all that trouble, as to oblige her to produce those things which are preferable to our taste? But let us suppose that men had multiplied to such a degree, that the natural products of the earth no longer sufficed for their support; a supposition which, by the way, would prove that this kind of life would be very advantageous to the human species; let us suppose that, without forge or workshops, the instruments of husbandry had dropped from the heavens into the hands of savages, that these men had overcome that mortal aversion they all have for constant labor; that they had learned to foretell their wants at so great a distance of time; that they had guessed exactly how they were to break the earth, sow the grain and plant trees; that they had found out the art of grinding their corn, and improving by fermentation the juice of their grapes; all operations which must have been taught them by the gods, since we cannot conceive how they should make such discoveries of themselves; after all these fine presents, what man would be mad enough to cultivate a field, that may be robbed by the first comer, man or beast, who takes a fancy to the produce of it. And would any man consent to spend his days in labor and fatigue, when the rewards of his labor and fatigue became more and more precarious in proportion to his want of them? In a word, how could this situation engage men to cultivate the earth, as long as it was not parceled out among them, that is, as long as a state of nature subsisted.

Though we should suppose savage man as well-versed in the art of thinking, as philosophers make him; though we were, following them, to make him a philosopher himself, discovering by himself the sublimest truths, forming to himself, by the most abstract arguments, maxims of justice and reason drawn from the love of order in general, or from the known will of his Creator: in a word, though we were to suppose his mind as intelligent and enlightened as it would have had to be, and is in fact found to have been dull and stupid; what benefit would the species receive from all these metaphysical discoveries, which could not be communicated, but must perish with the individual who had made them? What progress could mankind make in the forests, scattered up and down among the other animals? And to what degree could men mutually improve and enlighten each other, when they had no fixed habitation, nor any need of each other's assistance; when the same persons scarcely met twice in their whole lives, and on meeting neither spoke to, or so much as knew each other.

Let us consider how many ideas we owe to the use of speech; how much grammar exercises and facilitates the operations of the mind; let us, besides, reflect on the immense pains and time that the first invention of languages must have required: let us add these reflections to the preceding; and then we may judge how many thousand ages must have been requisite to develop successively the operations, which the human mind is capable of producing.

I must now beg leave to stop one moment to consider the perplexities attending the origin of languages. I might here barely cite or repeat the researches made, in relation to this question, by the Abbé de Condillac,* which all fully confirm my system, and perhaps even suggested to me the first idea of it. But, as the manner in which this philosopher resolves the difficulties he himself raises concerning the origin of arbitrary signs shows that he supposes, what I doubt, namely a kind of society already established among the inventors of languages; I think it my duty, at the same time that I refer to his reflections, to give my own, in order to expose the same difficulties in a light suitable to my subject. The first that offers itself is how languages could become necessary; for as there was no correspondence between men, nor the least necessity for any, there is no conceiving the necessity of this invention, nor the possibility of it, if it was not indispensable. I might say, with many others, that languages are the fruit of the domestic intercourse between fathers, mothers, and children: but this, besides its not answering the difficulties, would be committing

* In the *Essai sur l'origine des connaissances humaines* (1746).

the same error as those, who reasoning on the state of nature, transfer to it ideas gathered in society, always consider families as living together under one roof, and their members as observing among themselves a union, equally intimate and permanent as that which exists among us, where so many common interests unite them; whereas in this primitive state, as there were neither houses nor cabins, nor any kind of property, everyone took up his lodging at random, and seldom continued above one night in the same place; males and females united without any premeditated design, as chance, occasion, or desire brought them together, nor had they any great occasion for language to make known what they had to say to each other. They parted with the same ease. (l) The mother suckled her children, when just born, for her own sake; but afterwards when habit had made them dear to her, for theirs; but they no sooner gained strength enough to run about in quest of food than they separated even from her, and as they scarcely had any other method of not losing each other, than that of remaining constantly in each other's sight, they soon came to a point of not even recognizing each other when they happened to meet again. I must further observe, that the child having all his wants to explain, and consequently more things to say to his mother, than the mother can have to say to him, it is he that must be at the chief expense of invention, and the language he makes use of must be in a great measure his own work; this makes the number of languages equal to that of the individuals who are to speak them; and this multiplicity of languages is further increased by their roving and vagabond kind of life, which allows no idiom time enough to acquire any consistency; for to say that the mother would have dictated to the child the words he must employ to ask her this thing and that, may well enough explain in what manner languages, already formed, are taught, but it does not show us in what manner they are first formed.

Let us suppose this first difficulty conquered: Let us

for a moment consider ourselves on this side of the immense space, which must have separated the pure state of nature from that in which languages became necessary, and let us, after allowing their necessity, examine how languages could begin to be established: a new difficulty this, still more stubborn than the preceding; for if men stood in need of speech to learn to think, they must have stood in still greater need of the art of thinking to invent that of speaking; and though we could conceive how the sounds of the voice came to be taken for the conventional interpreters of our ideas we should not be the nearer knowing who could have been the interpreters of this convention for such ideas, which, in consequence of their not corresponding to any sensible objects, could not be indicated by gesture or voice; so that we can scarcely form any tolerable conjectures concerning the birth of this art of communicating our thoughts, and establishing a correspondence between minds: a sublime art which, though so remote from its origin, philosophers still behold at such a prodigious distance from its perfection, that I never met with one of them bold enough to affirm it would ever arrive there, even though the revolutions necessarily produced by time were suspended in its favor; though prejudice could be banished from, or would at least consent to sit silent in the presence of our academies; and though these societies should consecrate themselves, entirely and during whole ages, to the study of this thorny matter.

The first language of man, the most universal and most energetic of all languages, in short, the only language he needed, before there was a necessity of persuading assembled multitudes, was the cry of nature. As this cry was never extorted but by a kind of instinct in the most urgent cases, to implore assistance in great danger, or relief in great sufferings, it was of little use in the common occurrences of life, where more moderate sentiments generally prevail. When the ideas of men began to extend and multiply, and a closer communication began to take place among them, they labored to devise more numerous signs, and a more extensive language: they multiplied the inflections of the voice, and added to them gestures, which are, in their own nature, more expressive, and whose meaning depends less on any prior determination. They therefore expressed visible and movable objects by gestures, and those which strike the ear by imitative sounds: but as gestures scarcely indicate anything except objects that are actually present or can be easily described, and visible actions; as they are not of general use, since darkness or the interposition of a material object renders them useless; and as besides they require attention rather than excite it; men at length bethought themselves of substituting for them the articulations of voice, which, without having the same relation to any determinate object, are, in quality of conventional signs, fitter to represent all our ideas; a substitution, which could only have been made by common consent, and in a manner pretty difficult to practice by men, whose rude organs were unimproved by exercise; a substitution, which is in itself still more difficult to be conceived, since such a common agreement would have required a motive, and speech therefore appears to have been exceedingly requisite to establish the use of speech.

We must suppose, that the words, first made use of by men, had in their minds a much more extensive signification, than those employed in languages of some standing, and that, considering how ignorant they were of the division of speech into its constituent parts, they at first gave every word the meaning of an entire proposition. When afterwards they began to perceive the difference between the subject and attribute, and between verb and noun, a distinction which required no mean effort of genius, the substantives for a time were only so many proper names, the infinitive was the only tense, and as to adjectives, great difficulties must have attended the development of the idea that represents them, since every adjective is an abstract word, and abstraction is an unnatural and very painful operation.

At first they gave every object a peculiar name, without

any regard to its genus or species, things which these
first originators of language were in no condition to distinguish; and every individual presented itself in isolation to their minds, as they are in the picture of nature.
If they called one oak A, they called another oak B:
so that their dictionary must have been more extensive
in proportion as their knowledge of things was more
confined. It could not but be a very difficult task to get
rid of so diffuse and embarrassing a nomenclature; as in
order to marshal the several beings under common and
generic denominations, it was necessary to be first acquainted with their properties, and their differences; to
be stocked with observations and definitions, that is to
say, to understand natural history and metaphysics, advantages which the men of these times could not have
enjoyed.

Besides, general ideas cannot be conveyed to the mind
without the assistance of words, nor can the understanding seize them except by means of propositions. This is
one of the reasons why mere animals cannot form such
ideas, nor ever acquire the perfectibility, which depends
on such an operation. When a monkey leaves without
the least hesitation one nut for another, are we to think
he has any general idea of that kind of fruit, and that
he compares its archetype with these two individual
bodies? No certainly; but the sight of one of these nuts
calls back to his memory the sensations which he has
received from the other; and his eyes, modified after some
certain manner, give notice to his palate of the modification it is in its turn going to receive. Every general idea
is purely intellectual; let the imagination tamper ever
so little with it, it immediately becomes a particular idea.
Endeavor to represent to yourself the image of a tree in
general, you never will be able to do it; in spite of all
your efforts it will appear big or little, with thin or thick
foliage, light or dark; and were you able to see nothing
in it, but what can be seen in every tree, such a picture
would no longer resemble any tree. Beings perfectly
abstract are perceivable in the same manner, or are only

conceivable by the assistance of speech. The definition of a triangle can alone give you a just idea of that figure: the moment you form a triangle in your mind, it is this or that particular triangle and no other, and you cannot avoid giving breadth to its lines and color to its area. We must therefore make use of propositions; we must therefore speak to have general ideas; for the moment the imagination stops, the mind can continue to function only with the aid of discourse. If therefore the first inventors could give no names to any ideas but those they had already, it follows that the first substantives could never have been anything more than proper names.

But when by means, which I cannot conceive, our new grammarians began to extend their ideas, and generalize their words, the ignorance of the inventors must have confined this method to very narrow bounds; and as they had at first too much multiplied the names of individuals for want of being acquainted with the distinctions called genus and species, they afterwards made too few genera and species for want of having considered beings in all their differences: to push the divisions far enough, they must have had more knowledge and experience than we can allow them, and have made more researches and taken more pains, than we can suppose them willing to submit to. Now if, even at this present time, we every day discover new species, which had before escaped all our observations, how many species must have escaped the notice of men, who judged of things merely from their first appearances! As to the primitive classes and the most general notions, it were superfluous to add that these they must have likewise overlooked: how, for example, could they have thought of or understood the words, matter, spirit, substance, mode, figure, motion, since even our philosophers, who for so long a time have been constantly employing these terms, can themselves scarcely understand them, and since the ideas annexed to these words being purely metaphysical, they could find no models of them in nature?

I stop at these first advances, and beseech my judges to

suspend their reading a little, in order to consider, what a great way language has still to go, in regard to the invention of physical substantives alone (though the easiest part of language to invent), to be able to express all the sentiments of man, to assume an invariable form, to bear being spoken in public, and to influence society. I earnestly entreat them to consider how much time and knowledge must have been requisite to find out numbers, abstract words, the aorists, and all the other tenses of verbs, the particles, and syntax, the method of connecting propositions and arguments, of forming all the logic of discourse. For my own part, I am so frightened by the difficulties that multiply at every step, and so convinced of the almost demonstrated impossibility of languages owing their birth and establishment to means that were merely human, that I must leave to whoever may please to take it up, the task of discussing this difficult problem, "Which was the more necessary, society already formed to invent languages, or languages already invented to form society?"

Whatever these origins may have been, we may at least infer from the little care which nature has taken to bring men together by mutual wants, and make the use of speech easy to them, how little she has done towards making them sociable, and how little she has contributed to anything which they themselves have done to become so. In fact, it is impossible to conceive, why, in this primitive state, one man should have more occasion for the assistance of another, than one monkey, or one wolf for that of another animal of the same species; or supposing that he had, what motive could induce another to assist him; or even, if he did so, how he, who wanted assistance, and he from whom it was wanted, could agree upon the conditions. I know we are continually told that in this state man would have been the most wretched of all creatures; and if it is true, as I fancy I have proved it, that he must have continued many ages without either the desire or the opportunity of emerging from such a state, their assertion could only serve to justify a charge against nature, and not any against the being which nature had thus constituted; But, if I thoroughly understand this term *wretched*, it is a word that either has no meaning, or signifies nothing but a privation attended with pain, and a suffering state of body or soul: now I would fain know what kind of misery can be that of a free being, whose heart enjoys perfect peace, and body perfect health? and which is most likely to become insupportable to those who enjoy it, a civil or a natural life? In civil life we can scarcely meet a single person who does not complain of his existence; many even throw away as much of it as they can, and the united force of divine and human laws can hardly put a stop to this disorder. Was ever any free savage known to have been so much tempted to complain of life, and do away with himself? Let us therefore judge with less pride on which side real misery is to be placed. Nothing, on the contrary, would have been so unhappy as savage man, dazzled by flashes of knowledge, racked by passions, and reasoning about a state different from that in which he saw himself placed. It was in consequence of a very wise providence, that the faculties, which he potentially enjoyed, were not to develop themselves, except in proportion as there offered occasions to exercise them, lest they should be superfluous or troublesome to him when he did not yet want them, or tardy and useless when he did. He had in his instinct alone everything requisite to live in a state of nature; in his cultivated reason he has barely what is necessary to live in a state of society.

It appears at first sight that, as there was no kind of moral relations between men in this state, nor any known duties, they could not be either good or bad, and had neither vices nor virtues, unless we take these words in a physical sense, and call vices, in the individual, the qualities which may prove detrimental to his own preservation, and virtues those which may contribute to it; in which case we should be obliged to consider him as most virtuous, who made least resistance against the simple impulses of nature. But without deviating from the usual meaning of these terms, it is proper to suspend the judgment we might form of such a situation, and be on our guard against prejudice, until, balance in hand, we have examined whether there are more virtues or vices among civilized men; or whether their virtues do them more good than their vices do them harm; or whether the improvement of their understanding is sufficient compensation for the mischief they do to each other, in proportion as they become better informed of the good they ought to do; or whether, on the whole, they would not be much happier in a condition, where they had nothing to fear or to hope from each other, than to have submitted to universal dependence, and to have obliged themselves to depend for everything upon those, who do not think themselves obliged to give them anything.

But above all things let us beware of concluding with Hobbes, that man, as having no idea of goodness, must be naturally bad; that he is vicious because he does not know what virtue is; that he always refuses to do any service to those of his own species, because he believes that none is due to them; that, in virtue of that right which he justly claims to everything he wants, he foolishly looks upon himself as proprietor of the whole universe. Hobbes very plainly saw the flaws in all the modern definitions of natural right: but the consequences, which he draws from his own definition, show that the sense in which he understands it is equally false. This author, to argue from his own principles, should say that the state of nature, being that in which the care of our own preservation interferes least with the preservation of others, was consequently the most favorable to peace, and the most suitable to mankind; whereas he advances the very reverse in consequence of his having injudiciously included in that care which savage man takes of his preservation, the satisfaction of numberless passions which are the work of society, and have made laws necessary. A bad man, says he, is a robust child. But this is not proving that savage man is a robust child; and though we were to grant that he was, what could this philosopher infer from such a concession? That if this man, when robust, depended on others as much as when feeble, there is no excess that he would not be guilty of. He would make nothing of striking his mother when she delayed ever so little to give him the breast; he would claw, and bite, and strangle without remorse the first of his younger brothers, that ever so accidentally jostled or otherwise disturbed him. But these are two contradictory suppositions in the state of nature, to be robust and dependent. Man is weak when dependent, and his own master before he grows robust. Hobbes did not consider that the same cause, which hinders savages from making use of their reason, as our jurisconsults pretend, hinders them at the same time from making an ill use of their faculties, as he himself pretends; so that we may say that savages are not bad, precisely because they don't know what it is to be good; for it is neither the development of the understanding, nor the curb of the law, but the calmness of their passions and their ignorance of vice that hinder them from doing ill: *tanto plus in illis proficit vitiorum Ignoratio, quam in his cognitio virtutis.** There is besides another principle that has escaped Hobbes, and which, having been given to man to moderate, on certain occasions, the ferocity of self-love, or the desire of self-preservation previous to the appearance of that love (o) tempers the ardor, with which he naturally pursues his private welfare, by an innate abhorrence to see beings suffer that resemble him. I shall not surely be contradicted, in granting to man the only natural virtue, which the most passionate detractor of human virtues could not deny him, I mean that of pity, a disposition suitable to creatures weak as we are, and liable to so many evils; a virtue so much the more universal, and withal useful to man, as it takes place in him before

---

* "So much more does ignorance of vice profit these than knowledge of virtue the others." (Justin, *Histories*, II, 2.)

all manner of reflection; and so natural, that the beasts themselves sometimes give evident signs of it. Not to speak of the tenderness of mothers for their young; and of the dangers they face to screen them from danger; with what reluctance are horses known to trample upon living bodies; one animal never passes unmoved by the dead carcass of another animal of the same species: there are even some who bestow a kind of sepulture upon their dead fellows; and the mournful lowings of cattle, on their entering the slaughterhouse, publish the impression made upon them by the horrible spectacle they are there struck with. It is with pleasure we see the author of the Fable of the Bees,* forced to acknowledge man a compassionate and sensitive being; and lay aside, in the example he offers to confirm it, his cold and subtle style, to place before us the pathetic picture of a man, who, with his hands tied up, is obliged to behold a beast of prey tear a child from the arms of his mother, and then with his teeth grind the tender limbs, and with his claws rend the throbbing entrails of the innocent victim. What horrible emotions must not such a spectator experience at the sight of an event which does not personally concern him? What anguish must he not suffer at his not being able to assist the fainting mother or the expiring infant?

Such is the pure impulse of nature, anterior to all manner of reflection; such is the force of natural pity, which the most dissolute manners have as yet found it so difficult to extinguish, since we every day see, in our theatrical representations, those men sympathize with the unfortunate and weep at their sufferings, who, if in the tyrant's place, would aggravate the torments of their enemies. Mandeville was aware that men, in spite of all their morality, would never have been better than monsters, if nature had not given them pity to assist reason: but he did not perceive that from this quality alone flow all the social virtues which he would dispute mankind

* Mandeville.

the possession of. In fact, what is generosity, what clemency, what humanity, but pity applied to the weak, to the guilty, or to the human species in general? Even benevolence and friendship, if we judge right, will appear the effects of a constant pity, fixed upon a particular object: for to wish that a person may not suffer, what is it but to wish that he may be happy? Though it were true that commiseration is no more than a sentiment, which puts us in the place of him who suffers, a sentiment obscure but active in the savage, developed but dormant in civilized man, how could this notion affect the truth of what I advance, but to make it more evident? In fact, commiseration must be so much the more energetic, the more intimately the animal, that beholds any kind of distress, identifies himself with the animal that labors under it. Now it is evident that this identification must have been infinitely more perfect in the state of nature, than in the state of reason. It is reason that engenders self-love, and reflection that strengthens it; it is reason that makes man shrink into himself; it is reason that makes him keep aloof from everything that can trouble or afflict him; it is philosophy that destroys his connections with other men; it is in consequence of her dictates that he mutters to himself at the sight of another in distress, You may perish for aught I care, I am safe. Nothing less than those evils, which threaten the whole community, can disturb the calm sleep of the philosopher, and force him from his bed. One man may with impunity murder another under his windows; he has nothing to do but clap his hands to his ears, argue a little with himself to hinder nature, that startles within him, from identifying him with the unhappy sufferer. Savage man lacks this admirable talent; and for want of wisdom and reason, is always ready foolishly to obey the first whispers of humanity. In riots and street brawls the populace flock together, the prudent man sneaks off. It is the dregs of the people, the market women, that part the combatants, and hinder gentlefolks from cutting one another's throats.

It is therefore certain that pity is a natural sentiment, which, by moderating in every individual the activity of self-love, contributes to the mutual preservation of the whole species. It is this pity which hurries us without reflection to the assistance of those we see in distress; it is this pity which, in a state of nature, takes the place of laws, manners, virtue, with this advantage, that no one is tempted to disobey her gentle voice: it is this pity which will always hinder a robust savage from plundering a feeble child, or infirm old man, of the subsistence they have acquired with pain and difficulty, if he has but the least prospect of providing for himself by any other means: it is this pity which, instead of that sublime maxim of rational justice, *Do to others as you would have others do to you,* inspires all men with that other maxim of natural goodness a great deal less perfect, but perhaps more useful, *Do good to yourself with as little prejudice as you can to others.* It is in a word, in this natural sentiment, rather than in finespun arguments, that we must look for the cause of that reluctance which every man would experience to do evil, even independently of the maxims of education. Though it may be the peculiar happiness of Socrates and other geniuses of his stamp to reason themselves into virtue, the human species would long ago have ceased to exist, had it depended entirely for its preservation on the reasonings of the individuals that compose it.

With passions so tame, and so salutary a curb, men, rather wild than wicked, and more attentive to guard against harm than to do any to other animals, were not exposed to any dangerous dissensions: as they kept up no manner of intercourse with each other, and were of course strangers to vanity, to respect, to esteem, to contempt; as they had no notion of what we call thine and mine, nor any true idea of justice; as they considered any violence they were liable to as an evil that could be easily repaired, and not as an injury that deserved punishment; and as they never so much as dreamed of revenge, unless perhaps mechanically and unpremeditatedly, as a dog who bites the stone that has been thrown at him; their disputes could seldom be attended with bloodshed, were they never occasioned by a more considerable stake than that of subsistence: but there is a more dangerous subject of contention, which I must not leave unnoticed.

Among the passions which ruffle the heart of man, there is one of a hot and impetuous nature, which renders the sexes necessary to each other; a terrible passion which despises all dangers, bears down all obstacles, and which in its transports seems proper to destroy the human species which it is destined to preserve. What must become of men abandoned to this lawless and brutal rage, without modesty, without shame, and every day disputing the objects of their passion at the expense of their blood?

We must in the first place allow that the more violent the passions, the more necessary are laws to restrain them: but besides that the disorders and the crimes, to which these passions daily give rise among us, sufficiently prove the insufficiency of laws for that purpose, we would do well to look back a little further and examine, if these evils did not spring up with the laws themselves; for at this rate, even if the laws were capable of repressing these evils, it is the least that might be expected from them, that they should check a mischief which would not exist without them.

Let us begin by distinguishing between what is moral and what is physical in the passion called love. The physical part of it is that general desire which prompts the sexes to unite with each other; the moral part is that which determines this desire, and fixes it upon a particular object to the exclusion of all others, or at least gives it a greater degree of energy for this preferred object. Now it is easy to perceive that the moral part of love is a factitious sentiment, engendered by society, and cried up by the women with great care and address in order to establish their empire, and secure command to that sex which ought to obey. This sentiment, being founded on certain notions of beauty and merit which a savage is not capable of having, and upon comparisons which he is not capable of making, can scarcely exist in him: for as his mind was never in a condition to form abstract ideas of regularity and proportion, neither is his heart susceptible of sentiments of admiration and love, which, even without our perceiving it, are produced by our application of these ideas; he listens solely to the dispositions implanted in him by nature, and not the taste which he never could have acquired; and any woman answers his purpose.

Confined entirely to what is physical in love, and happy enough not to know these preferences which sharpen the appetite for it, at the same time that they increase the difficulty of satisfying such appetite, men, in a state of nature, must be subject to fewer and less violent fits of that passion, and of course there must be fewer and less violent disputes among them in consequence of it. The imagination, which causes so many ravages among us, never speaks to the heart of savages, who peaceably wait for the impulses of nature, yield to these impulses without choice and with more pleasure than fury; and the need once satisfied, all desire is lost.

Nothing therefore can be more evident, than that it is society alone, which has added even to love itself as well as to all the other passions, that impetuous ardor, which so often renders it fatal to mankind; and it is so much the more ridiculous to represent savages constantly murdering each other to glut their brutality, as this opinion is diametrically opposite to experience, and the Caribbeans, the people in the world who have as yet deviated least from the state of nature, are to all intents and purposes the most peaceable in their amours, and the least subject to jealousy, though they live in a burning climate which seems always to add considerably to the activity of these passions.

As to the inductions which may be drawn, in respect to several species of animals, from the battles of the males, who in all seasons cover our poultry yards with blood, and in spring particularly cause our forests to ring again with the noise they make in disputing their females, we must begin by excluding all those species where nature has evidently established, in the relative power of the sexes, relations different from those which exist among us: thus from the battles of cocks we can form no induction that will affect the human species. In the species, where the proportion is better observed, these battles must be owing entirely to the fewness of the females compared with the males, or what amounts to the same, to the intervals of refusal, during which the female constantly refuses the advances of the males; for if the female admits the male but two months in the year, it is all the same as if the number of females were five-sixths less: now neither of these cases is applicable to the human species, where the number of females generally surpasses that of males, and where it has never been observed that, even among savages, the females had, like those of other animals, their stated times of heat and indifference. Besides, among several of these animals the whole species takes fire all at once, and for some days nothing is to be seen among them but confusion, tumult, disorder and bloodshed; a state unknown to the human species, where love is never periodical. We cannot therefore conclude from the battles of certain animals for the possession of their females, that the same would be the case of man in a state of nature; and even if we did, since these contests do not destroy the other species, there is at least equal room to think they would not be fatal to ours; and it is very probable that they would cause fewer ravages than they do in society, especially in those countries where, morality being as yet held in some esteem, the jealousy of lovers and the vengeance of husbands every day produce duels, murders, and even worse crimes; where the duty of an eternal fidelity serves only to propagate adultery; and the very laws of continence and honor necessarily increase dissoluteness, and multiply abortions.

Let us conclude that savage man, wandering about in the forests, without industry, without speech, without any fixed residence, an equal stranger to war and every social tie, without any need of his fellows, as well as without any desire of hurting them, and perhaps even without ever distinguishing them individually one from the other, subject to few passions, and finding in himself all he wants, let us, I say, conclude that savage man had no knowledge or feelings but such as were proper to that situation; that he felt only his real necessities, took notice of nothing but what it was his interest to see, and that his understanding made as little progress as his vanity. If he happened to make any discovery, he could the less communicate it as he did not even know his children. The art perished with the inventor; there was neither education nor improvement; generations succeeded generations to no benefit; and as all constantly set out from the same point, whole centuries rolled on in the rudeness and barbarity of the first age; the race was grown old, and man still remained a child.

If I have enlarged so much upon the supposition of this primitive condition, it is because I thought it my duty, considering what ancient errors and inveterate prejudices I have to extirpate, to dig to the very roots, and show in a true picture of the state of nature, how much even natural inequality falls short in this state of that reality and influence which our writers ascribe to it.

In fact, we may easily perceive that among the differences, which distinguish men, several pass for natural, which are merely the work of habit and the different kinds of life adopted by men living in a social way. Thus a robust or delicate constitution, and the strength and weakness which depend on it, are oftener produced by the hardy or effeminate manner in which a man has been brought up, than by the primitive constitution of his body. It is the same thus in regard to the forces of the mind; and education not only produces a difference between those minds which are cultivated and those which are not, but even increases the difference which is found among the former in proportion to their culture; for let a giant and a dwarf set out in the same road, the giant at every step will acquire a new advantage over the dwarf. Now, if we compare the prodigious variety in the education and way of living of the various orders of men in a civil state, with the simplicity and uniformity that prevail in the animal and savage life, where all the individuals feed on the same food, live in the same manner, and do exactly the same things, we shall easily conceive how much the difference between man and man in the state of nature must be less than in the state of society, and how greatly every social inequality must increase the natural inequalities of mankind.

But even if nature in the distribution of her gifts should really affect all the preferences that are imputed to her, what advantage could the most favored derive from her partiality, to the prejudice of others in a state of things which admits hardly any kind of relation between them? Of what service can beauty be, where there is no love? What will wit avail people who don't speak, or cunning those who have no business? Authors are constantly crying out, that the strongest would oppress the weakest; but let them explain what they mean by the word oppression. One man will rule with violence, another will groan under a constant subjection to all his caprices: this is indeed precisely what I observe among us, but I don't see how it can be said of savage men, into whose heads it would be a hard matter to drive even the meaning of the words domination and servitude. One man might indeed seize the fruits which another had gathered, the game which another had killed, the cavern which another had occupied for shelter; but how is it possible he should ever exact obedience from him, and what chains of dependence can there be among men who possess nothing? If I am driven from one tree, I have nothing to do but look out for another; if one place is made uneasy to me, what can hinder me from taking up my quarters elsewhere? But suppose I should meet a man so much superior to me in strength, and withal so depraved, so lazy and so barbarous as to oblige me to provide for his subsistence while he remains idle; he must resolve not to take his eyes from me a single moment, to bind me fast before he can take the least nap, lest I should kill him or give him the slip during his sleep: that is to say, he must expose himself voluntarily to much greater troubles than what he seeks to avoid, than any he gives me. And after all this, let him abate ever so little of his vigilance; let him at some sudden noise but turn his head another way; I am already buried in the forest, my fetters are broken, and he never sees me again.

But without insisting any longer upon these details, everyone must see that, as the bonds of servitude are formed merely by the mutual dependence of men one upon another and the reciprocal necessities which unite them, it is impossible for one man to enslave another, without having first reduced him to a condition which, as it does not exist in a state of nature, must leave every man his own master, and render the law of the strongest altogether vain and useless.

Having proved that inequality in the state of nature is scarcely felt, and that it has very little influence, I must now proceed to show its origin and trace its progress, in the successive developments of the human mind. After having showed that *perfectibility*, the social virtues, and the other faculties, which natural man had received as potentialities, could never be developed of themselves, that they needed the fortuitous concurrence of several foreign causes, which might never arise, and without which he must have eternally remained in his primitive condition, I must proceed to consider and bring together the different accidents which may have perfected the human understanding while debasing the species, and made man wicked by making him sociable, and from so remote a time bring man at last and the world to the point at which we now see them.

I must own that, as the events I am about to describe might have happened many different ways, I can determine my choice only by mere conjecture; but aside from the fact that these conjectures become reasons, when they are the most probable that can be drawn from the nature of things and the only means we can have of discovering truth, the consequences I mean to deduce from mine will not be merely conjectural, since, on the principles I have just established, it is impossible to form any other system, that would not supply me with the same results, and from which I might not draw the same conclusions.

This will make it unnecessary for me to dwell on the manner in which the lapse of time compensates for the slight probability of events; on the surprising power of very trivial causes, when their action is constant; on the impossibility, on the one hand, of destroying certain hypotheses, while on the other we cannot give them the degree of certainty of facts; on its being the business of history, when two facts are proposed, as real, and connected by a chain of intermediate facts which are either unknown or considered as such, to furnish such facts as may actually connect them; and the business of philosophy, when history is silent, to point out similar facts which may answer the same purpose; finally, on the power of similarity, in regard to events, to reduce facts to a much smaller number of different classes than is generally imagined. It suffices me to offer these matters to the consideration of my judges; it suffices me to have conducted my inquiry in such a manner as to save the general reader the trouble of considering them at all.

SECOND PART

The first man, who after enclosing a piece of ground, took it into his head to say, *this is mine,* and found people simple enough to believe him, was the real founder of civil society. How many crimes, how many wars, how many murders, how many misfortunes and horrors, would that man have saved the human species, who pulling up the stakes or filling up the ditches should have cried to his fellows: Beware of listening to this impostor; you are lost, if you forget that the fruits of the earth belong equally to us all, and the earth itself to nobody! But it is highly probable that things had by then already come to such a pass, that they could not continue much longer as they were; for as this idea of property depends on several prior ideas which could only spring up gradually one after another, it was not formed all at once in the human mind: men must have made considerable progress; they must have acquired a great stock of industry and knowledge, and transmitted and increased it from age to age before they could arrive at this last point of the state of nature. Let us therefore take up things at an earlier stage, and collect into one point of view, and in their most natural order, the slow succession of events and discoveries.

Man's first feeling was that of his existence, his first care that of preserving it. The productions of the earth yielded him all the assistance he required, instinct prompted him to make use of them. Hunger and other appetites made him at different times experience different modes of existence; one of these excited him to perpetuate his species; and this blind propensity, quite void of anything like pure love or affection, produced nothing but an act that was merely animal. Their need once gratified, the sexes took no further notice of each other, and even the child was nothing to his mother, the moment he could do without her.

Such was the condition of infant man; such was the life of an animal confined at first to pure sensations, and so far from harboring any thought of forcing her gifts from nature, that he scarcely availed himself of those which she offered to him of her own accord. But difficulties soon arose, and there was a necessity for learning how to surmount them: the height of some trees, which prevented his reaching their fruits; the competition of other animals equally fond of the same fruits; the fierceness of many that even aimed at his life; these were so many circumstances, which obliged him to apply to bodily exercise. There was a necessity for becoming active, swift-footed, and sturdy in battle. The natural arms, which are stones and the branches of trees, soon offered themselves to his reach. He learned to surmount the obstacles of nature, to fight when necessary with other animals, to fight for his subsistence even with other men, or indemnify himself for the loss of whatever he found himself obliged to yield to a stronger.

In proportion as the human species grew more numerous, and extended itself, its difficulties likewise multiplied and increased. The difference of soils, climates and seasons succeeded in forcing them to introduce some difference in their way of living. Bad harvests, long and severe winters, and scorching summers which parched up all the fruits of the earth, required a new resourcefulness and activity.* On the seashore, and the banks of rivers, they invented the line and the hook, and became fishermen and fish-eaters. In the forests they made themselves bows and arrows, and became huntsmen and warriors. In the cold countries they covered themselves with the skins of the beasts they had killed; thunder, a volcano, or some happy accident made them acquainted with fire, a new resource against the rigors of winter: they discovered the method of preserving this element, then that of reproducing it, and lastly the way of preparing with it the flesh of animals, which heretofore they had devoured raw.

This reiterated applying of various things to himself, and to one another, must have naturally engendered in the mind of man the idea of certain relations. These relations, which we express by the words, great, little, strong, weak, swift, slow, fearful, bold, and the like, compared occasionally, and almost without thinking of it, produced in him some kind of reflection, or rather

---

* The French word *industrie* combines both meanings.

a mechanical prudence, which pointed out to him the precautions most essential to his safety.

The new knowledge resulting from this development increased his superiority over other animals, by making him aware of it. He applied himself to learning how to ensnare them; he played them a thousand tricks; and though several surpassed him in strength or in swiftness, he in time became the master of those that could serve him, and a sore enemy to those that could do him mischief. Thus it was that the first look he gave into himself produced the first emotion of pride in him; thus it was that at a time he scarcely knew how to distinguish between the different orders of beings, in considering himself the highest by virtue of his species he prepared the way for his much later claim to preeminence as an individual.

Though other men were not to him what they are to us, and he had scarcely more intercourse with them than with other animals, they were not overlooked in his observations. The conformities, which in time he was able to perceive between them, and between himself and his female, made him presume of those he did not perceive; and seeing that they all behaved as he himself would have done in similar circumstances, he concluded that their manner of thinking and feeling was quite conformable to his own; and this important truth, when once engraved deeply on his mind, made him follow, by an intuition as sure and swift as any reasoning, the best rules of conduct, which for the sake of his own safety and advantage it was proper he should observe towards them.

Instructed by experience that the love of well-being is the sole spring of all human actions, he found himself in a condition to distinguish the few cases, in which common interest might authorize him to count on the assistance of his fellows, and those still fewer, in which a competition of interests should make him distrust them. In the first case he united with them in the same herd, or at most by some kind of free association which obliged none of its members, and lasted no longer than the transitory necessity that had given birth to it. In the second case every one aimed at his own private advantage, either by open force if he found himself strong enough, or by ruse and cunning if he felt himself the weaker.

Such was the manner in which men were gradually able to acquire some gross idea of mutual engagements and the advantage of fulfilling them, but this only as far as their present and obvious interest required; for they were strangers to foresight, and far from troubling their heads about a distant futurity, they gave no thought even to the morrow. Was a deer to be taken? Every one saw that to succeed he must faithfully stand to his post; but suppose a hare to have slipped by within reach of any one of them, it is not to be doubted that he pursued it without scruple, and when he had seized his prey never reproached himself with having made his companions miss theirs.

We may easily conceive that such an intercourse scarcely required a more refined language than that of crows and monkeys, which flock together almost in the same manner. Inarticulate exclamations, a great many gestures, and some imitative sounds, must have been for a long time the universal language of mankind, and by joining to these in every country some articulate and conventional sounds, of which, as I have already said, it is not very easy to explain the first institution, there arose particular languages, but rude, imperfect, and such nearly as are to be found at this day among several savage nations. Hurried on by the rapidity of time, the abundance of things I have to say, and the almost imperceptible progress of the first improvements, my pen flies like an arrow over numberless ages; for the slower the succession of events, the more quickly are they told.

At length, these first advances enabled man to make others at a greater rate. He became more industrious in proportion as his mind became more enlightened. Men, soon ceasing to fall asleep under the first tree, or take shelter in the first cave, hit upon several kinds of hatchets of hard and sharp stones, and employed them to dig the ground, cut down trees, and with the branches build huts, which they afterwards bethought themselves of plastering over with clay or mud. This was the epoch of a first revolution, which produced the establishment and distinction of families, and which introduced a species of property, and already along with it perhaps a thousand quarrels and battles. As the strongest however were probably the first to make themselves cabins, which they knew they were able to defend, we may conclude that the weak found it much shorter and safer to imitate, than to attempt to dislodge them: and as to those, who were already provided with cabins, no one could have any great temptation to seize upon that of his neighbor, not so much because it did not belong to him, as because he did not need it; and as he could not make himself master of it without exposing himself to a very sharp fight with the family that was occupying it.

The first developments of the heart were the effects of a new situation, which united husbands and wives, parents and children, under one roof; the habit of living together gave birth to the sweetest sentiments the human species is acquainted with, conjugal and paternal love. Every family became a little society, so much the more firmly united, as mutual attachment and liberty were its only bonds; and it was now that the sexes, whose way of life had been hitherto the same, began to adopt different ways. The women became more sedentary, and accustomed themselves to stay at home and look after the children, while the men rambled abroad in quest of subsistence for the whole family. The two sexes likewise by living a little more at their ease began to lose somewhat of their usual ferocity and sturdiness: but if on the one hand individuals became less able to engage separately with wild beasts, they on the other were more easily got together to make a common resistance against them.

In this new state of things, the simplicity and solitariness of man's life, the paucity of his wants, and the instruments which he had invented to satisfy them leaving him a great deal of leisure, he employed it to supply himself with several conveniences unknown to his ancestors; and this was the first yoke he inadvertently imposed upon himself, and the first source of evils which he prepared for his descendants; for besides continuing in this manner to soften both body and mind, these conveniences having through use lost almost all their ability to please, and having at the same time degenerated into real needs, the privation of them became far more intolerable than the possession of them had been agreeable; to lose them was a misfortune, to possess them no happiness.

Here we may a little better discover how the use of speech was gradually established or improved in the bosom of every family, and we may likewise form conjectures concerning the manner in which divers particular causes may have propagated language, and accelerated its progress by rendering it every day more and more necessary. Great inundations or earthquakes surrounded inhabited districts with water or precipices. Portions of the continent were by revolutions of the globe torn off and split into islands. It is obvious that among men thus collected, and forced to live together, a common idiom must have started up much sooner, than among those who freely wandered through the forests of the mainland. Thus it is very possible that the inhabitants of the islands, after their first essays in navigation, brought among us the use of speech; and it is very probable at least that society and languages commenced in islands, and even were highly developed there, before the inhabitants of the continent knew anything of either.

Everything now begins to wear a new aspect. Those who heretofore wandered through the woods, by taking to a more settled way of life, gradually flock together, coalesce into several separate bodies, and at length form in every country a distinct nation, united in character and manners, not by any laws or regulations, but by the same way of life, and alimentation, and the common influence of the climate. Living permanently near each other could not fail eventually to create some connection between different families. The transient commerce required by nature soon produced, among the youth of both sexes living in neighboring huts, another kind of commerce, which besides being not less agreeable is rendered more durable by mutual association. Men begin to consider different objects, and to make comparisons; they imperceptibly acquire ideas of merit and beauty, and these soon give rise to feelings of preference. By seeing each other often they contract a habit, which makes it painful not to see each other always. Tender and agreeable sentiments steal into the soul, and are by the smallest opposition wound up into the most impetuous fury: jealousy kindles with love; discord triumphs; and the gentlest of passions requires sacrifices of human blood to appease it.

In proportion as ideas and feelings succeed each other, and the head and the heart become active, men continue to shake off their original wildness, and their connections become more intimate and extensive. They now began to assemble round a great tree: singing and dancing, the genuine offspring of love and leisure, became the amusement or rather the occupation of the men and women, free from care, thus gathered together. Everyone began to notice the rest, and wished to be noticed himself; and public esteem acquired a value. He who sang or danced best; the handsomest, the strongest, the most dexterous, or the most eloquent, came to be the most respected: this was the first step towards inequality, and at the same time towards vice. From these first distinctions there arose on one side vanity and contempt, on the other envy and shame; and the fermentation raised by these new leavens at length produced combinations fatal to happiness and innocence.

Men no sooner began to set a value upon each other, and know what esteem was, than each laid claim to it, and it was no longer safe for any man to refuse it to another. Hence the first duties of politeness, even among savages; and hence every voluntary injury became an affront, as besides the hurt which resulted from it as an injury, the offended party was sure to find in it a contempt for his person often more intolerable than the hurt itself. It is thus that every man, punishing the contempt expressed for him by others in proportion to the value he set upon himself, the effects of revenge became terrible, and men learned to be sanguinary and cruel. Such precisely was the degree attained by most of the savage nations with whom we are acquainted. And it is for want of sufficiently distinguishing ideas, and observing at how great a distance these people were from the first state of nature, that so many authors have hastily concluded that man is naturally cruel, and requires a civil government to make him more gentle; whereas nothing is more gentle than he in his primitive state, when placed by nature at an equal distance from the stupidity of brutes, and the pernicious enlightenment of civilized man; and confined equally by instinct and reason to providing against the harm which threatens him, he is withheld by natural compassion from doing any injury to others, so far from being led even to return that which he has received. For according to the axiom of the wise Locke, *Where there is no property, there can be no injury.*

But we must take notice, that the society now formed and the relations now established among men required in them qualities different from those which they derived from their primitive constitution; that as a sense of morality began to insinuate itself into human actions, and every man, before the enacting of laws, was the only judge and avenger of the injuries he had received, that goodness of heart suitable to the pure state of nature by no means was suitable for the new society; that it was necessary punishments should become severer in the same proportion that the opportunities of offending became more frequent, and the dread of vengeance add strength to the too weak curb of the law. Thus, though men had become less patient, and natural compassion had already suffered some alteration, this period of the development of the human faculties, holding a just mean between the indolence of the primitive state and the petulant activity of egoism, must have been the happiest and most durable epoch. The more we reflect on this state, the more convinced we shall be, that it was the least subject of any to revolutions, the best for man, (p) and that nothing could have drawn him out of it but some fatal accident, which, for the common good, should never have happened. The example of savages, most of whom have been found in this condition, seems to confirm that mankind was formed ever to remain in it, that this condition is the real youth of the world, and that all ulterior improvements have been so many steps, in appearance towards the perfection of individuals, but in fact towards the decrepitness of the species.

As long as men remained satisfied with their rustic huts; as long as they were content with clothes made of the skins of animals, sewn with thorns and fish bones; as long as they continued to consider feathers and shells as sufficient ornaments, and to paint their bodies different colors, to improve or ornament their bows and arrows, to fashion with sharp-edged stones some little fishing boats, or clumsy instruments of music; in a word, as long as they undertook such works only as a single person could finish, and stuck to such arts as did not require the joint endeavors of several hands, they lived free, healthy, honest and happy, as much as their nature would admit, and continued to enjoy with each other all the pleasures of an independent intercourse; but from the moment one man began to stand in need of another's assistance; from the moment it appeared an advantage for one man to possess enough provisions for two, equality vanished; property was introduced; labor became necessary; and boundless forests became smiling fields, which had to be watered with human sweat, and in which slavery and misery were soon seen to sprout out and grow with the harvests.

Metallurgy and agriculture were the two arts whose invention produced this great revolution. With the poet, it is gold and silver, but with the philosopher, it is iron and corn, which have civilized men, and ruined mankind. Accordingly both one and the other were unknown to the savages of America, who for that very reason have still remained savages; nay other nations seem to have continued in a state of barbarism, as long as they continued to exercise one only of these arts without the other; and perhaps one of the best reasons that can be assigned, why Europe has been, if not earlier, at least more constantly and highly civilized than the other quarters of the world, is that it both abounds most in iron and is most fertile in corn.

It is very difficult to conjecture how men came to know anything of iron, and the art of employing it: for we are not to suppose that they should of themselves think of digging the ore out of the mine, and preparing it for smelting, before they knew what could be the result of such a process. On the other hand, there is the less reason to attribute this discovery to any accidental fire, as mines are formed nowhere but in barren places, bare of trees and plants, so that it looks as if nature had taken pains to keep from us so mischievous a secret. Nothing therefore remains but the extraordinary chance of some volcano, which belching forth metallic substances already fused might have given the spectators the idea of imitating that operation of nature. And we must further suppose in them great courage and foresight to undertake so laborious a work, and have, at so great a distance, an eye to the advantages they might derive from it; qualities scarcely suitable but to minds more advanced than those can be supposed to have been.

As to agriculture, the principles of it were known a long time before the practice of it took place, and it is hardly possible that men, constantly employed in drawing their subsistence from trees and plants, should not have early hit on the means employed by nature for the generation of vegetables; but in all probability it was very late before their industry took a turn that way, either because trees which with hunting and fishing supplied them with food, did not require their attention; or because they did not know the use of grain; or because they had no instruments to cultivate it; or because they were destitute of foresight in regard to future necessities; or lastly, because they lacked means to hinder others from running away with the fruit of their labors. We may believe that on their becoming more industrious they began their agriculture by cultivating with sharp stones and pointed sticks a few vegetables or roots about their cabins; and that it was a long time before they knew the method of preparing wheat, and were provided with instruments necessary to raise it in large quantities; not to mention the necessity there is, in order to follow this occupation and sow lands, to consent to lose something now to gain a great deal later on; a precaution very foreign to the turn of man's mind in a savage state, in which, as I have already remarked, he can hardly foresee in the morning what he will need at night.

For this reason the invention of other arts must have been necessary to oblige mankind to apply themselves to that of agriculture. As soon as some men were needed to smelt and forge iron, others were wanted to maintain them. The more hands were employed in manufactures, the fewer hands were left to provide subsistence for all, though the number of mouths to be supplied with food continued the same; and as some required commodities in exchange for their iron, the rest at last found out the method of making iron serve for the multiplication of commodities. Thus were established on the one hand husbandry and agriculture, and on the other the art of working metals and of multiplying the uses of them.

The tilling of the land was necessarily followed by its distribution; and property once acknowledged, the first rules of justice ensued: for to secure every man his own, every man had to be able to own something. Moreover, as men began to extend their views toward the future, and all found themselves in possession of goods capable of being lost, there was none without fear of reprisals for any injury he might do to others. This origin is so much the more natural, as it is impossible to conceive how property can flow from any other source but work; for what can a man add but his labor to things which he has not made, in order to acquire a property in them? It is the labor of the hands alone, which giving the husbandman a title to the produce of the land he has tilled gives him a title to the land itself, at least until he has gathered in the fruits of it, and so on from year to year; and this enjoyment forming a continued possession is easily transformed into property. The ancients, says Grotius, by giving to Ceres the epithet of legislatrix, and to a festival celebrated in her honor the name of Thesmophoria, insinuated that the distribution of lands produced a new kind of right; that is the right of property different from that which results from the law of nature.

Things thus circumstanced might have remained equal, if men's talents had been equal, and if, for instance, the use of iron and the consumption of commodities had always held an exact proportion to each other; but as nothing preserved this balance, it was soon broken. The man that had most strength performed most labor; the most dexterous turned his labor to best account; the most ingenious found out methods of lessening his labor; the husbandman required more iron, or the smith more grain, and while both worked equally, one earned a great deal by his labor, while the other could scarcely live by his. Thus natural inequality insensibly unfolds itself with that arising from men's combining, and the differences among men, developed by the differences of their circumstances, become more noticeable, more permanent in their effects, and begin to influence in the same proportion the condition of individuals.

Matters once having reached this point, it is easy to imagine the rest. I shall not stop to describe the successive inventions of other arts, the progress of language, the trial and employment of talents, the inequality of fortunes, the use or abuse of riches, nor all the details which follow these, and which every one may easily supply. I shall just give a glance at mankind placed in this new order of things.

Behold then all our faculties developed; our memory and imagination at work; egoism involved; reason rendered active; and the mind almost arrived at the utmost bounds of that perfection it is capable of. Behold all our natural qualities put in motion; the rank and lot of every man established, not only as to the amount of property and the power of serving or hurting others, but likewise as to genius, beauty, strength or skill, merits or talents; and as these were the only qualities which could command respect, it was found necessary to have or at least to affect them. It became to the interest of men to appear what they really were not. To be and to seem became two very different things, and from this distinction sprang haughty pomp and deceitful knavery, and all the vices which form their train. On the other hand, man, heretofore free and independent, was now, in consequence of a multitude of new needs, brought into subjection, as it were, to all nature, and especially to his fellows, whose slave in some sense he became, even by becoming their master; if rich, he stood in need of their services, if poor, of their assistance; even mediocrity itself could not enable him to do without them. He must therefore have been continually at work to interest them in his happiness, and make them, if not really, at least apparently find their advantage in laboring for his: this rendered him sly and artful in his dealings with some, imperious and cruel in his dealings with others, and laid him under the necessity of using ill all those whom he stood in need of, as often as he could not awe them into compliance and did not find it his interest to be useful to them. In fine, an insatiable ambition, the rage of raising their relative fortunes, not so much through real necessity as to overtop others, inspires all men with a wicked inclination to injure each other, and with a secret jealousy so much the more dangerous, as to carry its point with the greater security it often puts on the mask of benevolence. In a word, competition and rivalry on the one hand, and an opposition of interests on the other, and always a secret desire of profiting at the expense of others. Such were the first effects of property, and the inseparable attendants of nascent inequality.

Riches, before the invention of signs to represent them, could scarcely consist in anything but lands and cattle, the only real goods which men can possess. So, when estates increased so much in number and in extent as to take in whole countries and touch each other, it became impossible for one man to aggrandize himself but at the expense of some other; at the same time, the supernumerary inhabitants, who were too weak or too indolent to make such acquisitions in their turn, impoverished without having lost anything, because while everything about them changed they alone remained the same, were obliged to receive or force their subsistence from the hands of the rich. And from that began to arise, according to their different characters, domination and slavery, or violence and rapine. The rich on their side scarcely began to taste the pleasure of commanding, when they preferred it to every other; and making use of their old slaves to acquire new ones, they no longer thought of anything but subduing and enslaving their neighbors; like those ravenous wolves, who having once tasted human flesh, despise every other food, and thereafter want only men to devour.

It is thus that the most powerful or the most wretched, respectively considering their power and wretchedness as a kind of right to the possessions of others, equivalent in their minds to that of property, the equality once broken was followed by the most terrible disorders. It is thus that the usurpations of the rich, the pillagings of the poor, and the unbridled passions of all, by stifling the cries of natural compassion, and the still feeble voice of justice, rendered men avaricious, wicked and ambitious. There arose between the title of the strongest and that of the first occupier a perpetual conflict, which always ended in battle and bloodshed. The new state of society became the most horrible state of war: Mankind thus debased and harassed, and no longer able to retrace its steps, or renounce the fatal acquisitions it had made; laboring, in short, merely to its confusion by the abuse of those faculties, which in themselves do it so much honor, brought itself to the very brink of ruin.

Attonitus novitate mali, divesque miserque,
effugere optat opes; et quae modo voverat, odit.*

But it is impossible that men should not sooner or later have made reflections on so wretched a situation, and upon the calamities with which they were overwhelmed. The rich in particular must have soon perceived how much they suffered by a perpetual war, of which they alone supported all the expense, and in which, though all risked life, they alone risked any property. Besides, whatever color they might pretend to give their usurpations, they sufficiently saw that these usurpations were in the main founded upon false and precarious titles, and that what they had acquired by mere force, others could again by mere force wrest out of their hands, without leaving them the least room to complain of such a proceeding. Even those, who owed all their riches to their own industry, could scarce ground their acquisitions upon a better title. It availed them nothing to say, It was I built this wall; I acquired this spot by my labor. Who traced it out for you, another might object, and what right have you to expect payment at our expense for doing that we did not oblige you to do? Don't you know that numbers of your brethren perish, or suffer grievously for want of what you have too much of, and that you should have had the express and unanimous consent of mankind to ap-

---

* Both rich and poor, shocked at their newfound ills, would fly from wealth, and hate what they had sought. (Ovid, *Metamorphoses*, XI, 127.)

propriate to yourself more of the common subsistence, more than you needed for yours? Destitute of valid reasons to justify, and sufficient forces to defend himself; crushing individuals with ease, but with equal ease crushed by banditti; one against all, and unable, on account of mutual jealousies, to unite with his equals against enemies united by the common hopes of pillage; the rich man, thus pressed by necessity, at last conceived the deepest project that ever entered the human mind: this was to employ in his favor the very forces that attacked him, to make allies of his enemies, to inspire them with other maxims, and make them adopt other institutions as favorable to his pretensions, as the law of nature was unfavorable to them.

With this view, after laying before his neighbors all the horrors of a situation, which armed them all one against another, which rendered their possessions as burdensome as their wants, and in which no one could expect any safety either in poverty or riches, he easily invented specious arguments to bring them over to his purpose. "Let us unite," said he, "to secure the weak from oppression, restrain the ambitious, and secure to every man the possession of what belongs to him: Let us form rules of justice and of peace, to which all may be obliged to conform, which shall give no preference to anyone, but may in some sort make amends for the caprice of fortune, by submitting alike the powerful and the weak to the observance of mutual duties. In a word, instead of turning our forces against ourselves, let us collect them into a sovereign power, which may govern us by wise laws, may protect and defend all the members of the association, repel common enemies, and maintain a perpetual concord and harmony among us."

Many fewer words of this kind would have sufficed to persuade men so uncultured and easily seduced, who had besides too many quarrels among themselves to live without arbiters, and too much avarice and ambition to live long without masters. All gladly offered their necks to the yoke, thinking they were securing their liberty;

for though they had sense enough to perceive the advantages of a political constitution, they had not experience enough to see beforehand the dangers of it. Those among them who were best qualified to foresee abuses were precisely those who expected to benefit by them; even the soberest judged it requisite to sacrifice one part of their liberty to insure the rest, as a wounded man has his arm cut off to save the rest of his body.

Such was, or must have been the origin of society and of law, which gave few fetters to the weak and new power to the rich; irretrievably destroyed natural liberty, fixed for ever the laws of property and inequality; changed an artful usurpation into an irrevocable right; and for the benefit of a few ambitious individuals subjected the rest of mankind to perpetual labor, servitude, and misery. We may easily conceive how the establishment of a single society rendered that of all the rest absolutely necessary, and how, to withstand united forces, it became necessary for the rest of mankind to unite in their turn. Societies once formed in this manner, soon multiplied or spread to such a degree, as to cover the face of the earth; and not to leave a corner in the whole universe, where a man could throw off the yoke, and withdraw his head from under the often ill-conducted sword which he saw perpetually hanging over it. The civil law being thus become the common rule of citizens, the law of nature no longer obtained except between the different societies, where under the name of the law of nations, it was modified by some tacit conventions to render commerce possible, and supply the place of natural compassion, which, losing by degrees all that influence over societies which it originally had over individuals, no longer exists but in some great souls, who consider themselves as citizens of the world, force the imaginary barriers that separate people from people, after the example of the sovereign being from whom we all derive our existence, and include the whole human race in their benevolence.

Political bodies, thus remaining in a state of nature

among themselves, soon experienced the inconveniencies which had obliged individuals to quit it; and this state became much more fatal to these great bodies, than it had been before to the individuals which now composed them. Hence those national wars, those battles, those murders, those reprisals, which make nature shudder and shock reason; hence all those horrible prejudices, which make it a virtue and an honor to shed human blood. The worthiest men learned to consider cutting the throats of their fellows as a duty; at length men began to butcher each other by thousands without knowing for what; and more murders were committed in a single action, and more horrible disorders at the taking of a single town, than had been committed in the state of nature during ages together upon the whole face of the earth. Such are the first effects we may conceive to have arisen from the division of mankind into different societies. Let us return to their institution.

I know that several writers have assigned other origins to political society; as for instance, the conquests of the powerful, or the union of the weak; and it is no matter which of these causes we adopt in regard to what I am going to establish. That which I have just laid down, however, seems to me the most natural, for the following reasons. First, because, in the first case, the right of conquest being in fact no right at all, it could not serve as a foundation for any other right, the conqueror and the conquered ever remaining with respect to each other in a state of war, unless the conquered, restored to the full possession of their liberty, should freely choose their conqueror for their chief. Until then, whatever capitulations might have been made between them being founded upon violence, and thus *ipso facto* null and void, there could not have existed in this hypothesis either a true society, or a political body, or any other law but that of the strongest. Secondly, because these words *strong* and *weak,* are, in the second case, ambiguous; for during the interval between the establishment of the right of property or prior occupancy, and that of political government, the meaning of these terms is better expressed by the words *poor* and *rich,* as before the establishment of laws men in reality had no other means of subjecting their equals, but by invading their property, or by parting with some of their own property to them. Thirdly, because the poor having nothing but their liberty to lose, it would have been the height of madness in them to give up willingly the only blessing they had left without obtaining some consideration for it; whereas the rich being sensitive if I may say so, in every part of their possessions, it was much easier to do them mischief, and therefore more incumbent upon them to guard against it; and because, in fine, it is but reasonable to suppose that a thing has been invented by him to whom it could be of service, rather than by him to whom it must prove detrimental.

Government in its infancy had no regular and permanent form. For want of a sufficient fund of philosophy and experience, men could see no further than the present inconveniencies, and never thought of providing for future ones except as they arose. In spite of all the labors of the wisest legislators, the political state still continued imperfect, because it was in a manner the work of chance; and, as the foundations of it were ill laid, time, though sufficient to reveal its defects and suggest the remedies for them, could never mend its original faults. It was always being mended; whereas they should have begun as Lycurgus did at Sparta, by clearing the ground and removing all the old materials, so that they could then put up a good edifice. Society at first consisted merely of some general conventions which all the members bound themselves to observe, and the performance of which the whole body guaranteed to every individual. Experience was necessary to show the great weakness of such a constitution, and how easy it was for those who infringed it to escape the conviction or chastisement of faults, of which the public alone was to be both the witness and the judge; the laws could not fail of being eluded a thousand ways; inconveniencies and disorders could not but multiply continually, until it was at last found necessary to think of committing to private persons the dangerous trust of public authority, and to magistrates the care of enforcing obedience to the decisions of the people. For to say that chiefs were elected before the confederacy was formed, and that the ministers of the laws existed before the laws themselves, is a supposition too ridiculous to deserve serious refutation.

It would be equally unreasonable to imagine that men at first threw themselves into the arms of an absolute master, without any conditions or consideration on his side; and that the first means contrived by jealous and unconquered men for their common safety was to run headlong into slavery. In fact, why did they give themselves superiors, if it was not to be defended by them against oppression, and protected in their lives, liberties, and properties, which are in a manner the elements of their being? Now in the relations between man and man, the worst that can happen to one man being to see himself at the mercy of another, would it not have been contrary to the dictates of good sense to begin by making over to a chief the only things they needed his assistance to preserve? What equivalent could he have offered them for so great a right? And had he presumed to exact it on pretense of defending them, would he not have immediately received the answer in the fable: What worse will an enemy do to us? It is therefore past dispute, and indeed a fundamental maxim of all political law, that people gave themselves chiefs to defend their liberty and not to be enslaved by them. *If we have a Prince,* said Pliny to Trajan, *it is in order that he may keep us from having a master.*

Politicians argue in regard to the love of liberty with the same sophistry that philosophers do in regard to the state of nature; by the things they see they judge of things very different which they have never seen, and they attribute to men a natural inclination to slavery, on account of the patience with which the slaves within their notice bear the yoke; not reflecting that it is with

liberty as with innocence and virtue, the value of which
is not known but by those who possess them, and the
taste for which is lost when they are lost. I know the
charms of your country, said Brasidas to a satrap who
was comparing the life of the Spartans with that of the
Persepolites; but you cannot know the pleasures of
mine.

As an unbroken courser erects his mane, paws the
ground, and rages at the bare sight of the bit, while a
trained horse patiently suffers both whip and spur, just so
the barbarian will never reach his neck to the yoke which
civilized man carries without murmuring, but prefers
the most stormy liberty to a peaceful slavery. It is not
therefore by the servile disposition of enslaved nations
that we must judge of the natural dispositions of man
for or against slavery, but by the prodigies done by every
free people to secure themselves from oppression. I know
that the former are constantly crying up that peace and
tranquillity they enjoy in their irons, and that *miserrimam
servitutem pacem appellant*:* But when I see the latter
sacrifice pleasures, peace, riches, power, and even life
itself to the preservation of that one treasure so disdained
by those who have lost it; when I see freeborn animals
through a natural abhorrence of captivity dash their
brains out against the bars of their prison; when I see
multitudes of naked savages despise European pleasures,
and brave hunger, fire and sword, and death itself to
preserve their independence, I feel that it is not for slaves
to argue about liberty.

As to paternal authority, from which several have derived absolute government and every other mode of society, it is sufficient, without having recourse to Locke
and Sidney, to observe that nothing in the world differs
more from the cruel spirit of despotism than the gentleness of that authority, which looks more to the advantage
of him who obeys than to the utility of him who com-

---

* "They call the most wretched slavery peace." (Tacitus,
Histories, IV, 17.)

mands; that by the law of nature the father continues master of his child no longer than the child stands in need of his assistance; that after that term they become equal, and that then the son, entirely independent of the father, owes him no obedience, but only respect. Gratitude is indeed a duty which we are bound to pay, but which benefactors cannot exact. Instead of saying that civil society is derived from paternal authority, we should rather say that it is to the former that the latter owes its principal force. No one individual was acknowledged as the father of several other individuals, until they settled about him. The father's goods, which he can indeed dispose of as he pleases, are the ties which hold his children to their dependence upon him, and he may divide his substance among them in proportion as they shall have deserved by a continual deference to his commands. Now the subjects of a despotic chief, far from having any such favor to expect from him, as both themselves and all they have are his property, or at least are considered by him as such, are obliged to receive as a favor what he relinquishes to them of their own property. He does them justice when he strips them; he treats them with mercy when he suffers them to live.

By continuing in this manner to test facts by right, we should discover as little solidity as truth in the voluntary establishment of tyranny; and it would be a hard matter to prove the validity of a contract which was binding only on one side, in which one of the parties should stake everything and the other nothing, and which could only turn out to the prejudice of him who had bound himself. This odious system is even today far from being that of wise and good monarchs, and especially of the kings of France, as may be seen by divers passages in their edicts, and particularly by that of a celebrated piece published in 1667 in the name and by the orders of Louis XIV. "Let it therefore not be said that the Sovereign is not subject to the laws of his Realm, since the contrary is a maxim of the law of nations which flattery has sometimes attacked, but which good princes have always defended as the tutelary divinity of their Realms. How much more reasonable is it to say with the sage Plato, that the perfect happiness of a State consists in the subjects obeying their prince, the prince obeying the laws, and the laws being equitable and always directed to the good of the public?" I shall not stop to consider whether, liberty being the noblest faculty of man, it is not degrading our nature, lowering ourselves to the level of brutes, who are the slaves of instinct, and even offending the author of our being, to renounce without reserve the most precious of his gifts, and to submit to committing all the crimes he has forbidden us, merely to gratify a mad or a cruel master; and whether that sublime craftsman must be more irritated at seeing his work dishonored than at seeing it destroyed. I shall only ask what right those, who were not afraid thus to degrade themselves, could have to subject their posterity to the same ignominy, and renounce for them, blessings which come not from their liberality, and without which life itself must appear a burden to all those who are worthy to live.

Pufendorf says that, as we can transfer our property from one to another by contracts and conventions, we may likewise divest ourselves of our liberty in favor of other men. This, in my opinion, is a very poor way of arguing; for, in the first place, the property I cede to another becomes a thing quite foreign to me, and the abuse of which can no way affect me; but it concerns me greatly that my liberty is not abused, and I cannot, without incurring the guilt of the crimes I may be forced to commit, expose myself to become the instrument of any. Besides, the right of property being of mere human convention and institution, every man may dispose as he pleases of what he possesses: but the case is otherwise with regard to the essential gifts of nature, such as life and liberty, which every man is permitted to enjoy, and of which it is doubtful at least whether any man has a right to divest himself: by giving up the one, we degrade our being; by giving up the other we annihilate it as much as it is our power to do so; and as no temporal enjoyments can indemnify us for the loss of either, it would be an offense against both nature and reason to renounce them for any consideration. But though we could transfer our liberty as we do our property, it would be quite different with regard to our children, who enjoy the father's property only by the transmission of his right; whereas liberty being a blessing, which as men they hold from nature, their parents have no right to strip them of it; so that, just as to establish slavery it was necessary to do violence to nature, so it was necessary to alter nature to perpetuate such a right; and the jurisconsults, who have gravely pronounced that the child of a slave is born a slave, have in other words decided that a man will not be born a man.

It therefore appears to me incontestibly true, that not only governments did not begin by arbitrary power, which is but the corruption and extreme term of government, and at length brings it back to the law of the strongest against which governments were at first the remedy; but even that, supposing they had begun in this manner, such power being illegal in itself could never have served as a foundation for social law, nor of course for the inequality it instituted.

Without embarking now upon the inquiries which still remain to be made into the nature of the fundamental pact underlying every kind of government, I shall accept the common opinion, and confine myself here to holding the establishment of the political body to be a real contract between the multitude and the chiefs elected by it. A contract by which both parties oblige themselves to the observance of the laws that are therein stipulated, and form the ties of their union. The multitude having, in regard to their social relations, concentrated all their wills in one, all the articles, in regard to which this will expresses itself, become so many fundamental laws, which oblige without exception all the members of the State, and one of which regulates the choice and power of the magistrates appointed to look to the execution of the rest. This power extends to everything that can maintain the constitution, but extends to nothing that can alter it. To this power are added honors, that may render the laws and their ministers respectable; and the ministers are distinguished by certain prerogatives, which may recompense them for the heavy burdens inseparable from a good administration. The magistrate, on his side, obliges himself not to use the power with which he is entrusted except in conformity to the intention of his constituents, to maintain every one of them in the peaceable possession of his property, and upon all occasions prefer the public good to his own private interest.

Before experience had shown, or knowledge of the human heart had made the abuses inseparable from such a constitution foreseeable, it must have appeared so much the more perfect, as those appointed to look to its preservation had themselves had most interest in it; for magistracy and its rights being built solely on the fundamental laws, as soon as these ceased to exist, the magistrates would cease to be legitimate, the people would no longer be bound to obey them, and, as the essence of the State did not consist in the magistrates but in the laws, each one would rightfully regain his natural liberty.

A little reflection would afford us new arguments in confirmation of this truth, and the nature of the contract might alone convince us that it cannot be irrevocable: for if there were no superior power capable of guaranteeing the fidelity of the contracting parties and of obliging them to fulfill their mutual engagements, they would remain sole judges in their own cause, and each of them would always have a right to renounce the contract, as soon as he discovered that the other had broke the conditions of it, or that these conditions ceased to suit his private convenience. Upon this principle, the right of abdication may probably be founded. Now, to consider, as we do, only what is human in this institution, if the magistrate, who has all the power in his own hands, and who appropriates to himself all the advantages of the contract, has nonetheless a right to renounce his authority; how much better a right should the people, who pay for all the faults of its chief, have to renounce their dependence upon him. But the shocking dissensions and disorders without number, which would be the necessary consequence of so dangerous a privilege, show more than anything else how much human governments stood in need of a more solid basis than that of mere reason, and how necessary it was for the public tranquillity, that the will of the Almighty should interpose to give to sovereign authority a sacred and inviolable character, which should deprive subjects of the fatal right to dispose of it. If mankind had received no other advantages from religion, this alone would be sufficient to make them adopt and cherish it, since it is the means of saving more blood than fanaticism has been the cause of spilling. But let us resume the thread of our hypothesis.

The various forms of government owe their origin to the various degrees of inequality which existed between individuals at the time of their institution. Where a man happened to be preeminent in power, virtue, riches, or credit, he became sole magistrate, and the State assumed a monarchical form. If several of pretty equal eminence stood out over all the rest, they were jointly elected, and this election produced an aristocracy. Those whose fortune or talents were less unequal, and who had deviated less from the state of nature, retained in common the supreme administration, and formed a democracy. Time demonstrated which of these forms suited mankind best. Some remained altogether subject to the laws; others soon bowed their necks to masters. The former labored to preserve their liberty; the latter thought of nothing but invading that of their neighbors, jealous at seeing others enjoy a blessing which they themselves had lost. In a word, riches and conquest fell to the share of the one, and virtue and happiness to that of the other.

In these various modes of government the offices at first were all elective; and when riches did not decide, the preference was given to merit, which gives a natural ascendancy, and to age, which is the parent of deliberateness in council, and experience in execution. The ancients among the Hebrews, the Gerontes of Sparta, the Senate of Rome, nay, the very etymology of our word *Seigneur*, show how much grey hairs were formerly respected. The oftener the choice fell upon old men, the oftener it became necessary to repeat it, and the more the trouble of such repetitions became sensible; intrigues took place; factions arose, the parties grew bitter; civil wars blazed forth; the lives of the citizens were sacrificed to the pretended happiness of the State; and things at last came to such a pass, as to be ready to relapse into their primitive confusion. The ambition of the principal men induced them to take advantage of these circumstances to perpetuate the hitherto temporary offices in their families; the people already inured to dependence, accustomed to ease and the conveniences of life, and too much enervated to break their fetters, consented to the increase of their slavery for the sake of securing their tranquillity; and it is thus that chiefs, become hereditary, contracted the habit of considering their offices as a family estate, and themselves as proprietors of those communities, of which at first they were but mere officers; of calling their fellow-citizens their slaves; of numbering them, like cattle, among their belongings; and of calling themselves the peers of gods, and kings of kings.

By pursuing the progress of inequality in these different revolutions, we shall discover that the establishment of laws and of the right of property was the first term of it; the institution of magistrates the second; and the third and last the changing of legal into arbitrary power; so that the different states of the rich and poor were authorized by the first epoch; those of the powerful and weak by the second; and by the third those of master and slave, which formed the last degree of inequality, and the term in which all the rest at last end, until new revolutions entirely dissolve the government, or bring it back nearer to its legal constitution.

To conceive the necessity of this progress, we are not so much to consider the motives for the establishment of the body politic, as the forms it assumes in its realization; and the faults with which it is necessarily attended: for those vices, which render social institutions necessary, are the same which render the abuse of such institutions unavoidable. And as laws (Sparta alone excepted, whose laws chiefly regarded the education of children, and where Lycurgus established such manners and customs, as made laws almost needless) are in general less strong than the passions, and restrain men without changing them, it would be no hard matter to prove that every government, which carefully guarding against all alteration and corruption should scrupulously comply with the purpose of its establishment, was set up unnecessarily; and that a country, where no one either eluded the laws, or made an ill use of magistracy, required neither laws nor magistrates.

Political distinctions are necessarily led in with civil distinctions. The inequality between the people and the chiefs increases so fast as to be soon felt by individuals, and appears among them in a thousand shapes according to their passions, their talents, and circumstances. The magistrate cannot usurp any illegal power without making himself creatures with whom he must share it. Besides, citizens only allow themselves to be oppressed in proportion as hurried on by a blind ambition, and looking rather below than above them, they come to love authority more than independence. When they submit to fetters, it is only to be the better able to fetter others in their turn. It is no easy matter to reduce to obedience a man who does not wish to command; and the most astute politician would find it impossible to subdue those men who only desire to be independent. But inequality easily gains ground among base and ambitious souls, ever ready to run the risks of fortune, and almost indifferent whether they command or obey, as she proves either favorable or adverse to them. Thus then there must have been a time, when the eyes of the people were bewitched to such a degree, that their rulers needed only to have said to the lowest of men, "Be great you and all your posterity," to make him immediately appear great in the eyes of everyone as well as in his own; and his descendants took still more upon them, in proportion to their distance from him: the more distant and uncertain the cause, the greater the effect; the longer line of drones a family produced, the more illustrious it was reckoned.

Were this a proper place to enter into details, I could easily explain in what manner inequalities of credit and authority become unavoidable among private persons (s) the moment that, united into one body, they are obliged to compare themselves one with another, and to note the differences which they find in the continual intercourse every man must have with his neighbor. These differences are of several kinds; but riches, nobility or rank, power and personal merit, being in general the principal distinctions, by which men in society measure each other, I could prove that the harmony or conflict between these different forces is the surest indication of the good or bad original constitution of any State: I could show that among these four kinds of inequality, personal qualities being the source of all the rest, riches is that in which they ultimately terminate, because, being the most immediately useful to the prosperity of individuals, and the most easy to communicate, they are made use of to purchase every other distinction. By this observation we are enabled to judge with tolerable exactness, how much any people has deviated from its primitive institution, and what steps it has still to make to the extreme term of corruption. I could show how much this universal desire of reputation, of honors, of preference, with which we are all devoured, exercises and compares our talents and our forces; how much it excites and multiplies our passions; and, by creating an universal competition, rivalry, or rather enmity among men, how many disappointments, successes, and catastrophes of every kind it daily causes among the innumerable aspirants whom it engages in the same competition. I could show that it is to this itch of being spoken of, to this fury of distinguishing ourselves which seldom or never gives us a moment's respite, that we owe both the best and the worst things among us, our virtues and our vices, our sciences and our errors, our conquerors and our philosophers; that is to say, a great many bad things and a very few good ones. I could prove, in short, that if we behold a handful of rich and powerful men seated on the pinnacle of fortune and greatness, while the crowd grovel in obscurity and want, it is merely because the first prize what they enjoy but in the same degree that others are deprived of it; and that, without changing their condition, they would cease to be happy the minute the people ceased to be miserable.

But these details would alone furnish sufficient matter for a more considerable work, in which we might weigh the advantages and disadvantages of every species of government, relatively to the rights of man in a state of nature, and might likewise unveil all the different faces under which inequality has appeared to this day, and may hereafter appear to the end of time, according to the nature of these several governments, and the revolutions which time must unavoidably occasion in them. We should then see the multitude oppressed by domestic tyrants in consequence of those very precautions taken by them to guard against foreign masters. We should see oppression increase continually without its being ever possible for the oppressed to know where it would stop, nor what lawful means they had left to check its progress. We should see the rights of citizens, and the liberties of nations extinguished by slow degrees, and the groans and protestations and appeals of the weak treated as seditious murmurings. We should see policy confine to a mercenary portion of the people the honor of defending the common cause. We should see taxes made necessary, the disheartened husbandman desert his field even in time of peace, and quit the plough to gird on the sword. We should see fatal and whimsical rules laid down for the code of honor. We should see the champions of their country sooner or later become her enemies, and perpetually holding their daggers to the breasts of their fellow-citizens. Nay the time would come when they might be heard to say to the oppressor of their country:

Pectore si fratris gladium juguloque parentis
Condere me jubeas, gravidaeque in viscera partu
*Conjugis, invita peragam tamen omnia dextra.**

From the vast inequality of conditions and fortunes, from the great variety of passions and of talents, of useless arts, of pernicious arts, of frivolous sciences, would issue clouds of prejudices equally contrary to reason, to happiness, to virtue. We should see the chiefs foment everything that tends to weaken men united in societies by dividing them; everything that, while it gives society an air of apparent harmony, sows in it the seeds of real dissension; everything that can inspire the different classes with mutual distrust and hatred by an opposition of their rights and interests, and so strengthen that power which controls them all.

It is from the midst of this disorder and these revolutions, that despotism, gradually rearing up her hideous head, and devouring in every part of the State all that still remained sound and untainted, would at last succeed in trampling upon the laws and the people, and establish itself upon the ruins of the republic. The times immediately preceding this last alteration would be times of calamity and trouble; but at last everything would be swallowed up by the monster; and the people would no longer have chiefs or laws, but only tyrants. From this fatal moment all regard to virtue and manners would likewise disappear; for despotism, *cui ex honesto nulla*

---

* "If you order me to plunge my sword into my brother's breast and into my father's throat and into the vitals of my wife heavy with child, I shall do, nevertheless, all these things even though my hand is unwilling." (Lucan, *Pharsalia*, I, 376–8.)

*est spes,** tolerates no other master, wherever it reigns; the moment it speaks, probity and duty lose all their influence, and the blindest obedience is the only virtue to slaves.

This is the last term of inequality, the extreme point which closes the circle and meets that from which we set out. It is here that all private men return to their primitive equality, because they are nothing; and that, subjects having no longer any law but the will of their master, nor the master any other law but his passions, all notions of good and principles of justice again disappear. This is when everything returns to the sole law of the strongest, and of course to a new state of nature different from that with which we began, inasmuch as the first was the state of nature in its purity, and this one the consequence of excessive corruption. There is, in other respects, so little difference between these two states, and the contract of government is so much dissolved by despotism, that the despot is master only so long as he continues the strongest, and that, as soon as they can expel him, they may do it without his having the least right to complain of their violence. The insurrection, which ends in the death or deposition of a sultan, is as juridical an act as any by which the day before he disposed of the lives and fortunes of his subjects. Force alone upheld him, force alone overturns him. Thus all things take place and succeed in their natural order; and whatever may be the upshot of these hasty and frequent revolutions, no one man has reason to complain of another's injustice, but only of his own indiscretion or bad fortune.

By thus discovering and following the lost and forgotten road, which man must have followed in going from the state of nature to the social state, by restoring, together with the intermediate positions which I have been just indicating, those which want of time obliges me to omit, or which my imagination has failed to suggest, every attentive reader must unavoidably be struck

---

* "in which there is no hope afforded by honesty."

at the immense space which separates these two states.
In this slow succession of things he may meet with the
solution of an infinite number of problems in morality
and politics, which philosophers are puzzled to solve.
He will perceive that, the mankind of one age not being
the mankind of another, the reason why Diogenes could
not find a man was, that he sought among his contemporaries the man of a bygone period: Cato, he will then
see, fell with Rome and with liberty, because he did
not suit the age in which he lived; and the greatest of
men served only to astonish that world, which would
have cheerfully obeyed him, had he come into it five
hundred years earlier. In a word, he will find himself
in a condition to understand how the soul and the passions of men by insensible alterations change as it were
their very nature; how it comes to pass, that in the long
run our wants and our pleasures seek new objects; that,
original man vanishing by degrees, society no longer
offers to the eyes of the sage anything but an assemblage
of artificial men and factitious passions, which are the
work of all these new relations, and have no foundation
in nature. What reflection teaches us on that score, observation entirely confirms. Savage man and civilized
man differ so much at the bottom of their hearts and in
their inclinations, that what constitutes the supreme
happiness of the one would reduce the other to despair.
The first sighs for nothing but repose and liberty; he
desires only to live, and to be exempt from labor; nay,
the ataraxy of the most confirmed Stoic falls short of his
profound indifference to every other object. Civilized
man, on the other hand, is always in motion, perpetually
sweating and toiling, and racking his brains to find out
occupations still more laborious: he continues a drudge
to his last minute; nay, he courts death to be able to live,
or renounces life to acquire immortality. He pays court
to men in power whom he hates, and to rich men whom
he despises; he sticks at nothing to have the honor of
serving them; he boasts proudly of his baseness and their
protection; and proud of his slavery, he speaks with dis-

dain of those who have not the honor of sharing it. What a spectacle must the painful and envied labors of a European minister of state form in the eyes of a Caribbean! How many cruel deaths would not this indolent savage prefer to such a horrid life, which very often is not even sweetened by the pleasure of doing good? But to see the purpose of so many cares, his mind would first have to affix some meaning to these words *power* and *reputation*; he should be apprized that there are men who set value on the way they are looked on by the rest of mankind, who know how to be happy and satisfied with themselves on the testimony of others rather than upon their own. In fact, the real source of all those differences is that the savage lives within himself, whereas social man, constantly outside himself, knows only how to live in the opinion of others; and it is, if I may say so, merely from their judgment of him that he derives the consciousness of his own existence. It is foreign to my subject to show how this disposition engenders so much indifference toward good and evil, notwithstanding such fine discourses on morality; how everything, being reduced to appearances, becomes mere art and mummery; honor, friendship, virtue, and often vice itself, of which we at last learn the secret of boasting; how, in short, ever asking others what we are, and never daring to ask ourselves, in the midst of so much philosophy, humanity and politeness, and such sublime moral codes, we have nothing but a deceitful and frivolous exterior, honor without virtue, reason without wisdom, and pleasure without happiness. It is sufficient that I have proved that this is certainly not the original state of man, and that it is merely the spirit of society, and the inequality which society engenders, that thus change and transform all our natural inclinations.

I have endeavored to reveal the origin and progress of inequality, the institution and abuse of political societies, as far as these things are capable of being deduced from the nature of man by the mere light of reason, and independently of those sacred maxims which give the sanction of divine right to sovereign authority. It follows from this survey that inequality, almost non-existent among men in the state of nature, derives its force and its growth from the development of our faculties and the progress of the human mind, and at last becomes permanent and lawful by the establishment of property and of laws. It likewise follows that moral * inequality, authorized, solely by positive right, † clashes with natural right, whenever it is not in proportion to physical ‡ inequality; a distinction which sufficiently determines what we are to think of that kind of inequality which obtains in all civilized nations, since it is evidently against the law of nature that children should command old men, and fools lead the wise, and that a handful should gorge themselves with superfluities, while the starving masses lack the barest necessities of life.

---

* "Moral" should here be interpreted as meaning "social," or "artificial."

† i.e., established laws.

‡ i.e., "natural."

NOTES

~~~~~~~~~~~~~~~~~~~~~~~~~~~~~~

(i)   A celebrated author,* by calculating the goods and the evils of human life and comparing the two sums, found that the last greatly exceeded the first, and that everything considered life to man was no such valuable present. I am not surprised at his conclusions; he drew all his arguments from the constitution of man in a civilized state. Had he looked back to man in a state of nature, it is obvious that the result of his inquiries would have been very different; that man would have appeared to him subject to very few evils but those of his own making, and that he would have acquitted nature. It has cost us much trouble to make ourselves so miserable. When on the one hand we consider the immense labors of mankind, so many sciences brought to perfection, so many arts invented, so many powers employed, so many abysses filled up, so many mountains leveled, so many rocks rent to pieces, so many rivers made navigable, so many tracts of land cleared, lakes emptied, marshes drained, enormous buildings raised upon the earth, and the sea covered with ships and sailors; and on the other weigh with ever so little attention the real advantages that have resulted from all these works to mankind; we canont help being amazed at the vast disproportion observable between these things, and deplore the blindness of man, which, to feed his foolish pride and I don't know what vain self-admiration, makes him eagerly court and pursue all the miseries he is capable of feeling, and which beneficent nature had taken care to keep at a distance from him.

* This author was Maupertuis, whose theory appeared in the *Essai de philosophie morale* (1749).

That men are wicked, a sad and constant experience renders the proof of it unnecessary; man, however, is naturally good; I think I have demonstrated it; what then could have depraved him to such a degree, unless the changes that have happened in his constitution, the advantages he has made, and the knowledge he has acquired. Let us admire human society as much as we please, it will not be the less true that it necessarily leads men to hate each in proportion as their interests clash; to do each other apparent services, and in fact heap upon each other every imaginable mischief. What are we to think of a commerce, in which the interest of every individual dictates to him maxims diametrically opposite to those which the interest of the community recommends to the body of society; a commerce, in which every man finds his profit in the misfortunes of his neighbor? There is not, perhaps, a single man in easy circumstances, whose death his greedy heirs, nay and too often his own children, do not secretly wish for; not a ship at sea, the loss of which would not be an agreeable piece of news for some merchant or another; not a house which a debtor would not be glad to see reduced to ashes with all the papers in it; not a nation, which does not rejoice at the misfortunes of its neighbors. It is thus we find our advantages in the ill fortune of our fellows, and that the loss of one man almost always constitutes the prosperity of another. But, what is still more dangerous, public calamities are ever the objects of the hopes and expectations of innumerable individuals. Some desire sickness, others mortality; some war, some famine. I have seen monsters of men weep for grief at the appearance of a plentiful season; and the great and fatal conflagration of London, which cost so many wretches their lives or their fortunes, may have made the fortune of more than ten thousand persons. I know that Montaigne finds fault with Demades the Athenian for having caused to be punished a workman who, selling his coffins very dear, was a great gainer by the deaths of his fellow-citizens. But Montaigne's reason being, that by the same rule every man should be punished, it is plain that it confirms my argument. Let us therefore look through our frivolous displays of benevolence at what passes in the inmost recesses of the heart, and reflect on what must be that state of things, in which men are forced with the same breath to caress and to destroy each other, and in which they are born enemies by duty, and knaves by interest. Perhaps somebody will object that society is so formed that every man gains by serving the rest. That would be fine, if he did not gain still more by injuring them. There is no legitimate profit that is not exceeded by what may be made illegitimately, and we always gain more by hurting our neighbors than by doing them good. It is only a matter of finding a way to do it with impunity; and this is the end to which the powerful employ all their strength, and the weak all their cunning.

Savage man, when he has dined, is at peace with all nature, and the friend of all his fellows. Does a dispute sometimes happen about a meal? He seldom comes to blows without having first compared the difficulty of conquering with that of finding his subsistence elsewhere; and, as pride has no share in the squabble, it ends in a few cuffs; the victor eats, the vanquished retires to seek his fortune, and all is quiet again. But with man in society it's quite another story; in the first place, necessaries are to be provided, and then superfluities; delicacies follow, and then immense riches, and then subjects, and then slaves. He does not enjoy a moment's relaxation; what is most extraordinary, the less natural and pressing are his wants, the more headstrong his passions become, and what is still worse, the greater is his power of satisfying them; so that after a long run of prosperity, after having swallowed up many treasures and ruined many men, our hero will end up by cutting every throat, until he at last finds himself the sole master of the universe. Such is in miniature the moral picture, if not of human life, at least of the secret ambitions in the heart of every civilized man.

Compare without prejudice the state of social man with that of the savage, and find out, if you can, how many inlets, besides his wickedness, his wants, his miseries, the former has opened to pain and death. If you consider the afflictions of the mind which prey upon us, the violent passions which waste and exhaust us, the excessive labors with which the poor are overburdened, the still more dangerous indolence, to which the rich give themselves up and which kill the one through want, and the other through excess. If you reflect a moment on the monstrous mixture, and pernicious manner of seasoning so many dishes; on the putrefied food; on the adulterated medicines, the tricks of those who sell them, the mistakes of those who administer them, the poisonous qualities of the vessels in which they are prepared; if you but think of the epidemics bred by bad air among great numbers of men crowded together, or those occasioned by our delicate way of living, by our passing back and forth from the inside of our houses into the open air, the putting on and taking off our clothes with too little precaution, and by all those conveniences which our boundless sensuality has changed into necessary habits, and the neglect or loss of which afterwards costs us our life or our health; if you set down the conflagrations and earthquakes, which devouring or overturning whole cities destroy the miserable inhabitants by thousands; in a word, if you sum up the dangers with which all these causes are constantly menacing us, you will see how dearly nature makes us pay for the contempt we have showed for her lessons.

I shall not here repeat what I have elsewhere said of the calamities of war; I only wish that sufficiently informed persons were willing or bold enough to make public the detail of the villainies committed in armies by the contractors for food and for hospitals; we should then plainly discover that their monstrous frauds, scarcely concealed, destroy more soldiers than actually fall by the sword of the enemy, so as to make the most gallant armies melt away. The number of those who every year perish at sea, by famine, by the scurvy, by pirates, by shipwrecks, would furnish matter for another very shocking calculation. Besides it is plain, that we are to place to the account of the establishment of property and therefore to that of society, the assassinations, poisonings, highway robberies, and even the punishments for these crimes; punishments, it is true, requisite to prevent greater evils, but which, by making the murder of one man prove the death of two, double in fact the loss to the human species. How many are the shameful methods to prevent the birth of men, and cheat nature? Either by those brutal and depraved appetites which insult her most charming work, appetites which neither savages nor mere animals ever knew, and which could only spring in civilized countries from a corrupt imagination; or by those secret abortions, the worthy fruits of debauch and vicious notions of honor; or by the exposure or murder of multitudes of infants, victims of the poverty of their parents, or the barbarous shame of their mothers; or finally by the mutilation of those wretches, part of whose existence, with that of their whole posterity, is sacrificed to vain singsong, or, which is still worse, the brutal jealousy of some other men: a mutilation, which, in the last case, is doubly outrageous to nature, both by the treatment of those who suffer it, and by the service to which they are condemned.* But what if I undertook to show the human species attacked in its very source, and even in the holiest of all ties, in forming which nature is never listened to until fortune has been consulted, and social disorder confusing all virtue and vice, continence becomes a criminal precaution, and a refusal to give life to beings like oneself, an act of humanity? But without tearing open the veil which hides so many horrors, it is enough to point out the disease for which others will have to find a remedy.

Let us add to this the great number of unwholesome trades which shorten life, or destroy health; such as the digging and preparing of metals and minerals, especially lead, copper, mercury, cobalt, arsenic, realgar; † those other dangerous trades, which every day kill so many men, for example, tilers, carpenters, masons, and quarrymen; let us, I say, unite all these things, and then we shall discover in the establishment and perfecting of societies the reasons for that diminution of the species, which so many philosophers have taken notice of.

Luxury, which nothing can prevent among men who are avid for their own comforts and the deference of others, soon puts the finishing hand to the evils which society had begun; and on pretense of giving bread to the poor, whom it should never have made such, impoverishes all the rest, and sooner or later depopulates the State.

Luxury is a remedy much worse than the disease which it pretends to cure; or rather is in itself the worst of all diseases; both in great and small States. To maintain those crowds of servants and wretches which it creates, it crushes and ruins

---

* A passage on arranged marriages, which first appeared in the posthumous edition of 1782, is here omitted.

† Arsenic monosulphide; found in the dust of certain caves.

the farmer and the townsman; not unlike those scorching south winds, which covering both plants and foliage with devouring insects rob the useful animals of subsistence, and carry famine and death with them wherever they blow.

From society and the luxury engendered by it, spring the liberal and mechanical arts, commerce, letters, and all those superfluities which make industry flourish, and enrich and ruin nations. The reason for such ruin is very simple. It is plain that agriculture, by its very nature, must be the least lucrative of all arts, because its products being of the most indispensable necessity for all men, their price must be proportionate to the abilities of the poorest. From the same principle it may be gathered, that in general arts are lucrative in the inverse ratio of their usefulness, and that in the end the most necessary must come to be the most neglected. From this we may form a judgment of the true advantages of industry, and of the real effects of its progress.

Such are the evident causes of all the miseries into which opulence at length precipitates the most celebrated nations. In proportion as industry and arts spread and flourish, the despised husbandman, loaded with taxes necessary for the support of luxury, and condemned to spend his life between labor and hunger, leaves his fields to seek in town the bread he should take to it. The more our capital cities strike with wonder the stupid eye of the common people, the greater reason is there to weep, the countryside abandoned, fields lie uncultivated, and the high roads crowded with unfortunate citizens turned beggars or robbers, and doomed, sooner or later to lay down their wretched lives on the wheel or the dunghill. It is thus, that while States grow rich on one hand, they grow weak, and are depopulated on the other; and the most powerful monarchies, after innumerable labors to enrich and depopulate themselves, fall at last a prey to some poor nation, which has yielded to the fatal temptation of invading them, and then grows opulent and weak in its turn, until it is itself invaded and destroyed by some other.

I wish somebody would condescend to inform us what could have produced those swarms of barbarians, which during so many ages overran Europe, Asia, and Africa? Was it to the activity of their arts, the wisdom of their laws, the excellence of their State they owed so prodigious an increase?

I wish our learned men would be so kind as to tell us, why instead of multiplying to such a degree, these fierce and brutal men, without sense or science, without restraint, without education, did not murder each other every minute in quarreling for the spontaneous productions of their fields and woods? Let them tell us how these wretches could have the assurance to look in the face such skillful men as we were, with so fine a military discipline, such excellent codes, and such wise laws. Why, in short, since society has been perfected in the northern climates, and so much pains have been taken to instruct the inhabitants in their duties to one another, and the art of living happily and peaceably together, do we no longer see them produce anything like those numberless hosts, which they formerly used to send forth? I am afraid that somebody may at last take it into his head to answer me by saying, that truly all these great things, namely arts, sciences and laws, were very wisely invented by men, as a salutary plague, to prevent the too great multiplication of mankind, lest this world, which was given us should at length become too small for its inhabitants.

What then? Must societies be abolished? Must *meum* and *tuum* be annihilated, and must man go back to living in forests with the bears? This would be a deduction in the manner of my adversaries, which I choose to anticipate rather than permit them the shame of drawing it. O you, by whom the voice of heaven has not been heard, and who think your species destined only to finishing in peace this short life; you, who can lay down in the midst of cities your fatal acquisitions, your restless spirits, your corrupted hearts and unbridled desires, take up again, since it is in your power, your ancient and primitive innocence; retire to the woods, there to lose the sight and remembrance of the crimes committed by your contemporaries; nor be afraid of debasing your species, by renouncing its enlightenment in order to renounce its vices. As for men like me, whose passions have irretrievably destroyed their original simplicity, who can no longer live upon grass and acorns, or without laws and magistrates; all those who were honored in the person of their first parent with supernatural lessons; those, who discover, in the intention to give immediately to human actions a morality which otherwise they must have been so long in acquiring, the reason of a precept indifferent in itself, and utterly inexplicable in every other system; those, in a word, who are convinced that the divine voice has called all men to the enlightenment and happiness of the celestial intelligences; all such will endeavor to deserve the eternal reward promised their obedience, by practicing those virtues to the practice of which they oblige themselves in learning to know them. They will respect the sacred bonds of those societies to which they belong; they will love their fellows, and will serve them to the utmost of their power; they will religiously obey the laws, and all those who make or administer them; they will above all things honor those good and wise princes who find means to prevent, cure, or palliate the crowd of evils and abuses always ready to overwhelm us; they will animate the zeal of those worthy chiefs, by showing them without fear of flattery the importance of their talk, and the rigor of their duties. But they will not for that reason have any less contempt for a social organization which cannot subsist without the assistance of so many men of worth, who are oftener wanted than found; and from which, in spite of all their cares, there always spring more real calamities than even apparent advantages.

(k) This appears to me as clear as daylight, and I cannot conceive whence our philosophers can derive all the passions they attribute to natural man. Except the bare physical necessities, which nature herself requires, all our other needs are merely the effects of habit, before which they were not needs, or of our cravings; and we don't crave that which we are not in a condition to know. Hence it follows that as savage man longs for nothing but what he knows, and knows nothing but what he actually possesses or can easily acquire, nothing can be so calm as his soul, or so confined as his understanding.

(l)* Mr. Locke, in fine, proves at most that there may be in man a motive to live with the woman when she has a

---

* Only the last part of this note is given here. Rousseau is replying to Locke's contention that men and women naturally stayed together in families because of the dependency of their young.

child; but he by no means proves that there was any necessity for his living with her before her delivery and during the nine months of her pregnancy: if a pregnant woman comes to be indifferent to the man by whom she is pregnant during these nine months, if she even comes to be entirely forgotten by him, why should he assist her after her delivery? Why should he help her to rear a child, which he does not know to be his, and whose birth he neither foresaw nor planned? It is evident that Mr. Locke supposes the very thing in question: for we are not inquiring why man should continue to live with the woman after her delivery, but why he should continue to attach himself to her after conception. The appetite satisfied, man no longer stands in need of any particular woman, nor the woman of any particular man. The man does not have the slightest concern, nor perhaps the slightest notion of what must follow his act. One goes this way, the other that, and there is little reason to think that at the end of nine months they should remember ever to have known each other: for this kind of remembrance, by which one individual gives the preference to another for the act of generation, requires, as I have proved in the text, a greater degree of progress or corruption in the human understanding, than man can be supposed to have attained in the state of animality we here speak of. Another woman therefore may serve to satisfy the new desires of the man fully as conveniently as the one he has already known; and another man in like manner satisfy the woman's, supposing her subject to the same appetite during her pregnancy, a thing which may be reasonably doubted. But if in the state of nature, the woman, when she has conceived, no longer feels the passion of love, the obstacle to her associating with men becomes still greater, since she no longer has any occasion for the man by whom she is pregnant, or for any other. There is therefore no reason on the man's side for his coveting the same woman, nor on the woman's for her coveting the same man. Locke's argument therefore falls to the ground, and all the logic of this philosopher has not secured him from the mistake committed by Hobbes and others. They had to explain a fact in the state of nature; that is, in a state in which every man lived by himself without any connection with other men, and no one man had any motives to associate with any other,

nor perhaps, which is still more serious, men in general to
herd together; and it never came into their heads to look
back beyond the times of society, that is to say, those times
in which men have always had motives for herding together,
and in which one man has often motives for associating with
a particular man, or a particular woman.

(o) We must not confuse selfishness with self-love; they
are two very distinct passions both in their nature and in their
effects. Self-love is a natural sentiment, which inclines every
animal to look to his own preservation, and which, guided
in man by reason and qualified by pity, is productive of humanity and virtue. Selfishness is but a relative and factitious
sentiment, engendered in society, which inclines every individual to set a greater value upon himself than upon any
other man, which inspires men with all the mischief they
do to each other, and is the true source of what we call
honor.

This position well understood, I say that selfishness does
not exist in our primitive state, in the true state of nature;
for every man in particular considering himself as the only
spectator who observes him, as the only being in the universe
which takes any interest in him, as the only judge of his own
merit, it is impossible that a sentiment arising from comparisons, which he is not in a condition to make, should
spring up in his mind. For the same reason, such a man
must be a stranger to hatred and spite, passions which only
the opinion of our having received some affront can excite;
and as it is contempt or an intention to injure, and not the
injury itself that constitutes an affront, men who don't know
how to set a value upon themselves, or compare themselves
one with another, may do each other a great deal of mischief,
as often as they can expect any advantage by doing it, without ever offending each other. In a word, man seldom considering his fellows in any other light than he would animals
of another species, may plunder another man weaker than
himself, or be plundered by another that is stronger, without
considering these acts of violence otherwise than as natural
events, without the least emotion of insolence or spite, and
without any other passion than grief at his failure, or joy at
his good success.

(p) It is very remarkable, that for so many years past that the Europeans have been toiling to make the savages of different parts of the world conform to their manner of living, they have not as yet been able to win over one of them, not even with the assistance of the Christian religion; for though our missionaries sometimes make Christians, they never make civilized men of them. There is no getting the better of their invincible reluctance to adopt our manners and customs. If these poor savages are as unhappy as some people would have them, by what inconceivable depravity of judgment is it that they so constantly refuse to be governed as we are, or to live happy among us; whereas we read in a thousand places that Frenchmen and other Europeans have voluntarily taken refuge, nay, spent their whole lives among them, without ever being able to quit so strange a kind of life; and that even very sensible missionaries have been known to regret with tears the calm and innocent days they had spent among those men we so much despise. Should it be observed that they are not enlightened enough to judge soundly of their condition and ours, I must answer, that the valuation of happiness is not so much the business of the understanding as of feeling. Besides, this objection may still more forcibly be turned against ourselves; for our ideas are more remote from that disposition of mind requisite for us to conceive the relish, which the savages find in their way of living, than the ideas of the savages are from those by which they may conceive the relish we find in ours. In fact, very few observations are enough to show them that all our labors are confined to two objects, namely the conveniences of life and the esteem of others. But how shall we be able to imagine that kind of pleasure, which a savage takes in spending his days alone in the heart of a forest, or in fishing, or in blowing into a wretched flute without ever being able to fetch a single note from it, or ever giving himself any trouble to learn how to make a better use of it? *

(s) Nay, this rigorous equality of the state of nature, even if it were practicable in civil society, would clash with distributive justice; and as all the members of the State owe it

---

* The remainder of this note is not given here.

services in proportion to their talents and abilities, they should be distinguished in proportion to their services. It is in this sense we must understand a passage of Isocrates, in which he extols the primitive Athenians for having distinguished which of the two following kinds of equality was the more useful, that which consists in sharing the same advantages indifferently among all the citizens, or that which consists in distributing them to each according to his merit. These able politicians, adds the orator, banishing that unjust inequality which makes no difference between the good and the bad, inviolably adhered to that which rewards and punishes every man according to his merit. But in the first place there never existed a society so corrupt as to make no difference between the good and the bad; and in those points concerning morals, where the law can prescribe no measure exact enough to serve as a rule to magistrates, it is with the greatest wisdom that in order not to leave the fate or the rank of citizens at their discretion, it forbids them to judge of persons, and leaves actions alone to their discretion. There are no *mores*, except those as pure as those of the old Romans, that can bear censors, and such a tribunal among us would soon throw everything into confusion. It belongs to public esteem to mark a difference between good and bad men; the magistrate is judge only as to strict law; whereas the multitude is the true judge of manners; an upright and even an intelligent judge in that respect; a judge which may indeed sometimes be imposed upon, but can never be corrupted. The rank therefore of citizens ought to be regulated, not according to their personal merit, for this would be putting it in the power of magistrates to make almost an arbitrary application of the law, but according to the real services they render to the State, since these will admit of a more exact estimation.